The Luck *of* Friendship

The Luck of Friendship
The Letters of Tennessee Williams and James Laughlin

EDITED BY

Peggy L. Fox *and* Thomas Keith

W. W. NORTON & COMPANY

Independent Publishers Since 1923

NEW YORK | LONDON

For information about permission to reproduce selections from this book, write to Permissions,
W. W. Norton & Company, Inc., 500 Fifth Avenue, New York, NY 10110

For information about special discounts for bulk purchases, please contact
W. W. Norton Special Sales at specialsales@wwnorton.com or 800-233-4830

Manufacturing by LSC Communications Harrisonburg
Book design by Marysarah Quinn
Production manager: Lauren Abbate

Library of Congress Cataloging-in-Publication Data

Names: Williams, Tennessee, 1911–1983, author. | Laughlin, James, 1914–1997, author. |
Fox, Peggy L., editor. | Keith, Thomas, 1961– editor.
Title: The luck of friendship : the letters of Tennessee Williams and James Laughlin / edited
by Peggy L. Fox and Thomas Keith.
Description: First edition. | New York : W. W. Norton & Company, [2018] |
Includes bibliographical references and index.
Identifiers: LCCN 2018000448 | ISBN 9780393246209 (hardcover)
Subjects: LCSH: Williams, Tennessee, 1911–1983—Correspondence. |
Laughlin, James, 1914–1997—Correspondence. | Dramatists, American—20th century—
Correspondence. | Publishers and publishing—United States—Correspondence. | Authors
and publishers—United States—History—20th century.
Classification: LCC PS3545.I5365 Z48 2018 | DDC 812/.54 [B] —dc23
LC record available at https://lccn.loc.gov/2018000448

W. W. Norton & Company, Inc., 500 Fifth Avenue, New York, N.Y. 10110
www.wwnorton.com

W. W. Norton & Company Ltd., 15 Carlisle Street, London W1D 3BS

1 2 3 4 5 6 7 8 9 0

Contents

Introduction

The Long and the Short of It:
*Four Decades of One of the Most Unlikely Friendships
in American Literature*

JAMES LAUGHLIN always maintained that meeting Tennessee Williams at Lincoln Kirstein's Manhattan apartment in December 1942 was pure happenstance. The improbably tall (six feet six) Laughlin and the rather shy, much shorter (by more than a foot) playwright bonded over their veneration of Hart Crane's poetry, and a friendship was off and running that would last until Tennessee's death in 1983. If one were to judge by the letters in this volume, that scenario is at least possible. But was it just a chance encounter?

Laughlin, whose family's fortune derived from the Jones & Laughlin Steel Corporation of Pittsburgh, had begun New Directions, a small literary publishing venture, only seven years earlier while a sophomore at Harvard. And although he still retained a whiff of the *enfant terrible* who wrote storm-the-barricades introductions to his signature "annuals" (as he called the nominally yearly anthology, *New Directions in Prose and Poetry*), his firm was increasingly respected and considered the place to be published by anyone who aspired to be part of the "advance guard" of American literature.

Meanwhile Thomas Lanier Williams, son of a middle-class St. Louis family—his father had Nantucket Coffins and aristocratic Laniers in his family tree, while his Ohio-born mother had cultivated Southern graces and a Mississippi accent[1]—was starting to make a name for himself as a playwright. In 1939 four one-act plays, under the collective title *American Blues*, had won a small prize from the prestigious Group Theatre in New York City. This led to an agent, Audrey Wood, then an up-and-coming representative for dramatic works. Williams was on the ascendant despite the fact that his first major effort, *Battle of Angels*, failed in spectacular fashion in Boston the following year—smoke pots were poorly rigged, causing the audience to flee the theater coughing. But Tennessee (as Williams began calling himself in 1938) yearned to be considered a poet, as did the publisher he was about to meet. Each man had been well prepared to meet the other by Lincoln Kirstein, who—when he wasn't cofounding the New York City Ballet with George Balanchine—was a literary impresario. Tennessee wrote to his family on December 6, 1942, that he was to meet a publisher that night "who is interested in bringing out a volume of my verse. . . . I hope we get along amiably at this first meeting." Laughlin considered a recommendation from Kirstein, whom he had admired since he had been allowed into the older man's advanced literary circle at Harvard, to be all he needed to know about a young poet. The stage, as it were, had been admirably set.

This volume, composed of letters selected from a correspondence spanning four decades, is the chronicle of two men, preeminent in their respective fields, whose not-so-secret longings to be taken seriously as poets drew them to each other. They forged an unlikely bond

---

1. The financial woes of the fictional Wingfield family of *The Glass Menagerie* created the impression (not refuted by Tennessee) that the Williams family was downwardly mobile with an absentee father. During Tennessee's adolescence, however, the family was financially secure if dysfunctional due to his father's temper and drinking. His parents finally separated after Tennessee had left home, and, when he became successful, Tennessee provided support for his mother. *Menagerie* is an emotional rather than a situational autobiography.

that survived the extremes of critical acclaim and critical rejection, good sales and bad, manic highs and depression (for both), serious relationships and passing liaisons. Tennessee designated New Directions and James Laughlin as his publisher of choice based largely on the impression formed at that first meeting, a commitment that never wavered. Their joint story, while admittedly only a small part of the life of either man, provides a window into the literary history of the mid-twentieth century and reveals not only the self-destructive tendencies of a great artist but also his lifelong perseverance to remain both a poet and an experimental playwright, supported in his endeavors by the publisher he considered his one true friend.

A little more than a week after their encounter at Lincoln Kirstein's apartment, Tennessee wrote to Jay—as he most often addressed Laughlin in writing, though the man himself preferred J, just the capital letter, no period—expressing a desire to get together to discuss the poetry (letter of 12/15/42). He sent J his only verse play, *Dos Ranchos*, also titled *The Purification*, and later some poems. In one of the few letters from Laughlin that has survived from this period (Tennessee's copies of the originals mostly disappeared over the years during his many moves, and J did not reliably make carbons of letters until after 1946), J responds fervently: "I am very excited with the poems you sent. It seems to me you ARE a poet" (1/20/43). A selection of poems under the group title "The Summer Belvedere" was accepted for *Five Young American Poets* (1944), the last New Directions anthology of that title.

Tennessee's early letters are notable for their enthusiasm, openness, and willingness to do what was necessary to be a professional writer across several genres. All the while J was supplying Tennessee with New Directions books and introducing him to the work of authors such as Delmore Schwartz and Henry Miller. Despite the fact that Tennessee was actually three years older than J, Tennessee was in awe, and possibly a little in love, with the handsome, sophisticated publisher. During his largely unsuccessful stint as a screenwriter at MGM, Tennessee confessed to J that "I have a little picture gallery in my office of persons of importance in my life. . . . As my first real publisher, I would like to include one of you . . . preferably on skis" (7/23/43).

The growing bond between the two men was further cemented in 1944 when Laughlin recommended Tennessee to the American Academy and Institute of Arts and Letters for a grant of one thousand dollars, calling him "the most talented and promising young writer whom we publish" (2/14/44). Tennessee thanked J for his "intercession," promising not to count his "birds of paradise" before they hatched but admitting that the award would be "a small convenience that I could use" (2/26/44). But he *did* get the grant, which provided a much needed psychological validation that reverberated down the years—as his earnings from the productions of his plays increased and then skyrocketed, Tennessee would privately give support to a number of friends and artists and, in the end, would leave the bulk of his estate to his grandfather's alma mater, The University of the South, to benefit "creative writing."[2]

Throughout the summer of 1944, Tennessee kept dropping hints about his "new play," which he thought would be "too quiet" for J since it was a "sentimental family portrait" (9/25/44). The "new play" was *The Glass Menagerie*, and with its success the American theater was changed forever. J, who traveled to Chicago to see the play before it opened in New York, knew immediately that it had "an overwhelming theatrical power"[3] and wanted to publish *Menagerie* as soon as possible. This was Tennessee's fervent wish as well; however, there was a problem. Back in 1940, shortly after he had won the

2. The Sewanee Writers' Conference, established in 1989 at The University of the South, provides some scholarship support for all aspiring writers who attend. In addition, the millions of dollars that the university has received from publication royalties and theatrical fees for Tennessee's work have financed not only the Writers' Conference but also other needs of the school.
3. Interview with James Laughlin (11/3/95), conducted by Peggy L. Fox at Laughlin's home, Meadow House, Norfolk, Connecticut.

award from the Group Theatre, Tennessee accepted an advance of one hundred dollars from Bennett Cerf, the president of Random House, against his "next work." Now, in early February 1945, Tennessee asked Audrey Wood to extricate him from this commitment since Cerf had shown no interest in *Battle of Angels* or anything else he had written. If Tennessee occupied the moral high ground, Cerf maintained the lower legal space. Tennessee wrote to J, "I need not tell you again how happy that would make me [to have you publish *Menagerie*] for I would like all my shy intrusions on the world of letters to be thru N.D." (2/6/45). J offered to pay Cerf one hundred dollars to reimburse the earlier advance, but Cerf stalled until after the New York opening and then pounced, moving very quickly to exercise his option on the play. Random House did publish *Menagerie* but allowed it to go out of print when sales dropped after the first year. J immediately secured the rights.[4] The play finally appeared in the New Directions New Classics series in 1949, and it continues to be published by New Directions to this day.

Tennessee's inability to extricate himself from the Random House contract was a small setback, but in the end the professional relationship between Tennessee Williams and New Directions was strengthened. Despite repeated offers from other publishers, Tennessee would never publish his plays, poems, or stories with anyone else (without J's express permission, as in the case of the *Memoirs*). He would often tell J that one reason he wanted always to publish with New Directions was so that any money J made from publishing his work could go toward subsidizing other young writers. And J let Tennessee know of his appreciation, writing when paperback reprint

---

4. A contract between Williams and Laughlin for *The Glass Menagerie* exists, dated 2/5/45. However, because of the Random House imbroglio, it could not be acted upon at the time. An exchange of letters between James Laughlin and Donald Klopfer of Random House (11/29/48 and 12/16/48) confirms that Random House would sell New Directions the plates for *Menagerie* (for seventy-five dollars) but that Random House would retain the anthology rights to the play. In his letter of December 16, 1948, Laughlin mentioned that: "We have, of course, made a separate contract with Tennessee's agent, for the basic royalty to be paid him on our edition."

rights to *Streetcar* were sold that he was happy about this "windfall, because my share of it will permit me to print two or three books by promising newcomers which I would not otherwise have been able to do" (7/25/51).

Despite their shared disappointment that New Directions was not the original publisher of *Menagerie*, J and Tennessee already had other projects in progress. *Battle of Angels* was published in the spring 1945 double issue of *Pharos*, a magazine J founded, in part to involve his young wife, Margaret Keyser Laughlin, in his literary pursuits. The magazine did not last (nor did the marriage), but that issue was Tennessee's first book-length publication. Already New Directions was preparing a volume of one-act plays, published later that year as *27 Wagons Full of Cotton & Other One-Act Plays*. New Directions did publish all the plays post-*Menagerie*, but an important motif in these letters is J's encouragement of Tennessee as an author across genres— as a poet and short-story writer independent of his success as a playwright. In a 1945 note, written while he was in Utah at his fledgling ski resort at Alta, J enjoined Tennessee to write another story "as good as 'One Arm.'" After spending an evening together, Tennessee wrote with feeling of his dependence on J's good opinion: "<u>You</u> are my literary <u>conscience</u>—the only one outside of myself" (mid-1945). Later on he implored J to be honest with him about poems recently sent: "If you hate them, for God's sake Jay, don't hesitate to say so! I depend so much on your critical opinion as there are times when my own seems to fail me. . . . Honesty about failure is the only help for it" (8/17/49).

And just as J was a sounding board for Tennessee, the young playwright responded warmly to J's poetry. Tennessee wrote to J: "The little blue book [*A Small Book of Poems*] is with me and I think it contains your very loveliest poem. . . . The level of work is higher, I think, than in *Some Natural Things* [an earlier volume of J's poems]" (7/9/48). At this stage in their relationship the two men were already confidants. Tennessee candidly acknowledged his homosexuality, saying, "So let us exchange fatherly advices. No, I don't want to be 'saved'" (1/25/46). He even drolly suggested that J travel to New Orleans and relieve him of unwanted female companionship, while simultaneously encouraging J to enjoy an extramarital affair (with Gertrude Freedman Huston, an appealing young war widow who, more than four decades later, would become J's third wife). They were two young(ish) men lamenting to each other about their disorderly sex lives.

The twin triumphs of *The Glass Menagerie* in 1945 and *A Streetcar Named Desire* in late 1947 forever changed the material reality of Tennessee's life, and he experienced the "Catastrophe of Success," as he called the "vacuity of a life without struggle" in his essay of 1947, often published with *The Glass Menagerie*. Not only was life no longer a struggle, but also now all the giants of the theater world (and eventually Hollywood) were clamoring to know the young playwriting sensation. Eventually J would pull back a bit from Tennessee's celebrity life. I once asked J if he felt that maintaining a certain distance from Tennessee and his circle made their relationship last, and he replied that theirs was "a more professional relationship" because he didn't "hang out with those buzzards [the celebrity seekers]." He went on to say that his being "ostensibly, a serious publisher" meant something to Tennessee. Although J's support was crucial to Tennessee's integrity as an author, even that was not sufficient protection for the playwright. Over the years the crushing combination of a desperate need to churn out another Broadway success and the concomitant fear of failure drove Tennessee to those stress relievers of drink and pills, sadly with predictable results for his personal and professional life.

J sailed for Europe in November 1947, hoping that a stay on the Continent might repair his disintegrating marriage. His canny aunt Leila Laughlin Carlisle paid for a nurse for the two young children so that the parents might be able to spend more time together. Thus J missed the opening of *Streetcar* on December 3, though he got a glowing report from someone on the New Directions staff, very likely the young novelist Hubert Creekmore, who was more or less running the New York operation at the time: "*Streetcar* opened last night to tumultuous approval . . . and the final [act] left them— and me—wilted, gasping, weak, befoozled, drained . . . and then an uproar of applause which went on and on" (12/4/47).[5]

However, as Tennessee readied himself for his own transatlantic crossing at the end of December, he would write not about the tremendous reception of the play but in consternation about the jacket of the just published *Streetcar*: "My first reaction to the book cover was adverse. I think it was the color more than the design. It's a sort of shocking pink which reminds me of a violet scented lozenge" (12/29/47). By the third try the jacket was changed to red, providing a vivid backdrop for the striking stick-figure design, and author/publisher harmony was restored. But this flap highlights another recurring theme of the letters: the *appearance* of the books.

J loved fine printing, and in the next year he encouraged Tennessee to authorize a limited edition of the short play about the death of D. H. Lawrence, *I Rise in Flame, Cried the Phoenix*, "printed by those boys who do that gorgeous hand printing up at the Cummington Press in Massachusetts" (12/18/48). Because he knew how much these aspects of publication mattered to Tennessee, over the years J would continue to suggest typefaces and paper and to comment on cover design. Many of the early jackets for Tennessee's plays, including *Streetcar*, were designed by Alvin Lustig,[6] whom Tennessee had met in California during his brief screenwriting career and whose work he greatly admired. But after Lustig's death, the eternal struggle

---

5. The single unattributed page found in Laughlin's correspondence file (and reproduced in this volume on page 92) has been previously attributed to Tennessee himself, but the various publishing details, such as recommending the binding up of all the remaining five thousand sets of sheets, could not have come from Tennessee.

6. Alvin Lustig was an American artist and designer whose startling jacket designs— especially for the New Directions New Classics series—would become the iconic face of New Directions' books for a generation. He died in 1955.

between an opinionated author and his publisher would continue, last surfacing in the mid-seventies when Tennessee strongly objected to the way in which his own painting was reproduced for the jacket of his second book of poems, *Androgyne, Mon Amour* (resolved only by repeated—and expensive—redoing of the color separations). Tennessee was one of very few authors who received special treatment and do-overs from a notoriously frugal publisher.

The first book-length publication of Tennessee's short stories came in the fall of 1948 when *One Arm & Other Stories* appeared in a limited edition. J's highly indulgent treatment of Tennessee as author was again on display as the playwright urged: "Please remember not to let *One Arm* be displayed for sale in bookstores. . . . I hope that the book will be distributed as we planned, entirely by subscription" (10/12/48). This counterintuitive approach to book sales was occasioned by the direct treatment of a gay hustler in the hard-hitting title story. But the caution on Tennessee's part was less from a fear of book banning or censorship than from the certain disapproval of his overbearing mother once she saw the story. J would continue to support Tennessee's less-than-mainstream subject matter throughout his career, replying to him that he greatly liked a new story, "Kingdom of Earth": "This is something to which I would apply my phrase of 'clean dirt.' To me, there is salacious sex, such as you find in magazines like the *Ladies' Home Journal*, and there is good, clean honest sex, such as you find in Henry Miller and Lawrence [and] in a story like that one" (12/18/48). Tennessee and J were on the same page.

The wide-ranging nature of their relationship was signaled by Tennessee's sensitive advice to J over the defection—to the ever-rapacious Random House—of New Directions' first best-selling author, Paul Bowles, whose novel *The Sheltering Sky*, published in 1949, had been brought to New Directions by Tennessee. "The only serious loss, for you, is through becoming angry and bitter, which I think you can avoid by thinking very objectively about the predicament of a writer such as Paul" (4/5/50), Tennessee would counsel, elaborating on the difficulties of a writer trying to live on meager earnings. The irony in the advice is that it would increasingly become Tennessee who could not be mollified by reason and who would see conspiracy and even treachery in those who most wished him well, as when, in a fit of paranoia, he fired his longtime and fiercely loyal agent, Audrey Wood, in 1971. J, in contrast, became with age increasingly tolerant of restive authors, even encouraging some to try larger publishers if they wished, with the promise that New Directions would publish them again if this strategy "didn't work out."

It was at this juncture that a most important ingredient was added to the New Directions publishing mix: Robert MacGregor, a former correspondent for United Press in Moscow and Beijing and decorated World War II veteran, was hired on June 19, 1950, in what Ian MacNiven, in his thorough and engaging biography of James Laughlin, *"Literchoor Is My Beat,"* called "the most momentous personnel decision of J's publishing career."[7] Not only was MacGregor competent and trustworthy, but also his presence added a steadying hand to both the running of the office and the handling of production. He was well versed in the theater, and he was gay—from the point MacGregor joined New Directions for the entire time the offices remained at 333 Sixth Avenue, New Directions would share the eleventh floor with Theatre Arts Books, the concern owned by MacGregor and his life partner, George Zournas. Soon a new correspondent entered the exchange of letters, as MacGregor not only began to handle many of the details of preparing the scripts of Tennessee's plays for publication but also became a valued friend to Tennessee and Frank Merlo, who was Tennessee's lover and companion for nearly fourteen years beginning in 1948. Much more than J, MacGregor became part of the fabric of Tennessee's New York life.

For a variety of personal reasons, following his divorce from Mar-

---

7. Ian S. MacNiven, *"Literchoor Is My Beat": A Life of James Laughlin, Publisher of New Directions* (New York: Farrar, Straus & Giroux, 2014), p. 270.

garet Keyser in 1951, J took a salaried job with the Ford Foundation, offered by his friend Robert Maynard Hutchins, formerly the wunderkind president and then chancellor of the University of Chicago. J would run Intercultural Publications, which produced *Perspectives USA*, a magazine of J's creation intended to promote American culture and creative achievement. Now that MacGregor was in place to take over the New Directions helm whenever J was not available, it was much easier for J to undertake the travel necessary to produce *Perspectives* in English, French, German, and Italian and later to prepare supplements for *The Atlantic Monthly* on other cultures (such as India and Burma [now Myanmar]) for American readers.

Although in mid-1952 Tennessee was still sending "affectionate greetings to Gertrude [J's steady companion since their meeting in 1945]" (7/24/52), by 1953 another name became prominent in the letters. Maria Britneva first entered the correspondence in 1948 when she came to the United States after meeting Tennessee in London theater circles. She was amusing and vivacious, though unfortunately without the talent or discipline for the stage career she aspired to. When it became clear that Tennessee was definitely not in the market for a wife, she transferred her affections to J, who, when I asked him what her appeal was, said that he "found her amusing . . . [but] I just realized that she wouldn't suit me. She would want to be tearing around all over the world spending money." After Maria announced their engagement in London in 1953, J, using his work on *Perspectives* as an excuse, faded away to India. Tennessee and MacGregor exchanged worried letters until Maria joined Tennessee in Rome, saying she had been "brutally jilted," as Tennessee reported to MacGregor, concluding that "we have inherited Maria for the summer" (5/29/54). While Tennessee extended sympathy and understanding to both parties, he was obviously pained that an alliance that would have kept two of his most fervent supporters close at hand had collapsed. News of Maria would continue to weave in and out of the correspondence.

One of the most fascinating aspects of Tennessee's side of the correspondence was the disclosure of his need to keep writing as the only way to maintain his sanity: "Perhaps I ought to stop writing," he told J, "but then I would explode from sheer ennui" (4/1/51). And later he would add, "It would be a good thing if I could stop altogether for a while, but I find my daily existence almost unbearably tedious without beginning it at the typewriter" (4/5/53). J, on the other hand, proclaimed his conviction that Tennessee's writing was no mere escape from boredom but a glorious thing, his dedication to it heroic: "Your poems, on the contrary, have a way of getting right into the marrow of life. They are charged with authentic emotion and they tell a story which people can understand and identify themselves with" (4/4/55). Later it would be J who would provide meaningful support to Tennessee when the plays were no longer Broadway hits: "You've had a rough life, not the glamorous ease that is supposed to go with success, but look at the wonders that have come out of it. And I don't just mean the great plays and the beautiful poems and the stories that cut through to the truth, but also the hundreds of kind things you have done for people, and can still do. You are a good human being, Tenn, and don't forget it" (3/29/63).

In addition to his fondness for Tennessee's poetry and prose, J was also a first reader on virtually all of the plays after *Menagerie* and could be counted on to respond with not only praise but also unflinching honesty. After saying that *The Rose Tattoo* "packs a real wallop . . . I think it will be very strong on the stage" (11/3/50), J analyzed its strengths and weaknesses as well as its differences from *Menagerie* and *Streetcar*, concluding with a practical discussion of how the Italian lines should be checked and handled in the published version. The comprehensive nature of J's responses would be repeated again and again. For example, J found fault with the production of *Camino Real* but understood (as few others seemed to at the time) what Tennessee was trying to accomplish: "The real feeling of the play, its philosophical depth and tragic beauty, never managed to

cut through all that scrambling around" (3/26/53). Tennessee's gratitude was heartfelt: "I want to thank you for the never-failing appreciation you have for anything good in my work. Your letter meant
a great deal to me, since I went through a pretty black period after
those notices came out" (4/5/53). When he read *Cat on a Hot Tin Roof*,
J found it "shattering . . . as strange and true as Dostoevski" (1/16/55);
of *Suddenly Last Summer* he said in wonder, "It's some kind of magic,
to make something so poetic and beautiful out of such a frightening
theme" (1/20/58). He showed his understanding of Tennessee's over-
all purpose in his writing by commenting on *Sweet Bird of Youth*'s
essence, "The corruption is in all of us, and our only chance is to recognize it, and live with it" (3/11/59). Even the lesser-known plays of
the late sixties and seventies such as *Out Cry*, the revision of *The Two-
Character Play*, received a thoughtful appraisal as J compared the two
versions: "I think the new version, with so many new good touches, is
even stronger: the abstract quality is not lost, but there is more fleshing out to dramatize the ideas, and it certainly is that, a play of ideas
as well as human passion" (3/6/73).

Much of the correspondence of the late 1950s was between Tennessee and Bob MacGregor concerning publishing details and is not
reproduced here. J was traveling for the Ford Foundation and in 1956
remarried, not yet to Gertrude Huston, but to Ann Resor, whose
parents had built the J. Walter Thompson Company into the largest advertising agency in the United States. In dynastic terms, the
Radcliffe-educated and patrician Ann was certainly considered more
suitable than Britneva or Huston by J's mother and aunt Leila, on
whose occasional largesse he still depended to shore up New Directions' unreliable finances. Tennessee's more than a decade of commercial success was winding down and he lamented that he was "tired
of writing and writing is tired of me" (7/26/60).

In a well-intentioned but ill-fated suggestion, MacGregor recommended that Tennessee see Dr. Max Jacobson, who had "done
marvels for me" (4/5/61). While MacGregor thought he was merely

taking "hormones and vitamins and enzymes" (JL interview, 11/3/95) and surmised that the same cocktail might benefit Tennessee, the infamous "Dr. Feelgood," whose patients included Senator and then President John F. Kennedy, was actually pumping his celebrity clientele full of amphetamines. Though Tennessee came to realize that he was cruising on "speed," he didn't appear to care. It did seem to perk him up and at least he *thought* he was doing some of his best writing.[8] A crucial difference between MacGregor and Tennessee was that MacGregor, a recovering alcoholic, had not touched liquor since long before he came to New Directions, while Tennessee, though warned not to combine alcohol with the "little brews" provided by Jacobson, only drank more as the sixties progressed until his body collapsed from the twin assaults. His brother Dakin stepped in and had him committed to the psychiatric division of Barnes Hospital in St. Louis for three months in 1969. Although this intervention probably saved his life, Tennessee never forgave Dakin and, except for a token sum, cut him out of his will. The year before his hospitalization, Tennessee's wry comment to J on this period of his life was: "I don't believe God is dead but I think he is inclined to pointless brutalities" (April 1968).

The Night of the Iguana (1961) was Tennessee's last successful Broadway play. Throughout the sixties and seventies, he continued to write and continued to expand his theatrical style—calling the double bill of the *Slapstick Tragedy* (1966) his "answer to Ionesco" (9/24/62). *The Night of the Iguana, The Milk Train Doesn't Stop Here Anymore* (1964), *In the Bar of a Tokyo Hotel* (1969), and even the last play produced on Broadway before his death, *Clothes for a Summer Hotel* (1980), would show the influence of Japanese drama to which he had been introduced by his friend Yukio Mishima (also published

---

8. Albert J. Devlin, ed., *Conversations with Tennessee Williams* (Jackson, MS: University Press of Mississippi, 1986), p. 343.

by New Directions). The letters still went back and forth, though perhaps not as frequently, with Tennessee, now out of the hospital, writing to "Bob and Jay" that "I suspect that I will die with my boots on, as it were, during the production of a play" (5/12/70). In fact, in 1971 when New Directions was beginning to collect all of Tennessee's plays into a uniform edition, he objected to the title "The Collected Works of . . ." as a bad omen of mortality and agreed to publication only under MacGregor's revised title, "The Theatre of Tennessee Williams."

J continued to applaud Tennessee's efforts, especially in verse—"Your poems move me in a way that those of no one else do" (5/22/72). Such encouragement provided Tennessee with much needed solace: "It was such a joy to receive that long, wonderful letter from you. You know how badly I need reassurance about my work" (July 1972). And J could validate Tenn (as J frequently addressed Tennessee in his letters) in a way no one else could: "when I look at the sturdy volumes of the 'theatre' set, it makes me feel that I have been part of something very important in the course of American drama and literature, something which was only possible because of your friendship and loyalty" (8/11/72). Yet, strangely, given that Tennessee was often so open about his own physical and psychological symptoms, J never mentioned that in 1970 he himself had been diagnosed with hereditary bipolar disorder, then known as manic depression—he would take lithium and other medications from that point on to manage his mood swings. Despite the fact that they had so often talked and written about their personal problems, it was as if J felt that his own clinical diagnosis would impose an impossible burden on a man and artist so fearful for his own precarious sanity.

But it was MacGregor's unexpected death in late 1974 from lung cancer, the same disease that had claimed Frank Merlo a decade earlier, that was a crushing blow to J and Tennessee alike. Laughlin had to resume his role as Tennessee's main New Directions correspondent. He wrote to Tennessee of his loss: "But it just isn't the same place down there in the Village without Bob, we miss his wisdom, and all his professional knowledge, and his wonderful sense of humor, and so many other little things each day" (1/17/75). Meanwhile the work went on. In 1975 I was hired to take care of contracts, copyrights, foreign rights, and whatever else needed doing. When Peter Glassgold, who had done most of the editorial work on the various volumes of *The Theatre of Tennessee Williams* that began coming out in the early seventies, wanted help with the Tennessee overload, I picked up the slack on the second volume of poems, *Androgyne, Mon Amour* (1977), and became in-house editor of a collection of Tennessee's introductions to the various plays and other occasional essays, published under the title *Where I Live* (1978). I saw Tennessee rarely, but once I had taken over all the work on Tennessee's oeuvre, I did on occasion go to lunch with him and J—a privileged fly on the wall as two old friends reminisced. Once, while J and I were going over proofs with Tennessee in the big corner office at 80 Eighth Avenue, the home of New Directions since late 1978, J commented on the negative critical reception—or lack of comprehension—that Tennessee's recent plays had faced, and Tennessee lamented, "But ahm an experiMENTal playwright . . . ah don't WANT to rewrite [those old plays]." J replied soothingly, "We know, Tennessee, we know."

In these latter years, the two had occasion to pay tribute to each other—Tennessee to J: "Very briefly and truly, I want to say this. You're the greatest friend that I have had in my life, and the most trusted" (8/13/78), and J to Tennessee: "I want to thank you again for coming to the affair at the PEN. I was in a state of nerves and you really helped me get through it" (9/26/79). Next Tennessee cabled a message to an event in Rochester where J was receiving an honorary degree (5/29/80), and J sent a greeting to Tennessee's seventieth birthday celebration (3/5/81). Tennessee even became annoyed when, through an oversight, he almost wasn't asked for a contribution to a Festschrift for J and New Directions—the initial issue of Brad Morrow's *Conjunctions*. But the tie between them had already frayed somewhat with J's withdrawal once again from New Directions affairs, brought about by his struggles with his bipolar illness and his reluctance to come into Manhattan. In addition, at the urging of his psychiatrist, Dr. Benjamin Wiesel, J had begun a series of college lecture tours, and his connection with the New Directions staff became somewhat tenuous.[9] Tennessee wrote to Frederick R. Martin, who had become vice president after MacGregor's death: "The semi-retirement of dear Jay and the loss of Bob MacGregor somehow interrupted the flow of communications between N.D. and me. Let's now try to restore it. A serious writer needs serious contacts to keep on the right track. . . . Please remember me to Jay who introduced me to the 'world of Letters.' I never want him to be ashamed of a work of mine that bears the N.D. imprimatur" (rcd. 10/30/81).

Of course, New Directions had continued to publish Tennessee's late plays such as *Vieux Carré* (1979), now considered a minor classic, and *A Lovely Sunday for Creve Coeur* (1980) as they appeared, despite their poor critical reception. Most editing problems were handled in the office, but in 1982 I appealed to J to prod Tennessee to restore cuts to *Clothes for a Summer Hotel* that had, I felt, eviscerated an already fragile play, whose original theatrical run had been compromised by a heavy-handed Broadway production and then dealt a lethal blow by a subway strike. J handled the situation as only he could, embedding his real concerns amid praise and encouragement: "I think many of the small corrections are excellent, they tighten it up. But I'm much troubled by your taking off 'A Ghost Play' as subtitle and the deletions and changes which play down or even eliminate that important part of the structure. It just isn't the same play

---

9. At this point, to maintain contact with J, I was sending a full packet of copies of correspondence and material to him each week and would receive in return an envelope of notes on quartered scrap paper, which were called, in the office, "Norfolk confetti."

if you take that out" (10/31/82). Tennessee, as if thinking of what he had written earlier about never wanting J to be ashamed of any of his work, immediately agreed, and the readying of the script for publication went forward. In late January 1983, I called Tennessee to tell him that I was sending over the galleys for *Clothes* for him to correct and told him about a "do" at the National Arts Club on February 25 honoring J. I said that I knew J would be enormously pleased if he could attend, but Tennessee said, somewhat vaguely, that he was going on a trip. Then I asked if he could possibly write something to be read and return it with the proofs. He said he'd try. I confirmed all this in a covering letter (1/26/83) and very shortly had the proofs back with the moving tribute that is the last item of this correspondence: "It was James Laughlin in the beginning and it remains James Laughlin now, with never a disruption or moment of misunderstanding in a friendship and professional relationship that has now lasted for forty years or more" (rcd. 2/4/83).

I sent the play to the printer and took off on a long-anticipated trip to China. In one of life's tragic ironies, Tennessee died the night before the ceremonial occasion. Although it was first thought—and reported—that he had been asphyxiated by an inhaled bottle cap, a suppressed medical examiner's report revealed that he had over-dosed, accidentally or intentionally, on Seconal.[10] J learned of his death the next morning. Shutting himself in his office, he wrote the poem "Tennessee/ has taken the sudden subway . . . ," which he read that night (2/25/83), turning an event intended to honor himself into a tribute to his friend.

After J asked me to edit his correspondence with Tennessee, I spent some time with the material and then in November 1995 went to his home in Connecticut to interview him about his relationship with Tennessee and ask questions that had come up as I pored over

---

10. John Lahr, *Tennessee Williams: Mad Pilgrimage of the Flesh* (New York: W. W. Norton, 2014), p. 588.

the letters. Over two days we talked, with a tape recorder running, about Tennessee—about what Tennessee was like as a person, about his writing and what J thought of it, about specific incidents, and about what New Directions meant to both James Laughlin and Tennessee Williams. Excerpts from the interview are used as section dividers throughout this volume. On Saturday afternoon, the interview finished, J asked me if I'd like a cup of tea. We went into the kitchen, where J, who *never* cooked, insisted on making the tea himself, as if to prove he could indeed boil water. I had brought the tape recorder with me, and once we sat down with our tea and Oreo cookies—J's favorite—I asked J to read the poem he had written in memory of Tennessee onto the tape. Haltingly, he complied:

Tennessee

called death the sudden subway and now he has taken that train
but there are so many good things to remember
first the young man in sloppy pants and a torn sweater
whom I met at Lincoln Kirstein's cocktail party
he was very shy and had hidden himself in a side room
I too was shy but we got talking
he told me that he wrote plays and that he loved Hart Crane
he carried the poems of Crane in his knapsack wherever he
    hitchhiked
then his first night of glory in Chicago
when he and Laurette Taylor made a new American theater
I remember happy days with him in London and Italy and
    Key West
and how often friends and writers who were down on their luck
told me how generously he had helped them
(but you would never hear it from him)
so many fine things to remember
that I can live again in my mind
until it is my turn to join him on the sudden subway.

And then J burst out: "Sentimental. SENTIMENTAL. . . . I was very upset by his death, he was a good friend . . . and I miss him." A tear rolled down his cheek. Our hands accidentally touched as I raised a teacup and he lifted an Oreo. We looked at each other, then turned and gazed out the window at the leafless birches.

Peggy L. Fox

Notes on the Text

THE EXTANT CORRESPONDENCE between Tennessee Williams and James Laughlin, whether original documents, carbon copies, or photocopies, consists of at least 261 letters, short notes, telegrams, and postcards. We have included 170 of them in this volume, 73 by Laughlin and 97 by Williams. Because Williams's relationship to his publisher, New Directions, is also part of the story of the friendship between Laughlin and Williams, we have included correspondence with Robert MacGregor from 1950 until his death in 1974. Editor, office manager, vice president when New Directions was incorporated, and from his arrival Laughlin's right-hand man, MacGregor developed a strong friendship with Williams over that twenty-four-year period. In a similar spirit, there are also communications to and from MacGregor's immediate successor, Frederick R. Martin, and Williams's last editor, Peggy L. Fox.

We have gathered the correspondence for this collection from seven archives. The editorial files in the New York City offices of New Directions contain original letters from Williams as well as carbon copies of letters and memos from Laughlin, MacGregor, Martin, and Fox. Laughlin's personal archive at his home in Norfolk, Connecticut, which held the majority of the original letters from Williams to Laughlin when we began this project, is now housed in the

James Laughlin/New Directions Archive at the Houghton Library of Harvard University, which is also the repository of correspondence belonging to the New Directions Publishing Corporation. Letters by Williams to Laughlin are also located at the Performing Arts Collection in the Butler Library at Columbia University, the Fred W. Todd Tennessee Williams Collection at the Historic New Orleans Collection, the Manuscripts Division at the UCLA Library Department of Special Collections, and the Williams Collection at the Harry Ransom Humanities Research Center, University of Texas at Austin, which also holds letters by Laughlin.

In our selection of correspondence we have tried to maintain a balance of the personal and professional aspects of the primary correspondents' relationship. Both men were staggeringly prolific, and their letters often extend to several pages. We have therefore edited or condensed many letters in this volume by the removal of day-to-day or pro forma business matters related to the publishing industry that do not illuminate the narrative. Deleted material is indicated by ellipses within square brackets. Any ellipses without brackets were put in by the author of the letter.

The formatting style follows closely the guidelines established by Hugh Witemeyer, editor of the first volume, *The Selected Letters of William Carlos Williams and James Laughlin* (1989), in this eight-volume series from W. W. Norton. A headnote precedes every letter with the number of the entry in the volume, the form of communication, and the number of pages. The epistolary forms are designated with the following abbreviations: TLS (typed letter signed), TL (typed letter unsigned), ALS (autograph letter signed), AL (autograph letter unsigned), TNS (typed note signed, which applies to internal and external memos originating from New Directions), and TN (typed note unsigned). The author's signatures are copied as written in each instance. For unsigned missives with typed names, which most often come from carbon copies of letters and memos by

Laughlin, the author's name appears in brackets. Typed names following autograph signatures are omitted.

All dates of composition are printed as written by the authors. When an author does not provide a date or year of composition, it is placed in brackets and is based on the best available evidence, internal or external. Because both men traveled around a great deal—though Williams far more frequently than Laughlin—after each date we have provided the location of composition in brackets. Determination of the latter is based on internal evidence, letterhead, and sources including journals, biographies, and other correspondence.

Editorial insertions within the correspondence are indicated by square brackets and are so placed for ease of reading. These are most often the completion of someone's name, the title of work referred to but not identified in the text, or a missing word. Angle brackets surround an author's handwritten insertion in an otherwise typed letter: < >. Typographical errors and misspellings, including proper names, have been silently corrected unless they appear to be a deliberate stylistic choice. Titles have been adjusted to standard formatting: The titles of books, full-length and one-act plays, magazines, paintings, and record albums appear in italics, while quotation marks surround the titles of poems, short stories, essays, and songs. We have standardized Williams's frequent use of short and long dashes as em dashes and maintained his style of using all capital letters for emphasis. For all correspondence we have removed line spaces between paragraphs and indented every paragraph.

The following abbreviations are used in the notes: JL for James Laughlin, TW for Tennessee Williams, ND for New Directions Publishing Corporation, RM for Robert MacGregor, FM for Frederick Martin, PF for Peggy L. Fox, *NDPP* (along with the number of the issue: *NDPP* 7, for example) for *New Directions in Prose and Poetry*, and *FYAP* (1944) for *Five Young American Poets* (1944) Third Series. ND, when followed by a year date, both enclosed in parentheses, indicates a New Directions title and its year of publication. The year set in parentheses following Williams play titles is most often the year of a play's official opening, including on Broadway but not out-of-town tryouts. The year in parentheses may also be the year of first publication, if there was no prior production at the time of publication, or for a collection of full-length or one-act plays. The year of composition or completion of a Williams play is identified as such within a note. In the case of his stories, poems, and novels, year dates are the date of trade publication.

Thomas Keith

Acknowledgments

BECAUSE I HAD BEEN EDITING the Tennessee Williams titles published by New Directions since the late 1970s, in 1994 James Laughlin asked me if I would undertake the Laughlin/Tennessee Williams volume of the ongoing series of his correspondence with the most famous of the authors he published at New Directions. I was honored, flattered, and, while feeling challenged, confident of being able to complete the task in a few years. But only months after I had accepted the commission, I was named vice president of New Directions and took charge of the day-to-day running of the corporation. While I was able to conduct and transcribe an extensive interview with Laughlin at his home in Norfolk, Connecticut, in 1995, it eventually became apparent that I would need help to complete the correspondence project, and I turned to Thomas Keith. As a young actor (who had come to New York to work at La MaMa Experimental Theatre Club), Thomas had a deep love for the works of Tennessee Williams. When he started doing part-time work at New Directions in 1987, it was natural that I should enlist his help in preparing Williams manuscripts for publication as part of the ambitious program of publishing Williams's previously unpublished work. In 1997, with Laughlin's approval that Thomas work as my coeditor on the letters project, we were able to make a preliminary selection and he began the job of entering all of the letters into the computer. However, Laughlin died later that year and my duties at New Directions took precedence over the work on this volume. From 2001 to 2009 Thomas worked full-time at New Directions where, after I turned the editing of Williams titles over to him in 2002, he was responsible for reissues of the most famous Williams titles and for editing much of Williams's unpublished work, including four volumes of previously unpublished or uncollected one-act plays. It was only after I retired in 2011 that we took up this project again.

By the time we recommitted ourselves, Thomas had become a well-known expert on all matters Tennessee, was a sought-after speaker and adviser for Tennessee Williams conferences and stage productions, and, as a consulting editor, was superintending all of Williams publications at New Directions. And as Laughlin's literary coexecutor and a trustee of both the New Directions Ownership Trust and the Private Literary Projects Trust under the will of James Laughlin, I had become much more familiar with Laughlin's life and the history of the corporation. Full disclosure: In 2004 I married Ian MacNiven, who had been chosen by the Laughlin trustees (Daniel Javitch, Laughlin's son-in-law and my literary coexecutor; Donald Lamm, former president and chairman of the board of W. W. Norton; and myself) to write the authorized biography of James Laughlin. Needless to say, my access to all the material needed for the commentary on the Laughlin letters was now unparalleled.

So it is with profound gratitude that I acknowledge and applaud the full partnership that developed between myself and Thomas Keith as this project evolved over the years—without his intervention and singular contributions, the book simply would not be. And I would also like to thank my husband, Ian MacNiven, who not only generously shared the fruits of his research for his much praised biography of Laughlin (*"Literchoor Is My Beat": A Biography of James Laughlin, Publisher of New Directions*, nominated for a National Book

Critics Circle Award in Biography in 2014) but also contributed his editorial expertise and experience in editing volumes of letters to make this a better book all around (love, support, and gourmet meals also much appreciated). My co-trustee Donald Lamm graciously read and offered very helpful suggestions on the Introduction. And I am grateful to Leila Laughlin Javitch and co-trustee Daniel Javitch for their support for this project over the years. Thanks also to dear friends Jan Fergus, Melinda Barnhardt Jud, Trudy Katzer, and Jane Keller, who have been my sounding boards for years.

Peggy L. Fox

THE COMPLETION OF THIS VOLUME has been made possible by the trustees of the Private Literary Projects Trust under the will of James Laughlin, by the heirs to the estate of Tennessee Williams— The University of the South—specifically their representatives Donna L. Pierce and Linda B. Lankewicz, and by the current chairman of the board of W. W. Norton, Drake McFeely, to all of whom we are grateful for their generosity and goodwill.

Our editor at W. W. Norton, John Glusman, deserves our heartfelt thanks. John provided sensitive and smart editorial insights that greatly improved the quality of this collection while he cheerfully kept us on track and the publication process in motion.

Special thanks are due to Leslie Morris, curator of modern books and manuscripts, Houghton Library, Harvard University, and in charge of the James Laughlin/New Directions Archive at the Houghton, where all of Laughlin's voluminous correspondence was transferred after his death, for generously and promptly supplying enhanced copies of the correspondence whenever requested. Thanks are also due to Cathy Henderson and Richard Workman at the Harry Ransom Humanities and Research Center at the University of Texas at Austin; Jennifer B. Lee, curator of the Performing Arts Collection at the Rare Book and Manuscript Library of Columbia University;

Mark Cave, curator of manuscripts/oral historian, at the Historic New Orleans Collection; and Genie Guerard, head of the Manuscripts Division at the UCLA Library, Department of Special Collections. And a special note of thanks goes to Mary de Rachewiltz, who supplied copies of Maria Britneva's letters to her, recording Britneva's and Williams's visit to de Rachewiltz's father, Ezra Pound.

As Peggy has mentioned, we benefited enormously from the expertise and generosity of Ian MacNiven concerning any questions we had relating to James Laughlin and New Directions. We are also grateful to our friend, the author, editor, and former New Directions editor in chief, Peter Glassgold, the longtime editor of Laughlin's poetry who recently completed the impressive *The Collected Poems of James Laughlin 1935–1997* (2014).

To say that we stand on the shoulders of Albert J. Devlin, Jr., and Nancy M. Tischler is insufficient to convey how important their work on the *Selected Letters of Tennessee Williams, Volume I* (2000) and *Volume II* (2003), is to the world of Tennessee Williams studies. Their meticulous research has informed every scholarly endeavor related to Tennessee Williams that has come since. Likewise, the significance of the two major biographies of Tennessee Williams, *Tom: The Unknown Tennessee Williams* (1995) by Lyle Leverich and *Tennessee Williams: Mad Pilgrimage of the Flesh* (2014) by John Lahr, cannot be overstated—while distinct in style and content, each has been a landmark for the public understanding of Williams's life and work.

Other essential reference works we relied upon include *The Notebooks of Tennessee Williams* (2006), edited by Margaret Bradham Thornton; *New Selected Essays: Where I Live* (2009), edited by John S. Bak; *The Collected Poems of Tennessee Williams* (2002), edited by David Roessel and Nicholas Moschovakis; and George Crandell's *Tennessee Williams: A Descriptive Bibliography* (1995). Drewey Wayne Gunn's *Tennessee Williams: A Bibliography* (2nd ed., 1991) is indispensable for accurately identifying and dating Williams productions as well as publications. For bibliographic information related to New Directions, *A New Directions Reader* (1964), edited by Hayden Carruth and J. Laughlin, and *Published for James Laughlin: A New Directions List of Publications, 1936–1997* (2008) by John A. Harrison, Rebecca Newth, and Anne Marie Candido have proved invaluable.

We gladly acknowledge the editors of the previous volumes in this series whose work has offered us substantial guidance: Hugh Witemeyer, *William Carlos Williams and James Laughlin: Selected Letters* (1989); Lee Bartlett, *Kenneth Rexroth and James Laughlin: Selected Letters* (1991); Robert Phillips, *Delmore Schwartz and James Laughlin: Selected Letters* (1993); David M. Gordon, *Ezra Pound and James Laughlin: Selected Letters* (1994); George Wickes, *Henry Miller and James Laughlin: Selected Letters* (1996); David D. Cooper, *Thomas Merton and James Laughlin: Selected Letters* (1997); and W. C. Bamberger, *Guy Davenport and James Laughlin: Selected Letters* (2007).

Warm gratitude goes to our friends and colleagues at New Directions: Barbara Epler, Laurie Callahan, Declan Spring, Sylvia Frezzolini Severance, Erik Rieselbach, Christopher Wait, Mieke Chew, and the late Daniel Allman and Griselda Ohannessian.

Among the extensive and supportive community of Tennessee Williams scholars Peggy and I have come to know and cherish over the decades, for their help with this volume we would like to thank particularly Michael Paller, Felicia Hardison Londré, and the intrepid Karen Kohlhaas, who discovered the earliest extant letter from Laughlin to Williams that had somehow found its way into the Audrey Wood Archive at the Harry Ransom Center. To many others whom we have relied upon for matters large and small in relation to this volume, we offer our thanks: Helen Thomaides, Lydia Brents, Jeff Shreve, and Brendan Curry at W. W. Norton, Mitch Douglas, Andreas Brown, John Lahr, Eric Bentley, Gregory Mosher, John Guare, Elaine Lustig Cohen, Dick Cavett, Brendan Fay, John Uecker, Donald Windham, Erin DiIorio, Jane D. Young, Paul J. Willis, David Kaplan, Jeremy Lawrence, and William Jay Smith, as well as Georges Borchardt, literary agent for the Williams Estate, and Tom Erhardt (retired) and Mel Kenyon of Casarotto Ramsay Associates, London, theatrical agency for the Williams Estate.

I am indebted to my partner, Arturo Noguera, for his steadfast encouragement. His good humor respecting all the passions and hobbyhorses I pursue is constant. From the time we first met, Peggy L. Fox's confidence in my abilities has led to much of the work that has brought joy into my life in the last thirty years. I thank her for that—if it's at all possible—and for our work together on this project.

Thomas Keith

Letters

SECTION I

⸺⸙⸺

PF: The first thing, of course, in your relationship with Tennessee is that you met him through Lincoln Kirstein, so why don't we start with how you knew Kirstein and that cocktail party where you first met Tennessee?

JL: Well, I'd always known Lincoln from college days because he was a member of the Ararat Thursday evening suppers in Boston. I was the only undergraduate in that group, and I kept very quiet. But I formed an enormous attachment for Lincoln because he was such a brilliant man and was doing such great work. The *Hound and Horn* or as Ezra called it, the *Bitch and Bugle*, was a wonderful magazine.

PF: So you knew him at Harvard. Did you keep in touch with him?

JL: Very off and on; I was in such awe of him. He was just such a god to me of what a man should be. He had me several times to his modest little apartment in New York for cocktail parties. That was when he was married to—I can't think of her name right now. I think it was a marriage of convenience. This particular time I saw off in an adjacent room this little man. He was hunched over, wearing a sweater and dirty gray pants.

And I said to myself, there's someone who needs company, and I went over and started talking to him. I liked him right away. We liked the same poets, like Hart Crane, and he started telling me about his work, and various contacts flowed out of that and he started sending me stuff.

« • »

Lincoln Kirstein: Founder of the School of American Ballet and *Dance Index* magazine (1907–1996).

Ezra: Ezra Pound, American poet (1885–1972). Pound was not only a teacher and mentor to James Laughlin, but also it was he who suggested that Laughlin become a publisher.

I can't think of her name: Fidelma Cadmus Kirstein (1906–1991). Painter, sister of the artist Paul Cadmus.

Hart Crane: American poet (1899–1932). Strongly influenced by Crane, TW was known to carry a tattered copy of Crane's poems with him wherever he went. Though he was ultimately buried in St. Louis, TW had made known his desire to be buried at sea in the Gulf of Mexico at the approximate spot where Crane committed suicide.

1. TLS—1

December 15, 1942 [New York]

DEAR JAY LAUGHLIN:

Lincoln tells me that your name is Jay, not James.

I hope you remember our talk about my poems at Lincoln's Sunday night recently.

Well, I have gotten most of the long ones into fairly presentable shape, but of the short ones there is a bewildering number to choose among. I am wondering if you plan to be in the town (Manhattan) any time soon so that instead of mailing the only existing copies of a great number of poems only a few of which may be acceptable to you—It would not be better for us to get together and sort of go over and discuss them informally[?]. With a sensitive poet in the grand manner, such a business might be a violent ordeal but with me I promise you it would be extremely simple and we would inevitably part on good terms even if you advised me to devote myself exclusively to the theatre for the rest of my life.

Any way that you want to do this is all right, just let me know. I might even be able to deliver them to you at your office in Norfolk if that seems a better plan.

Of course I am excited over the possibility and I do hope enough of the poems are sympathetic to you to make it work out.

Lincoln sends his love.

Cordially,

Tennessee

c/o Lincoln Kirstein, 637 Madison Ave., New York City.

≪ • ≫

Norfolk: The town in Connecticut where Laughlin's aunt, Leila Laughlin Carlisle, lived. After JL's first marriage in 1942, she renovated and enlarged a farmhouse across the road from her home, Robin Hill, for the young couple. JL continued to live at what came to be called Meadow House for the rest of his life. JL maintained the offices of New Directions on the property from 1936 to 1945 in a cottage with a converted stable attached. He then opened an office at 500 Fifth Avenue in New York City.

2. ALS—2

Dec. 21, 1942 [New York]

DEAR JAY LAUGHLIN—

I am enclosing the only existing copy of my verse play *Dos Ranchos* or *The Purification*. The agent has apparently not seen fit to have it typed because of its non-commercial nature. I feel, however, that it is more of a stage than a closet drama and might be better in production than reading. No music for the guitar accompaniment has been composed yet. It could be printed without the marginal directions which sound a bit crude, I'm afraid. Things in brackets are <u>suggested</u> cuts.

I feel that an inexpensive printing of this little play might be commercially rewarding because of the interest here in my dramatic writing. I think a pretty good sale would be assured in New York Shops.

The poems will come along later.

Carly Wharton has advanced some money on the D. H. Lawrence adaptation (long play and a production this season seems likely).

It is possible I can bring the poems up to Norfolk since you will not return to New York soon. Otherwise I will send as many as practicable through the mail.

Please take good care of this only copy for me.

Cordially,

Tenn. Williams

≪ • ≫

Dos Ranchos *or* The Purification: TW's only play in verse, *The Purification* was originally produced at the Pasadena Laboratory Theater, Pasadena, California, in July 1944. ND published the script in 27 *Wagons Full of Cotton and Other Plays* (ND 1945).

The agent: Audrey Wood (1905–1986). TW was approached by Wood after he won a prize of one hundred dollars as an honorable mention in a contest sponsored by the Group Theatre for four one-act plays submitted under the collective title *American Blues* (not the same group of plays published under that title in 1948), along with three full-length plays. Wood was TW's agent from 1939 until he broke off the relationship in 1971.

Carly Wharton: (1898–). Along with her business partner, Martin Gabel (1912–1986), Carly Wharton considered producing *You Touched Me!*, on Broadway but ultimately rejected the project.

The D. H. Lawrence adaptation: *You Touched Me!* Coauthored with Donald Windham, TW's only literary collaboration.

D. H. Lawrence: (1885–1930), English novelist, poet, critic, and painter. Inspired by Lawrence's ideas about sensuality and sex, TW wrote at least three one-act plays about Lawrence: *I Rise in Flame Cried the Phoenix*, *A Panic Renaissance in the Lobos Mountains*, and *Adam and Eve on a Ferry*.

Donald Windham: (1920–2010), American novelist. In addition to collaborating with TW on the play *You Touched Me!* he introduced TW to Lincoln Kirstein, Paul Cadmus, Gore Vidal, and George Platt Lynes, among others. Windham was the author of several novels, two plays, and a memoir; he also edited a volume of his correspondence with TW published by Holt, Rinehart & Winston in 1977. Though he often tried, TW could never interest JL in Windham's writing enough for JL to publish him at New Directions. Windham's roman à clef about TW, *The Hero Continues*, was published in 1960.

3. TL—1

Dec. 23, 1942 [Norfolk]

DEAR TENNESSEE—

I think the play is extremely interesting and very beautiful in places. The verse really has a lovely tone to it. Perhaps the plot is sort of melodramatic, but there is plenty of tradition for that.

I am now anxious to see the poems so that I can get a general idea of the situation and decide about the best method of publication.

A good play like that reinforces a book of verse, or it might go well in the annual, or it might even go by itself in the Poets series. But I would like to get an idea of the whole layout before trying to suggest anything.

Best wishes,

J Laughlin

« • »

the annual: New Directions in Prose and Poetry. In 1936, JL inaugurated his publishing house with an anthology bearing its name. Although it was informally known as "the annual," it did not necessarily appear each year in the early years, and after 1972 it became biennial. These anthologies were often a forum for new writing from ND's stable of authors as well as a showcase for new, international, and avant-garde writers. JL's first Annual contained contributions by William Carlos Williams, E. E. Cummings, Gertrude Stein, Henry Miller, Kay Boyle, Elizabeth Bishop, Louis Zukofsky, Jean Cocteau, Wallace Stevens, and Ezra Pound, among others.

the Poets series: Most likely a reference to the Poet of the Month series, which ran from 1941 to 1945; each monthly "issue" was a finely printed pamphlet devoted to an individual poet. See note following JL's letter to TW of October 20, 1955, for additional details.

4. TLS—1

January 12, 1943 [New York]

DEAR JAY LAUGHLIN:

I have gone about preparing these poems with more energy than method, but rather than delay any longer I am just going to stick a bunch of them in an envelope and shoot them off—the first contingent. Others will come along in a second dispatch.

I have made no effort to arrange them in any logical sequence, if such a sequence exists.

As I told you, I have had to combine the poetry with work on a play or I would have finished sooner and in much better order.

> Truly,
> T. W.

I have thought of several titles for a collection—*One Hand in Space, Dark Arm, Fiddler's Green*. That could be decided after you have read all the poems.

5. TLS—1

Jan 20 [1943] [Norfolk]

DEAR TENNESSEE—

I am very excited with the poems you sent. It seems to me you ARE a poet. Some of the stuff is rough, to be sure, but it's studded with nuggets. You have some of the wonderful quality of Éluard— strange insights that reduce to highly poetic images.

I'm keen on the stuff and want to do something about it. Will be down in NYC before long. We must get together and plan it out. I'll call Lincoln's office when I get to town and leave word where I am staying.

> Best wishes,
> JL

≪ • ≫

Éluard: Paul Éluard (1895–1954) was the pen name of the French poet Eugène Grindel, whose *The Dour Desire to Endure* (1950) and *Selected Writings* (1951) were published by ND.

6. TLS—1

1/31/43 [St. Louis, Missouri]

DEAR JAY:

Here is the list of books I wanted. All you have of Rimbaud, the Kafka, anything you recommend by E.M. Forster. Lately my enthusiasm has divided between Crane and Rimbaud but I don't think Crane would resent the division. Crane would drunkenly declare himself the reincarnation of Christopher Marlowe but I think it is more significant to observe that he was born less than ten years after the death of Rimbaud. A restless spirit like Rimbaud's wouldn't wait longer to find another earthly residence, though I wonder if he would choose to be a poet again—maybe as expiation—No, he wouldn't need that, not after that horrible last chapter of his life. Do you think one should write a play about him? A motion picture would be the ideal medium starting with "Morte a Dieu" and ending with the pitiful conversion in the hospital at Marseilles. Not with pious implications, however.

I am at work on your stories. In fact so intensely that when I stopped this evening I had a regular crise de nerfs. Vertigo, so that I couldn't stand up, a crazy feeling of panic, palpitations, nausea, chill—then finally an absolute drowsy peace with a wolfish appetite. I am now in that last phase, thank God. When I read the stuff tomorrow it will either be in my best vein or else pure gibberish. Unfortunately the subsequent paroxysms could signify either.

I will probably leave here in less than two weeks, for N.Y. if I receive favorable news of the play, otherwise for New Orleans or Mexico—but I will send you an address when I leave.

Letters from Margo and David, both raving of books you sent them. You have acquired two fanatic admirers in them. With your Lincoln-like aura it must be hard to avoid idolatry of this kind. People like David and Margo, too intelligently skeptical for the church and with more emotional excitability than they can put into social or sexual relationships and with professions not quite creative enough to absorb it, have need of discovering a modern Saint or Buddha, and sooner or later your mountain lodge will inevitably be a citadel of holiness.

10.

« • »

Rimbaud, Kafka, Forster: Arthur Rimbaud (1854–1891), French poet. ND published *A Season in Hell & The Drunken Boat* (1961) and *Illuminations and Other Prose Poems* (1957). Franz Kafka (1883–1924), German-language novelist born in Prague. ND published Edwin Muir's translation of *Amerika* (1946) as well as an anthology of criticism, *The Kafka Problem* (1946). E. M. Forster (1879–1970), English novelist. ND reissued Forster's novels *The Longest Journey* (1943) and *A Room with a View* (1943) as well as a book of criticism on Forster by Lionel Trilling.

Marlowe: Christopher Marlowe (1564–1593), English dramatist.

"Morte a Dieu": TW's imperfect French; he may have intended "Morte à Dieu," which is not idiomatic either but which approximates "Death to God." Possibly TW is hinting at episodes in Rimbaud's youth when he expressed such thoughts.

Margo: Margo Jones (1913–1955), American theater director and producer. Known as the "Texas Tornado," Jones directed the original productions of TW's *The Purification*, *Stairs to the Roof*, *You Touched Me!*, *The Glass Menagerie* (co-directed with Eddie Dowling), *Summer and Smoke*, and *The Last of My Solid Gold Watches*.

David: Possibly producer David Merrick (1911–2000) who was considering TW's play *Stairs to the Roof* at that time. Merrick would later produce TW's *Kingdom of Earth* on Broadway in 1968, under the title *The Seven Descents of Myrtle*, and the Broadway premiere of *Out Cry* in 1973. In 1975 Merrick produced TW's *The Red Devil Battery Sign*, which he closed in Boston.

mountain lodge: In early 1940, with money received from the estate of his late uncle, James Laughlin III, JL bought the lease to a pristine ski area in Little Cottonwood Canyon near Salt Lake City from the U.S. Forest Service. His enthusiasm for skiing went back to the time he spent at the Le Rosey School in Switzerland in 1927 to 1928. With Dick Durrance, one of the earliest American international ski champions, he completed the Alta Lodge and founded the Alta Ski Lift Company. Alta was both a passion and a retreat, and the ski lift company still remains in the Laughlin family.

7. TLS—1

Feb. 10, 1943 [New York]

DEAR JAY:

You said at our lunch that you would mention me to an editor at *The New Yorker* who might could use some of my lyrical triviata. That would be exceptionally convenient right now, so would you mind asking him to look at the stuff? I will pick out the things that seem slanted for the magazine. If you have a fairly good idea of the verse you wish to keep for the prospective anthology, would you send me back the poems you definitely won't require? I could use them for the above purpose perhaps. Also I have a bunch which quite obviously wouldn't have interested you but might do for this, some folk ballads and lyrics called "Blue Mountain Blues" or "The Songs that Saved Me from a Drunkard's Grave."

With spring coming on, I will probably write some more poetry and will concentrate on the long free verse things we both prefer.

I have a new job, as usher at the Strand theatre, a colorful little world of its own, which I enjoy exploring.

Best wishes always,

10.

≪ • ≫

prospective anthology: *Five Young American Poets* (1944) Third Series [*FYAP* (1944) hereafter].

8. TLS—1

April 1943 [Clayton, Missouri]

DEAR JAY:

How are you? As the custodian of my verse you have a great importance to me, and I am a little worried because I haven't heard anything from you. Will you drop me a line to assure me the poems are in a safe place and not in danger of loss?

I am poised in the mid-continent, briefly, trying to decide which way to jump. The west is the strongest attraction, but New York still has some strings on me.

Inadvertently, just before I left, I did run into one of your other poets. I went to a modern dance recital and afterwards to a cocktail party for one of the dancers, and there he was—Howard Moss. Along with two other sort of school-teacherish poets, the opposite of the Paul Goodman type. As a group at a party, poets of this type always remind me of ladies in a delicate condition, excused from making any social effort. I was sort of in between the dancers and the poets and tried to form a connection, so I got to talking to Moss. It came out that he was to be in your planned anthology. I said I was, too. This started a great disturbance. They all wanted to know if I was "the dark horse." I couldn't say whether I was or not, and the speculations became very heated. Up till then they had just been sitting there like brooding hens, but now they all hopped up talking at once, as though their eggs had hatched into something very alarming. It was too bad for the dancers, for in spite of their natural vivacity, they were thrown in obscurity from then on, and the chasm between the groups became abysmal. My fortuitous prominence was great fun.

I would like you to see a short play of mine just come out in Dodd-Mead's anthology, *The Best One-Act Plays of 1942*. If works of this genre interest you, I would like to submit some to you.—I am enclosing a new long poem.

Address above for about ten days,

Cordially,

Tennessee

« · »

Howard Moss: (1922–1987), American poet and editor. Moss was not published in the *Five Young American Poets* series after all. He later went on to be the editor of *The New Yorker*.

Paul Goodman: (1911–1972), American social critic and psychotherapist, published by ND in *Five Young American Poets* (1941) First Series and *The Break-Up of Our Camp* (1949).

short play: *The Last of My Solid Gold Watches* was published in *27 Wagons Full of Cotton and Other Plays* (ND 1945).

9. TLS—2.

[April 1943] [Clayton]

DEAR JAY:

What a relief to hear from you! I had a nightmarish suspicion that you and my verse had just dropped out of the world.

[. . .]

My agent has ordered me to remain here in Clayton another week or ten days till some mysterious negotiations with Hollywood have been concluded, at which time she will advise me whether to turn East or West. If I am allowed to go West, I will certainly pass through Salt Lake City, which I have never seen, and make an effort to see you.

I will enjoy writing the preface and will do it immediately.

Cordially,

10

P.S. I have written <u>two</u> prefaces, the first one seemed a little too serious and the second a little too frivolous, so I am letting you choose. I think the serious one is probably better.

My agent just wired me I am signed up in Hollywood, must go to New York first and then to the Coast. I will try to pass through Salt Lake City.

You can reach me either care of this address or Audrey Wood, 551 Fifth Ave., New York, until I have a place on the Coast.

≪ • ≫

two prefaces: Both were published as "Frivolous Preface" and "Serious Preface" for TW's section, "The Summer Belvedere," in *FYAP* (1944).

signed up in Hollywood: On April 30 Audrey Wood wired TW to inform him that she had secured a six-month contract with Metro Goldwyn Mayer as a screenwriter at the salary of two hundred fifty dollars a week.

10. TL—1

[May 1943] [Alta, Utah]

DEAR TENNESSEE—

Thanks for your prefaces. I like them BOTH in their different way. Why not run both. "Frivolous Preface" and "Serious Preface." It's a good angle, don't you think.

Hope you can stop off here on your way to the Coast. I haven't seen a soul literary for months. Not that I'm trying to insult you by including you in a category which includes Parker Tyler etc. But what I mean is that skiers are very nice but sort of one sided.

Wire ahead and I'll meet your train or plane or telephone l d Alta 4 when you get to town and I'll come down for you.

REALLY I only lost one ms in a truck and that was later found. So keep up your hopes.

hastily, & regards

j

I don't worry in the LEAST about Hoolywood spoiling you after the training you've been through. I rather like the place. I have a good friend there—Alvin Lustig—a Jewish boy who looks like Jesus and designs very well. Do you want to meet him?

≪ • ≫

Parker Tyler: (1904–1974), American poet and critic associated with Charles Henri Ford and his magazine *View*.

11. TLS—1

May 14, 1943 [Culver City, California]

DEAR JAY:

I was hoping to stop off in Salt Lake to see you on my way to the Coast, but I had to go by the Santa Fe which went way South of there.

I suppose you got the prefaces I wrote before leaving Clayton. I am enclosing a final draft of "The Summer Belvedere." That and a short poem called "Beanstalk Country" I had addressed previously to your editorial office in Norfolk, Conn.

Perhaps you will come to the Coast before returning East. If you do, please look me up here. If you're not already familiar with this fantastic filmland, perhaps I could show you about with some familiarity by that time. It is pretty fantastic to find myself writing a vehicle for Lana Turner, but I am getting paid what I think is a fabulous salary—at least when I compare it to the $18.50 a week I was making last winter ushering at the Strand, and I have a private office, a typewriter, and a lot of free time, so it is not, altogether, a bad deal. Also I have a motor scooter and an apartment on the beach at Santa Monica!

I have heard from Clark Mills. He has finished "The Circus" but hasn't sent the final draft off yet—I think it is going to be published as soon as he releases it. I do hope it's as good as those two or three superb poems of his.

Tennessee

≪ • ≫

"*The Summer Belvedere*": The title poem from TW's section in *FYAP* (1944).

"*The Beanstalk Country*": A poem first published in *FYAP* (1944).

a vehicle for Lana Turner: TW was assigned to write additional dialogue for the film *Marriage Is a Private Affair*, starring the popular World War II pin-up, platinum-blonde actress.

Clark Mills: American poet (1913–1986). After they met in a poetry club at Washington University in 1936, Mills greatly influenced TW's tastes in poetry, introducing him to the work of Hart Crane, as well as translations of Rimbaud, Baudelaire, and Lorca.

12. TLS—2

[late May/early June 1943] [Culver City]

DEAR JAY:

Your letter from Utah traveled back and forth across the continent before it reached me. What a pity they didn't book me through Salt Lake City. I am sure that skiers are the opposite of writers and both of us must be reaching corresponding degrees of satiety though I can't help thinking yours is better than mine. I would love to have gone there but they put me on the Santa Fe, through a beautiful blizzard in Arizona and New Mexico but way off the track of your skiers.

I could not decide between the two prefaces either. There is a paragraph about Joyce at which point the two could be joined—or if you like the serious and frivolous angle—that would do just as well, I think. Certainly I would be pleased to have them both printed if you can give me that much space in the volume.

This celluloid brassiere that I am making for Lana Turner is not unamusing; I have gone to movies so much, even ushering at them, that the script is almost automatic. I was somewhat disconcerted the other day—after writing many fiery dramatic speeches I thought I had better refresh my memory of the girl's technique, so they ran her latest picture for me in the projection room—I discovered she talked baby-talk!—but nicely.

Do you know Christopher Isherwood or like his work? I visited him last night in his monastery. He has gone into one in Holly-wood, of all places. It is a miniature copy, architecturally, of the Taj Mahal and when I entered about eight girls and three men, including one Hindu, were seated on cushions in a semi-circle about the fire-place, all with an absolutely expressionless silence. Which made me so uncomfortable that I turned to one of them and said, "Why is it that the word Krishnamurti comes into my mind?" It was the only thing Hindu I could think of, and I had no idea who or what it was. Turned out to be dreadful blunder, as they acidly explained that he was the follower of Annie Besant and she not hardly mentionable in their circles. The dead-pan atmosphere became even thicker—and Isherwood suggested we go out for a walk. I cannot surmise his real attitude toward "the family"—he is English enough not to speak his mind very frankly—but I am wondering a little if he is not going to write a wonderful story of what is going on there.

I would very much like to meet the designer you mention and I am hoping you will make the trip to L.A. Call me at the Studio when you get here.

If my teeth were not in such a bad condition already, I would have appreciated the 17th century couplet more deeply. At any rate, it reminded me to make an appointment with the dentist.

En Avant!

10

≪ • ≫

Joyce: James Joyce (1882–1941), Irish novelist and poet. ND published Joyce's novel *Stephen Hero* (1944) and a reissue of Joyce's play *Exiles* (1945).

Christopher Isherwood: (1904–1986), English novelist, short-story writer, playwright, and memoirist. ND published Isherwood's *The Berlin Stories* (1945), *The Memorial* (1946), *Lions and Shadows* (1947), and *All the Conspirators* (1958).

Krishnamurti: Jiddu Krishnamurti (1895–1986), Indian theosophist and author.

Annie Besant: (1847–1933), English author, theosophist, and political radical.

13. TL—1

[late May/early June 1943] [Alta, Utah]

DEAR TENN—

The Isherwood fandang sounds wonderful. For goodness sake write a story about it. That will go fine with Henry Miller's account of life with Dali at Caresse Crosby's Virginia chateau.

I hope to get down the end of this month so will delay all matters till then. Something which is constitutionally easy for me to do. Don't worry, wheels are rolling on the other end of the project. The book will get out OK.

It strikes me that I never sent you a contract. Hell, I'll bat off a short one now. All contracts are the balls, being twistable, turnable and evadable at all the joints, but we seem to go on with them anyway.

Two feet of new snow here yesterday. Them pore little flowers they just haven't got a chance.

Yrs,

J

≪ • ≫

Henry Miller: (1891–1980). ND publishes more than a dozen Miller titles, mostly his essays and nonfiction.

Dali: Salvador Domingo Felipe Jacinto Dalí i Domènech, known as Salvador Dalí, (1904–1989), a Spanish surrealist painter.

Caresse Crosby: (1891–1970), American patron of the arts. Crosby was known as "literary godmother to the Lost Generation of American expatriate writers in Paris."

14. TLS—1

June 9, 1943 [Culver City]

DEAR J:

I guess I return one of these signed contracts to you and keep the one with your signature on it. Hope this is correct. The check for the verse looks more impressive to me than an MGM pay-check and I feel like it ought to be framed.

I am writing Isherwood a mildly sardonic letter requesting another audience in the seraglio. He may boil with rage over the suggestion that I do an article about him and his sacred calling. On the other hand, he may be pleased. He says he hates the British but I have never known anybody so British unless it is that other Anglo-phobe, D. H. Lawrence. Don't be surprised at any reaction we get from him. Herr Issyvoo of Berlin Diary was a very sympathetic character but we must remember that all writers are pleasant only on paper, and rarely even then.—The juxtaposition with Dali is what he may find offensive. I like Dali's work, most of it, but I think it is fashionable to deplore it lately.

Ever,
Tennessee

≪ • ≫

Herr Issyvoo of Berlin Diary: "Issyvoo" was Isherwood's own rendering of the German pronunciation of his name.

Berlin Diary: Published as *The Berlin Stories*, containing the novels *The Last of Mr. Norris* and *Goodbye to Berlin* (ND 1945).

15. TLS—1

7/8/43 [Culver City]

DEAR JAY:

I have been looking for you to arrive on the Coast. What's happened?

I have been plunging into Hollywood society, sort of drafted into it by a visiting playwright, Horton Foote, the wonder boy from Texas who is re-writing a play under the Svengali influence of a movie producer. We have met Simone Simon, Geraldine Fitzgerald, to mention the most attractive.

I hope you get here before Horton leaves so that we can give you some intimate glimpses of the insanity here. You will be asked to contribute to or criticize all kinds of story-ideas for people like Charles Boyer. The only defense is pretending to be drunk or fallen asleep. These people, the Hollywood writers and producers, are regular vampires.

I had a long interview with Christopher Isherwood about the proposed article and learned plenty about him but nothing about Vedanta, which is just as well.

The title "Mornings on Bourbon Street" had been in my mind for a long time as I wanted to use it, possibly, for the collection, so I wrote the enclosed poem to fit it. It may seem a little sentimental or facile, in which case we won't bother about it.

But let me know if you are still coming here and when.

Ever,

Tennessee

≪ • ≫

Horton Foote: (1916–2009), American playwright and screenwriter.

a play: Foote's *Only the Heart*.

a movie producer: Jacques Thiery.

Simone Simon: (1910–2005), French film actress.

Geraldine Fitzgerald: (1913–2005), Irish-born American actress.

Charles Boyer: (1899–1978), French-born Hollywood actor.

Vedanta: In 1943 Isherwood joined the Vedanta Society monastery in Hollywood, and in 1945 would edit and contribute to *Vedanta for the Modern World*, a collection of essays on Vedanta philosophy.

"Mornings on Bourbon Street": A poem from *FYAP* (1944) and included in *In the Winter of Cities* (ND 1956), TW's first volume of poems.

16. TLS—2

July 23, 1943 [Culver City]

DEAR JAY:

It is wise of you to recognize the astringent value of life in the snow and mountains. Every artist needs such a place of refuge. New York makes you hard and grubby, California relaxes you too much. Reading back through my journal to the summer I was here before, Laguna Beach in 1939, just before the war broke out in Europe—those far-away days—I find myself observing that life here, on the beach, is like Gauguin's picture *Nave Nave Mahana*, "The Careless Days." I was disturbed at the time that life was too indolent and pleasurable and that I would almost welcome the return of interior storms after so much dreamy peace. Well, plenty of storms came along and I experienced, later, quite a nostalgia for the *Nave Nave Mahana*. During that summer I was care-taker on a chicken-ranch while the owners were away. For days I would forget to feed the chickens, life was so dreamy, then I would make up for it by feeding them too much. About half of them died, fell on their backs with their feet sticking rigidly up, and I left the ranch in disgrace for New Mexico.

When you first mentioned "The Ecuadorean Carrion" I thought it was the title of a long poem and it intrigued me immensely. Isn't it a good title? I feel a keen desire to see this material, Latin American poetry is so much softer and yet stronger than ours, they are not afraid of tender feelings and lavish color nor of the cruelty that goes with it, like the bullfights in Mexico where the fighters have an almost feminine or tender grace but destroy the bulls so remorselessly, with such wonderful music and brilliant colors. I think the cold British influence has done us in a little. We ought to look south of us, since we can't follow Crane with intensity enough to make it worth while.

I did not know you had relinquished your copy of the verse play until Margo Jones showed up with freshly typed copies of it in a very mysterious way and has gotten everybody at the Pasadena Playhouse very excited over it. I think she intercepted it on the way to the typist in New York, then fled for California with it. She has come out here to try out my plays with the hope of obtaining Hollywood money for New York productions.

I will see that you get a fresh copy, and apologize for the agent.

I have a little picture gallery in my office of persons of importance in my life, such as Crane and Chekhov and Katherine Anne Porter and this amazing new sponsor, Margo Jones. As my first real publisher, I would like to include one of you, if you have one to send me, preferably on skis.

My next picture assignment will probably be a folk-opera, the lyrics and libretto for it, on the saga of Billy The Kid. They despaired of getting me to write for Lana Turner, suitably, and until the right assignment comes along I am left to my own devices, happily.

I hope you haven't given up on the trip out here entirely. There may be parts of my longer poems that you think need revisions, such as the end of "The Dangerous Painters," which I think may slacken a bit in the end. If so, I have time now to do further work.

Salud!

Tennessee

« • »

Nave Nave Mahana: A scene of Tahitian life painted in 1896 by French impressionist painter Paul Gauguin (1848–1903).

"The Ecuadorean Carrion": TW is referring to an Ecuadorian poet, Alejandro Carrión, whose work was also included in *FYAP* (1944).

Chekhov: Anton Pavlovich Chekov (1860–1904), Russian playwright and short-story writer. TW often cited Chekhov as a great influence. In the late 1970s TW wrote what he called "a free adaptation" of Chekhov's *The Seagull* entitled *The Notebook of Trigorin* (1981).

Katherine Anne Porter: (1890–1980), American short-story writer and novelist.

"The Dangerous Painters": A poem included in *In the Winter of Cities*.

17. TLS—1

[Typed at the top of the page:] Read a terrific story called 'The White Boat' by Sidney Alexander and a nice piece by Kafka in Summer issue of *Accent*.

8–20–43 [Santa Monica, California]

DEAR JAY:

I'm very pleased with your choice of poems which is just about what mine would have been. Only two that I like more than casually were left out. "The Cataract" and "The Christus of Guadalajara." The first is probably colored by personal meanings, the second by a nostalgia for Mexico—anyhow my regard for your judgment as an editor is altogether unqualified, for nearly every time something is printed that I didn't look for, there is the name "New Directions." Now I have the feeling that if I refine my out-put, narrow it into pure and individual channels, then there will [be] a place for it. That is, of course, all the difference in the world from thinking—Even if I do it, who will care?

About the title of "The Fox"—Put after it (to D.H.L.).

You did not enclose the Lincoln-like portrait you mention. I hope it will come along later. Both of the two gentlemen already up in my gallery, Crane and Chekhov, looking brooding, but Margo and KAP [Katherine Anne Porter] are grinning like Cheshires. KAP writes me that she has some smiling pictures of Crane, snap-shots taken in her Mexican garden when they were neighbors. I have asked for them but no response. I think they would be of more than private value, as she says they show a side of his nature usually not remembered.

Right now I am taking a six weeks lay-off from Metro, but doing a job for Goldwyn on a picture for Teresa Wright. The Play from the Lawrence story will go on in the Cleveland Playhouse and in Pasadena also in the month of October. If these productions should result in a successful Broadway showing, it may interest you as a publisher.

Isherwood has temporarily withdrawn from his monastery and become a fellow beach-comber. I am trying to agree with him upon a subject for dramatic collaboration—and if you read any stories or books that you think would make a wonderful play—I want to write a really wonderful one or none at all—let me know!

Yours,

10

≪ • ≫

Sidney Alexander: (1866–1948), English poet, author, and clergyman.

Accent: Subtitled *A Quarterly of New Literature*, it was published from 1940 to 1945.

picture for Teresa Wright: (1918–2005), American film star of the 1940s. The picture was a screen treatment of TW's early play *Spring Storm*, which MGM did not purchase.

Cleveland Playhouse / The Play from the Lawrence story: Adapted from the eponymous D. H. Lawrence short story, *You Touched Me!* premiered at the Cleveland Playhouse on October 13, 1943, under the direction of Margo Jones, before opening on Broadway September 25, 1945, under the direction of Guthrie McClintic and Lee Shubert.

Pasadena: Margo Jones directed another production of *You Touched Me!* that rehearsed in November 1943 and opened at the Pasadena Playhouse on November 29.

SECTION II

———— ❧ ————

PF: About this same time Tennessee mentions Charles Henri, who, I assume, was Charles Henri Ford. What was his connection with New Directions at this time?

JL: Well, he was a friend. Charles Henri was the boyfriend of Tchelitchew, the painter.

PF: Oh, he's the one that Tennessee calls "Chilly Death."

JL: Right, he was the painter. He did the beautiful portrait of Ann in the living room, and Charles Henri was his boyfriend. Tchelitchew was a respectable person. He was a Russian nobleman. It was through him that I got to know Charles Henri. I liked Charles Henri. We did two little books of his.

≪ • ≫

Charles Henri Ford: (1913–2002) American poet. The brother of actress Ruth Ford and the boyfriend of the Russian surrealist painter Pavel Tchelitchew (1898–1957), Ford's volumes of poetry *The Garden of Disorder & Other Poems* (1939) and *Sleep in a Nest of Flames* (1949) were published by ND.

beautiful portrait of Ann: JL's second wife, Ann Clark Resor Laughlin (1925–1989), was the daughter of Stanley Burnet Resor and Helen Lansdowne, who had built the J. Walter Thompson Company into the largest advertising firm in the country.

Introduced by a common friend, the novelist and travel writer Santha Rama Rau, JL and Ann were married in 1956 and remained so until her death. In 1964 Ann inherited many modernist paintings collected by her mother, a major benefactor of the Museum of Modern Art. The lovely painting of Ann at age seventeen by Tchelitchew had been commissioned by her parents.

18. TLS—1

9/26/43 [Santa Monica]

DEAR JAY:

I have just gotten back from a bicycle trip down the coast taken during my studio lay-off. Your picture has come and has made a fine addition to my little gallery. Many many thanks!

The reason you got two copies of the play is that I took the precaution of wiring both Audrey and Margo as I didn't know for sure who had the copies. Apparently they both did. Will you get some copies of the books to me as soon as they come out? Of course I am crazy to see them.

Right now I am working on a little group of short stories called "Three Myths & A Malediction," which I may ask you to look at when finished.

That extra play copy you may return to me or to Audrey Wood, it doesn't matter which. I am back on the payroll at the studio but still working at home so you can address me here, 1647 Ocean Ave., Santa Monica.

Charles Henri's sister tells me that he and Chilly Death are leaving for Mexico City if they can overcome their fear of dysentery. I suppose Mexico City is going to become the Paris of Post–War II.

Yours,

Tennessee

≪ • ≫

my studio lay-off: TW was laid off from MGM for six weeks in early August 1943, following which he was not given an assignment and his six-month option was not renewed.

19. ALS—3

Dec. 20/43 [Taos, New Mexico]

DEAR JAY,

I have retreated like you to a place of snow, the snow-covered desert of Taos. Washes Hollywood off. In Hollywood I am a <u>worm</u>—
prostrate—crawling—here I feel alive again. Frieda Lawrence has
promised me a piece of her ranch in the Lobos to build on when I
am ready. I will be ready this spring if the play sells. Frieda is helping me with it, removing the Dame and all the war shit which isn't
Lawrence or me. Frieda is still a Valkyrie. The only exciting woman
I've known.

It is lovelier here in winter than other seasons. Cold but so dry it
feels good. Makes the blood run again and brighter. I was all, all gone
on the coast—this is my predestined home I believe. But I must leave
to be home in Clayton for Xmas to see the kid brother off on a hop
to China—& comfort the family.

There I will try to get some stories in shape for you, while waiting
news from N.Y.

The Creole Palace was fun, the most I had off the beach the whole
time I was in Calif.

I have just read an article by Henry Miller in a mag. Frieda has,
called *The Phoenix*—1938—He damns Proust and Joyce as dead writers of a dead world. A cruel allusion is made to Joyce's blindness 'as
symbolic'—which I find odious. However the article has a macabre
brilliance. I met Miller before I left—Red beard and I went out there.
He seemed very spry. Alert. Highly conscious.

Having read nothing but that unfortunate attack on Joyce—and
Proust—I should reserve my judgment, but I suspect he is too heartless to be a great artist. I will try and get hold of his works.

Strange that he admires Lawrence. Lawrence would hate him, I imagine.

They tell me there is some good skiing around here.

Ultimately we may compare notes.

En Avant

10.

If I get a home here I will form a hospice for poets—St. Bernard dogs with brandy flasks and everything! But God pity them when they get there! Evanôit!

≪ • ≫

Frieda Lawrence: Frieda von Richthofen Lawrence (1879–1956), German wife of the English novelist and short-story writer D. H. Lawrence. TW visited her Taos ranch for the first time in August 1939.

kid brother: Walter Dakin Williams (1919–2008), known as Dakin.

Creole Palace: A popular African American cabaret that operated in San Diego during World War II.

Evanôit!: This seems to be a construction from the French verb *s'évanouir* (to swoon, to faint), meaning roughly, "It makes one swoon."

20. TLS—1

1/12/44 [Clayton]

DEAR JAY:

I got your proofs [*FYAP* (1944)] this morning—made two small corrections—a line out of place, some mis-spellings—and returned them air-mail this afternoon. I was very happy over the appearance of the script, it was beautifully set-up and the spatial arrangements certainly an improvement.

So much of the time writing is like digging for water in a desert: it is wonderfully gratifying when there is a spring and someone offers you a cup to catch it.

My return home was a signal for great disturbances. My Grandmother died suddenly of a lung hemorrhage and father was hauled off to hospital with pneumonia and my kid brother sailed over-seas with the air-force, a mosquito net the only clue as to destination. Then I had an eye operation—but that was very successful and with the aid of a thick lens I see nearly as well as with the right eye. Gives me a terrifying appearance as it magnifies the eye—so much the better!

Since Taos and Frieda I have almost completely re-written *You Touched Me!* And I think it's much stronger. Will send you a copy of the pretentious foreword. It is meant to intimidate more guileless persons than you!—When I get all this off my hands, I will start on your stories.

Salud!

10

« • »

Grandmother: Rosina Otte Dakin (1863–1944), TW's maternal grandmother Rose, affectionately known as "Grand."

father: Cornelius Coffin Williams (1880–1957), TW's father. See the essay "The Man in the Overstuffed Chair" in *New Selected Essays: Where I Live* (ND 2009).

pretentious foreword: "Homage to Ophelia" remains unpublished.

21. TLS—1

2–26–44 [Clayton]

DEAR JAY:

I wrote you before, but lost it in the blizzard of papers on the table. As for the Academy—thanks for your intercession. Birds of paradise should not be counted before they're hatched but admittedly a thousand dollars is a small convenience that I could use—for a year in Mexico no less! I haven't heard anything from them. The future is spectral, but only from a distance. When you get up close it takes off the false face, and looks reasonably human.

I wrote everybody in N.Y. that I was leaving immediately for there—about two weeks ago. I'm still here. Sort of dread the blustering attitudes you have to assume in the city: imitation of someone much alive! I feel dreamy and drifty.—I see where Charles Henri is going into the book-publishing trade. Opening shot is something by André Breton with an exquisite title involving rabbits and cherry trees. I don't know Breton, but I think of [Charles Henri] Ford's Group as "The Odor of Lightning" school. They always choose the one attribute that a thing never possesses and attribute that to it. Startling effects are unquestionably obtained by this process, but as a desideratum in itself—how good is that? Still—I have admired some of Ford's own work much more than any of his followers. And do you know—Charles Henri has a good heart? He once did something very generous to my knowledge, a real self-sacrifice! Then two days later he was very insulting. Where do you stand with such people?

I suppose your books [*FYAP* (1944)] will be out soon, but I wish they would hurry. I could use them to political advantage in N.Y. this spring, using them as a letter of introduction to people like Stark Young who have esthetic principles but also influence, even on Broadway. I say I am not a professional writer, but I'm not above wanting to use their tricks—I have been reading something by Delmore Schwartz—*Shenandoah* I think is pedantic but another one—a play also—has a real <u>fresh</u> quality—I would like to meet him. Is he in New York?

Last night I had a wild dream about Saroyan!—of all things. I went to a play of his and it was so strange and beautiful that I cried, but there were only about five in the audience, and no critics. Saroyan was very humble and begged me for an honest opinion. I cried so that I couldn't tell him. We left the theatre together. Saroyan jumped over a high wall—I couldn't follow. Then he caught a fast train that rushed into a tunnel. I caught another follow[ing], just caught it by the back of the observation platform. Mine turned into a sleigh—I landed in a pile of snow with children—but thinking, though I am having a lot of fun, I ought to be with Saroyan—for he is going to a party at Tallulah Bankhead's!—Figure that one out!

Tenn.

≪ • ≫

the Academy: The American Academy and Institute of Arts and Letters. JL was instrumental in helping TW secure a grant of one thousand dollars from the Academy in May 1944.

André Breton: (1896–1966), French artist, poet, novelist, and essayist.

Stark Young: (1881–1963), American writer and critic.

Delmore Schwartz: (1913–1966), American poet, short-story writer, and critic. Schwartz had a long association with JL; ND published his major works, among them *In Dreams Begin Responsibilities* (1938) (which included the play to which TW is referring, *Dr. Bergen's Belief*) and *Summer Knowledge* (1967), a book of poems.

Saroyan: William Saroyan (1908–1981), American poet, short-story writer, novelist, and playwright. ND published reissues of *Madness in the Family* (1988), *The Man with the Heart in the Highlands* (1989), and *The Daring Young Man on the Flying Trapeze* (1997).

Tallulah Bankhead: (1903–1968), American stage and film actress. TW campaigned vigorously to get Bankhead to play the leading role of Myra in *Battle of Angels*, which she declined. Backstage after a performance of *The Little Foxes* years later, Bankhead purportedly said to TW, "Well, darling, I was luckier than Miriam Hopkins, who lost her mind and actually appeared in that abominable Battle-some-thing-or-other that you had the impertinence to write for me." Bankhead starred in a revival of *A Streetcar Named Desire* in the 1950s and appears as a character in TW's 1981 play about his 1940 summer in Provincetown, *Something Cloudy, Something Clear* (ND 1995).

22. TLS—1

3/7/44 [Clayton]

My dear boy!

Your books just reached me and I am delirious with them!

I have been mentally unstable all week from working on a blood and thunder tragedy, the sort that makes you all ice and fire one day and roar with laughter the next and sick with rage—then through the same cycle, pulverizing what is left of the central nervous system. But all in all it is more satisfactory than anything I've worked on since the last act of *Battle*, for I love to hammer and bang and bellow like that. I'm just an old fashioned ham and may as well face it.

I was supposed to leave weeks ago for N.Y. but am waiting till I get the rough blocks knocked out. I don't trust myself in N.Y. I get to running around and thinking in urbane terms that are inimical to blood and thunder.

Assure your wife that I will love to have the play [*Battle of Angels*] in the magazine. It has been so much abused it ought to be given a chance to defend itself. Do you want someone to write a preface? Maybe Margaret Webster would, although she only knows the earlier version that was put on in Boston—which she directed there. I don't know what her current attitude is, but she is the most literate mind on Broadway—well—excepting Stark Young and Krutch. I think George Jean Nathan's comment "A cheap sex-shocker" ought to go on the cover! Along with more temperate reactions.

10

<P.S. I will mail you back copy of *Battle*>

≪ • ≫

your books: Probably a selection of current ND titles that JL sent to TW. JL often supplied his authors with copies of books by other ND writers.

blood and thunder tragedy: Possibly *Daughter of the American Revolution*, a generational drama that was a precursor to both *The Glass Menagerie* and *A Streetcar Named Desire*.

your wife . . . play in the magazine: JL married Margaret Keyser (1917–1994) in Salt Lake City, Utah, on March 24, 1942. They had met through the Salt Lake City/Alta skiing community. They had two children, Paul (1942) and Leila (1944), and were divorced in 1952. JL began the magazine *Pharos* partially to engage Margaret in his literary work. The first number containing *Battle of Angels* (Spring 1945) was a double issue, and the magazine lasted for only four issues.

Margaret Webster: (1905–1972), American-born British theater actress, producer, and director.

Krutch: Joseph Wood Krutch (1893–1970), American critic, author, and naturalist. Krutch was drama critic for *The Nation* from 1924 to 1952.

George Jean Nathan: (1882–1958), American critic and editor. Perhaps the most famous and respected drama critic in the first half of the twentieth century, Nathan proved a nemesis to TW, calling *The Rose Tattoo* TW's "latest peep show," and cheerfully telling the press that *The Glass Menagerie* was actually written by Nathan's friend, the play's director, Eddie Dowling.

23. TLS—1

[*March 1944*] [*New York*]

DEAR JAY:

The old fish-peddler Liebling woke me up early this morning on the phone saying he had a letter to read me. I was very indifferent as I supposed it was from the scooter people in California or something equally fatuous but disagreeable. Consequently I was a little thunderstruck when it turned out to be from Walter Damrosch of your estimable society informing me that they were going to present me on May 19th with a thousand dollars, at a suitable ceremony which they hoped I would attend by person or proxy. Words are a bit inexpressive about such feelings but I will venture to say that I am happy about it. And that I am grateful to you for your part in this dispensation. I am quite certain it was more your recommendation than whatever it was Liebling saw fit to send them. Audrey was out of town and while Liebling is a smart Broadway character, somewhat nicer than most, I doubt that his selections were very strategic. I think I've already told you what I will do. I will go to Mexico!—I have been here about a week, making the dizzy rounds of theatre people and shows but somehow feeling totally unoccupied, while in Saint Louis, where I saw no one and only went swimming, I felt horribly busy. Mother writes me that she has mailed *Battle* to you, I left it for her to do as she is one of those conscientious Puritans who never leave undone what ought to be done. They may drive you crazy but they are never lazy. I have written Peggy Webster. She is about to succeed Le Gallienne in the leading part of *The Cherry Orchard* so she may beg off. To write about what happened in Boston is a frightening assignment but I will undertake it. It will be hard without stepping on sensitive toes. The whole thing was an explosion of which nobody got a very lucid impression, least of all myself. I will try to describe the chaos, ambiguously enough to avoid offense. All of us who came with the Company meant well: it was Boston that was dirty.

Don and I are courting backers for *You Touched Me!* It may go on late this spring or early Fall. Sometime when I have a play that I am absolutely sure of, I will offer you a piece of it. But not this one. It will not offend anybody but I can't see making anybody a Croesus.

After the turmoil of this week and the next I may get back to work but don't expect I'll really do much till I retire on my thousand to some quieter precincts. Robeson as *Othello* made my blood run cold. Christ, what majesty!—All the rest here is piffle. Even *The Cherry Orchard* seems a little wilted. But life—life is good and exciting!

Tennessee

« • »

Mother: Edwina Estelle Dakin Williams (1884–1980).

Liebling: William Liebling, Audrey Wood's husband and cofounder of their literary agency, Liebling and Associates, later called the Ashley-Famous agency, and now International Creative Management (ICM).

Walter Damrosch: President of the American Academy and Institute of Arts and Letters from 1940 to 1948.

Le Gallienne: Eva Le Gallienne (1899–1991), American stage actress.

Robeson: Paul Robeson (1898–1976), American actor, poet, singer, and civil rights activist. Robeson played Othello on Broadway, opposite Uta Hagen as Desdemona, in 1943 to 1944.

24. TLS—2

4/2/44 [New York]

DEAR JAY:

I hesitate to send you this, because while the story of this play is interesting to me as a dreadful crisis in my life, I am afraid it will seem like much ado about nothing—especially the way I have written it up—to other people. You must judge about that, and don't print it if you think it will give a disgusting impression of vanity or martyrdom.

I saw poor Peggy Webster last night. I say 'poor' because she has just replaced Eva Le Gallienne in *Cherry Orchard* and is having, I think, a ghastly time with it. She has none of Le Gallienne's delicacy and charm on the stage. In fact, she has gotten heavier, her body and movements are rather masculine, she looked almost like a Princeton Triangle ingénue, and the loose flowing garments that Le G. wore so bewitchingly appeared on her incongruously like maternity garments. You see how mean I can be? For an essentially kind person? The only justice is that the part should have been given to a deserving actress who needed it—Peggy is a director. Well, we were both a bit embarrassed as this was the first meeting since *Battle*. Peggy seems willing to write a preface but cannot say <u>when</u>. I said, knowing your printers' dilatory habits, eventually might be soon enough. However if necessary I think she could be prodded into fairly early action. Since this crap of mine is so wordy, you may want only a short piece from her. Peggy loathes failure and her work on *Battle* was. What a failure! About the mag's name—as you say, names don't matter much.

The difficulty with *Pharos* is that phonetically it has antique sound of Egypt, a bit musty sounding, you know. Otherwise it is excellent. But Margaret is such a lovely name. Why not call it *Margaret's Magazine*? Or *Nerves*? No—that's awful! I give up.

But try and find something with a green quality if you can. I am beginning to hate N.Y. again already—I spent night before last in the Federal Pen. I was picked up crossing the park after midnight and didn't have my registration card on me. In fact I didn't possess one. Was turned over to the FBI and incarcerated for the night. I am now with a subpoena while my cards are being sent from Clayton. The night in the Pen was fearful! But I have made some good friends at the FBI—they are really very gentlemanly. New York is sweltering with suspicion and prurience and petty malice. It is sad to see one's friends caught here and becoming infected with it, especially when they came here as such fresh and sensitive individuals. I want to get them all out! The publicity woman for the "Academy" asked for some pictures: George Platt Lynes offered to make some free of charge. If they turn out good—he is a wonderful though somewhat chi-chi photographer—I will send you one for *Margaret's Mag* [*Pharos*].

The Acad. ceremony is May 19th! After that I will be at liberty. I will leave here and get back to real work.

God Bless you!

Tennessee

« • »

the story of this play: "A History with Parenthesis," his introduction to *Battle of Angels*.

George Platt Lynes: (1907–1955), American photographer. Lynes took publicity shots of TW (mentioned in the following letter), dressed in a costume of ragged clothes as a humorous depiction of the "starving artist."

25. TLS—1

4/14/44 [New York]

DEAR JAY:

These proofs [*FYAP* (1944)] forwarded from Saint Louis where they had been intercepted by my mother and enclosed with a little disapproving note suggesting the substitution of some verses I wrote in high school.

All is correct except for the poem "Dissection." This poem is the first draft of one I sent you later called "Cortege." I sent you the only copy of that correction—but I have tried here to reproduce it from memory in case you don't have the original. Did you like the <u>first</u> draft better? I don't at all. It seems altogether weaker, especially in the conclusion, as it does not establish the image of the cortege as the succession of betrayals. Read this over and see if you don't agree, that it is better.

Charles Henri called me yesterday. Said you had told him I had written you a long, enthusiastic letter about his verse! He wanted a copy of it, and said he would ask you for it. What will you do about that? Thought I should warn you as I am afraid there is really no such letter, though I made out like there was. (Over the phone.) He is completely "nigger."

A letter from Frieda Lawrence. She expects to get rich off the first Lady Chatterley.

Once again I am tied down to *You Touched Me!* and the producer here wants another re-writing. But she is very intelligent—Mary Hunter—and we are doing good with it. The money is not all raised but she thinks it will be. Having a thousand bucks coming next month, I feel an Olympian indifference.—I have seen and talked to Webster about the preface and she has lately written me that she wants to know <u>when</u> it is expected—signifies her willingness to do it. Let me know when and I will keep after her about it. She may write something stupid, however, for her object will be defense of her failure with it mostly.

I am going to send you glossy print of photo George P. Lynes took for award publicity. He did it free so insisted on freakish poses or out-fits.

I have a dreadful cold and will be a wreck by the time I get away from New York, which is what I am living for. Oh—by the way—I want you to be my literary executor. It would be dreadful if all my papers fell into the family's possession as they would burn the best because of impropriety. This letter authorizes you to seize all Mss. if I should kick the bucket before I could get them to you.—Not that that seems particularly imminent at the moment.

Tennessee

« • »

"*nigger*": See reference to Charles Henri Ford's "Negro charm" in letter of JL to TW of July 1944. TW considered these terms compliments to the white Ford.

Mary Hunter: American stage director and producer. Though Hunter went through many negotiations, she ultimately did not produce *You Touched Me!* on Broadway.

26. TLS—1

June 9, 1944 [New York]

DEAR JAY:

I have been out of touch with the world the past few weeks, on Fire Island, a narrow strip of dunes between the Atlantic and the Sound, getting in some good swimming and less interrupted work on plays. But the "season" commenced and the atmosphere of the place became even more hectic than Manhattan. So I am back here to select another retreat. I can't go too far away this summer as money is being raised on *You Touched Me!* and I am supposed to stand by for maybe rehearsals in August. I wonder if it is worth it, but there is more than myself to consider. I will probably go up on the Cape, till the situation is clearer.

I didn't know the magazine was coming out so soon. Charles Henri says the new issue of *View* will carry an announcement of it. Do you still want something from Webster? Personally I don't care whether she does it or not. I can imagine the apologetic tone that she would take, but I think if Margaret, your wife, feels it would increase the attention or sales, which it very well might, the article could be obtained from her. She said she was glad to do it, provided it wasn't expected too quickly. Now that *Cherry Orchard* has closed (she was playing Le Gallienne's role) I think she might be willing to undertake it right away. Write or wire me if you want it and I will approach her again.—I was worried about my preface. I was afraid it might have an hysterical, persecuted effect. If there are any touches of that, please cut them out. I hate such things. I did once have a competent prose style, but since writing plays it has gone to seed. It is now difficult for me to write straight prose, for I am morbidly conscious of rhythm. Everything has to have a regular beat, or it seems awkward to me. How does Eliot get his wonderful, free rhythms? It is the only thing I like very much about the new *Quartet*, the marvelous rhythmic freedom. I have got a copy to study the sound-effects, but they are so subtle you can hardly analyze them.—I am having a few short dramatic pieces typed up for distribution and will get you a copy. They are rather eclectic. One of them has a nice modern grotesqueness, a fiendish portrait of a fat southern matron. The general title is *The Little God* which I don't like—perhaps you can suggest one better.

Yep, I got the one grand and sent it home to Mother to put in the bank. I am still living on my Hollywood savings—think they will get me through the summer, then I'll have the award intact for flight to Mexico, if I'm not detained by "YTM"—which is written over and improved considerably. The end is much more active and lighter.

All the money raised is contingent upon our ability to sign up some name stars—which is a good thing. It requires names to put it over, and damned good acting. Margo is a mad girl, but adorable—She loves you. We all do!—

Tennessee

P.S. I told Charles Henri you had broken your wrist and his only comment was he hoped it didn't prevent you from signing checks! Typical *View* attitude. *Dance Index* is more sympathetic. *View*'s new issue is shocking! I think they are in pursuit of another "banning."

≪ • ≫

View: A literary magazine published from 1940 to 1947 by Charles Henri Ford and Parker Tyler.

Eliot: T. S. Eliot (1888–1965), American-born English poet. TW is referring to Eliot's *Four Quartets* (written between 1935 and 1941), published as a set in New York in 1943.

Dance Index: Donald Windham and TW both spent time working in the *Dance Index* office. This letter was written on *Dance Index* stationery.

27. TL—1

[June 1944] [Norfolk]

DEAR TENN—

2 wks mors of the damn splint so here is a short
one with the left

poem is nice ill try to place it in accent

george's photo very fine will frame it up
thanks a million we can use it in some
book some time

i think a little note from webster would be
fine just a few words for the use of the
name your own preface much better than
anything she could write.

the play is still being set up very slow
local printer

therell be some money coming for that so
let me know when you need it—$100 anyway

and where are the short stories?

be good to yourself

J

[This letter is reproduced here as typed by JL with one hand.]

28. TLS—2

[July 1944] [Provincetown, Massachusetts]

DEAR JAY:

Just between us, the play [*Battle of Angels*] was never copyrighted. I always put copyrighted on my Ms. though they never really are. I think it will suffice to follow that procedure—just put "protected by copyright" and lightning won't strike us for lying—I hope.

This is a very unreal sort of summer. Do you ever have periods like that in which reality seems to have entirely withdrawn? It is not necessarily unpleasant—it creates irresponsibility, more vagueness than usual—a new sense of proportions or the lack of them. Usually it only occurs in summer and on the ocean.—It happened to me once in California—Laguna Beach just before the war. I called it *Nave Nave Mahana*, after the painting by Gauguin. It doesn't interfere with work—I have done a good deal on a long play but it makes your work seem more smokey more cloudy than it even is. And you are impatient with words. They seem the most unreal things a man can work with. Sometimes a storm blows up and enormous birds rush over—that's what you are waiting and enduring for. In between times everything is unbelievably pink shrimpish. What comes, what is coming?

I have just returned from the beach and a fish supper—maybe I am writing in a sun-stroke.

I am still living here on my Hollywood savings, the one grand intact—I'm saving it for a probable flight to Mexico in the Fall. I may need the money for the play late this summer. When I do, I'll wire you for it.

Saw Charles and Chilly Death and Charles' mother—one day they drove up the Cape and took me to lunch. First time I ever saw a thoroughly intimidated southern matron. Chilly was on his high horse, complained so bitterly about lunch that Madame paid the entire bill to conciliate him.—This was the only high society incident of my season and I greedily absorbed enough of it to last me a while. Yes, I find the same charm you do in Charles—a negro charm I call it. I think he is rather like a piss-elegant mulatto, which is really quite charming. Since there is a heart underneath.

As for printing Charles' book, of course that is entirely a matter of your own discretion and choice. I find his work phenomenally uneven. I have read things which were right out of heaven and others—there is [a] Broadway term "from Dixie" which means real corn. However I think he is an important literary figure mostly through his magazine. If only he were not so biased against anything non-magical, *View*—because of its exploratory ardor—might be the only exciting magazine in America. (*Pharos* being still at the mercy of the Mormons.) I have great hopes for resurgence of experimental writing and journals and theatre after the war—*View* might have a prodigious future, if only Charles could achieve a more comprehensive taste and less egocentricity—I liked the last issue. If I go to Mexico, how about letting me dig up some Mexican material for an issue of *Pharos* if you can get it past the Mormons? Would I have to know Spanish?—I don't. But plan to study it.

I am planning to stay here through September, except, for a week of library research at Cambridge (Harvard)—It is too expensive to return to New York before I am ready to leave the East Coast. Perhaps you will come up on the Cape? I will have a cabin and could put you up here. Practically the entire lunatic fringe of Manhattan are among the summer colonists at P-town.

10

« • »

a long play: *The Gentleman Caller*, which TW later titled *The Glass Menagerie*.

negro charm: See note to TW letter to JL of 4/14/44.

at the mercy of the Mormons: The first issue of *Pharos* was delayed for almost a year because the Mormon printers in Utah felt that *Battle of Angels* was a "sinful text."

29. TLS—2

[summer 1944] [Provincetown]

DEAR JAY:

Got your letter and Webster's in the same post. <She wanted to know what I had written so she would not "repeat or contradict it." She says she will write something short.> I'm writing her to send her piece directly to you.

[. . .]

You ought to hear from Webster pretty quickly. Her address is Bay Head, Martha's Vineyard, Mass. Wire her if she is not meeting the dead-line. She is a hard-working woman, that is what I like about her.

Sorry this is so messy. The fog has gotten in the machine and it seems to be dissolving. I am delighted with the new item for my gallery!

Have been reading Henry Miller's *Tropics*—How can a thing be so brilliant and still not good?

> Tennessee
> My address is:
> Captain Jack's Wharf,
> Provincetown, Mass.

« • »

Henry Miller's Tropics: In a 1938 *Time* magazine interview, JL announced that he would publish *Tropic of Cancer*, first published in Paris by Obelisk Press in 1934 but widely considered obscene. This caused JL's aunt, Leila Laughlin Carlisle, to threaten to withdraw her periodic (but crucial) financial support of ND. *Tropic of Cancer* was finally published in the United States in 1961 by Barney Rosset's Grove Press.

Captain Jack's Wharf: Where TW lived in Provincetown during his first summer there in 1940 and later when he was working on *A Streetcar Named Desire* in 1947.

30. TLS—1

[summer 1944] [New York]

DEAR JAY:

I figured you weren't in a hurry for the play proofs [*Battle of Angels*] so I left them at your town office saying you would pick them up when you returned here. I will phone them today that you want them sent to Cambridge.

[. . .]

Have met an editor of *Town & Country* who thinks he might could use one of my stories so I dug them all out of the trunk for him last week and read them aloud. They are all so sloppy, but some have very interesting material and exciting passages. Trouble is characters are usually up to something nobody does out[side] of pirated or smuggled editions. Though it is all such sweeter and cleaner than Miller! I figure it would take two months' concentrated effort to get, say, eight of them into printable shape, but I may do that alternately with the poetic play I'm on. If only print seemed as alive to me as stage. Don't you worry over the dull look of most print?—everyone who has seen the new play *The Glass Menagerie* here likes it, though I doubt it is for the commercial theatre. Haven't gotten Margo's report on it yet. As the title suggests—it is about the delicate feelings in life—that got broken.

The weather is nice, my nerves are better, but I am still reluctant to go back to Clayton and work.

Tenn

≪ • ≫

The Glass Menagerie: The first mention to JL, by name, of the play that launched TW's Broadway career.

SECTION III

PF: When did you first see *Menagerie*, when it came to New York?

JL: No, he invited me to come to Chicago for the opening and that marvelous actress, what was her name? I don't remember.

PF: Laurette Taylor?

JL: Laurette Taylor. She was really something, and the man, too, the man was good. They put the play across in Chicago. It was a tremendous performance on both parts and that awakened the Chicago critics, and they wrote about Tennessee. I went out there. I don't know where we stayed or who else we saw, but it had an overwhelming theatrical power this play.

* * *

PF: In 1940 Tennessee had signed some agreement with Bennett Cerf?

JL: There was a contract.

PF: He knew there was a contract, and he knew there wasn't anything he could do about it, but he felt bad and he wrote to her [Tennessee's agent, Audrey Wood] and told her that

"Laughlin was to do everything else" and then there's a lovely paragraph where he gives his rationale—that he so much approved of your enterprise of encouraging young poets and he wanted to be involved in that and that Audrey had to understand that if sometimes this worked against his material advantage, that's the way he wanted it.

JL: That's good, that's true. He had a sense of helping young writers one way or another get published, maybe get some money, a deep sense of that, which came, I think, from his own insecurity. When he was in St. Louis he practically had no money.

≪ • ≫

Chicago for the opening: The out-of-town tryout for *The Glass Menagerie* opened at Chicago's Civic Theatre on December 26, 1944, in an icy gale.

Laurette Taylor: (1884–1946), American actress. Considered one of the greatest actresses of her generation, Taylor had been a star on Broadway since 1908. Her most famous portrayal was the ingénue in *Peg o' My Heart*, a sentimental Irish comedy written by her husband, Hartley J. Manners. After Manners's death in 1928, Taylor turned to alcohol, and her drinking was so severe she was often unemployable. After Eddie Dowling coaxed Taylor out of retirement, her portrayal of Amanda Wingfield went on to be considered the greatest Broadway performance of the twentieth century. Taylor's legendary performance as Amanda helped establish TW's reputation.

the man, too: Eddie Dowling [Joseph Nelson Goucher] (1889–1972), American actor, director, and producer. Codirector of *The Glass Menagerie*, Eddie Dowling, who also played Tom Wingfield, was a showman who bought plays as vehicles he could direct, star in, tour with, and on which he could make a profit.

the Chicago critics: Claudia Cassidy and Ashton Stevens championed the play and helped it stay open during a prolonged blizzard, essentially guaranteeing its transfer to Broadway.

Bennett Cerf: (1898–1971), American humorist and editor. In 1940, without telling his agent Audrey Wood, TW signed a contract with Cerf and Random House, which stipulated their option on the next work by TW at their discretion. Along with the contract TW was paid an advance of one hundred dollars. In the meantime TW committed himself to ND, promising that all of his writing would thereafter be published by JL. The conflict was resolved and Random House ended up printing the first edition of *The Glass Menagerie* in 1945. However, Random House would soon let the play go out of print; it was reissued by ND in the New Classics series in 1949 with an iconic cover by Alvin Lustig. The play has been published by ND ever since.

31. TLS—2

Nov. 1, 1944 [Clayton]

DEAR JAY:

It is quiet and sunny here. Fall just getting started, big rooms full of yellow light, sounds of women puttering about, all very reassuring and agreeable in this appalling world. Just before I left N.Y. I saw a picture *The Rainbow* (Soviet film, at the Stanley in Times Square). Such a powerful study of hatred and horror! I suppose this is an authentic picture of what is happening outside "the belvedere" and I felt quite shaken by it. If you have a strong stomach, see it! It is really an apology for hatred. With such savagery unleashed in the world I don't see how there can be peace again for hundreds of years. Those are the things one should be writing about. How to reconcile my world, or the world of—say—Charles Henri Ford—tender or private emotions or rare, esoteric fancies with what's going on outside. Micro with macro cosmos! Should one even try? Or blandly assume, as I suppose Charles does, that we are the really important ones with the significant concerns?—Have you read Parker Tyler's dissertation in the new *View*? There is where a superlative is reached in esthetic distance!—It is a good issue, incidentally, especially the "folk" pieces.

The work on *Menagerie* may start in two or three weeks. Just before I left town I had a frightening conversation with Dowling. He proposed that a happy ending be flashed on the screen at the close of the play—Laura with the brace removed ("orthopedics do such wonderful things!") and the gentleman caller standing again at the door!—That is the sort of thing the most intelligent producers spring on you!—He said it was just a suggestion, not a demand, "There is so much unhappiness in the world, Etc." that the audience shouldn't go away feeling depressed.—I am working out at the "Y" so I will go back in condition to fight off all such assaults. Fortunately Margo will be there. She will arrive in N.Y. in a few days.

Great distress here as we have received a 15 page letter from my brother in the Burma jungle announcing and justifying his conversion to Roman Catholicism. My grandfather, the Episcopal minister, has packed up and returned South. Wouldn't you think this generation would at last and at least be done with theological dogma? No!— my kid brother writes a long dissertation from the fighting front on "Transubstantiation" (accepts it literally) and "The Infallibility of the Pope" which he says has not been disproven!—Believe it or not, I am the bright one of the family!

Maybe I will get back before you leave—if Dowling wires me.

Hope you get back at [Delmore] Schwartz and all writers who bore each other. Don't let them do all the talking!

I talked to a woman who works for Vanguard at a cocktail party. She says you don't circularize the book-dealers enough. How about that?

I have to write a critique for new *View*. Think it will be on Lorca and Ramon Naya and "The Plastic Theatre."—Not on Shapiro. I could think of nothing pleasant to say about his *V-Letter* so I just won't do it.

Tennessee

« • »

my grandfather: The Reverend Walter E. Dakin (1857–1955), TW's maternal grandfather on whom the character of Nonno in *The Night of the Iguana* (1961) is based.

Lorca: Federico García Lorca (1898–1936), Spanish poet and playwright. ND published Lorca's *Selected Poems*, *Five Plays*, and several other titles.

Ramon Naya: Playwright and author of *Mexican Mural*, which was the first-prize winner in the 1939 Group Theatre play contest.

The Plastic Theatre: TW frequently used this term to help describe his ideas about how a playwright's responsibility goes beyond the words to engage the nonliterary elements of theater—music, sound, light, settings, dance—strategically within the physical environment to reach those moments that create meaning not found solely in the text of a play. In *The Glass Menagerie* TW incorporated many of his ideas about "The Plastic Theatre."

Shapiro [. . .] his V-Letter: Karl [Jay] Shapiro (1913–2000), American poet, critic, and editor. *Victory Letter* is a book of poems by Shapiro.

32. TLS—1

Dec. 15, 1944 [Clayton]

Dear Jay:

We catch the train tomorrow afternoon for Chicago and probably the most hectic week of my far from pacific career, so I am snatching these few relatively tranquil moments to say hello.—When I think of you on your mountain, among the everlasting snows,—well, it is like Kilimanjaro from the pestilential jungle! Stay on your mountain, boy!

I won't try to tell you how things are going. It's just in the lap of the gods. Too many incalculables—the brain-cells of an old woman, a cold-blooded banker's reckoning of chances, enigmas of audience and critics. It is really a glass menagerie that we are taking on the road and God only knows how much of it will survive the journey.

I have one great thing to be thankful for—and that is Margo, in whose apartment I'm writing. Without her in on this adventure I wouldn't have gotten this far along with it—she has been heroic.

Have just said goodbye to Audrey—she mentioned that she is getting in touch with your man Brecht and seems highly interested in him.

Anything new on *Battle*? Incidentally, Dowling is enthusiastic over it and has sent a copy to Tallulah Bankhead. <u>IF</u> the menagerie is successful, I think he would try to interest her in an early production of it and I think she'd be damned good as Myra. Maybe a little short on tenderness but plenty of richness and drama. If this materialized I would try another version of the script—eliminating two features that have always troubled me, the vague "book" and the prologue-epilogue. I hope you are making that suggested division in Act Two—that would help.

I have seen only one review of the poems [*FYAP* (1944)], in the *Herald Tribune*. It was pretty condescending but not really evil—as the *View* would have been. But I think *View* has killed their review—for lack of space in the Christmas issue.

Regardless of how things turn out on the present venture, I will be grateful for a chance to retire from the world and get back some composure. It has been months since my heart beat quietly!

Yours ever,
Tennessee

<Best to Margaret.
　　We open Dec. 26>

« • »

Brecht: Bertolt Brecht (1898–1956), German playwright and exile. ND published Brecht's *Private Life of the Master Race*, translated by Eric Bentley, in 1944. According to Bentley, JL was interested in taking on Brecht as an author and, though the playwright initially showed interest, eventually Brecht did not to respond to communications from JL or Audrey Wood.

we open Dec. 26: See note to Section III.

33. ALS—2

December 28, 1944 [Chicago]

Dear Jay—

Bob Carter, who wrote this review of the *Poets*, is a poet himself and a student at Chicago University. He has interviewed me in connection with the *Menagerie*. We got to talking about Rimbaud which I think he should especially read—*A Season in Hell*—I only know one line Bob has written but I think it is very lovely. "She gives him pleasure in the time it takes to break a bottle!"

Well, anyhow—

If you have an extra copy of any Rimbaud—wish you would send it to him.

The play went well in Chicago—three raves, two mixed reviews—but the best critics were on our side. And the audiences have been warm, however box office is bad and we'll probably move to New York soon.

Hope Bob's review pleases you as it did me—It was written <u>before</u> we met.

Best,

Tennessee

≪ • ≫

Bob Carter: Robert Carter (1927–2010) became a Jesuit priest, later founded the gay Catholic organization Dignity, and was cofounder of the National Gay and Lesbian Task Force.

Chicago University: University of Chicago.

the best critics: Ashton Stevens and Claudia Cassidy.

34. TLS—1

[received February 6, 1945] [Chicago]

DEAR JAY:

I am mailing at the same time a letter to Audrey with a signed copy of your contract. She has to see it first, but I have urged her strongly as possible to clear me of Random House. I am sure her concern will be primarily your ability to get the book out on time and distributed widely enough—there was such a long delay about the *Five Poets* due to your troubles with printers that I hope you can give us some assurance of a dependable date on this one. That is, while the play is still hot! On top of my strong letter and that assurance, I feel sure that Audrey will extricate me from Cerf. I need not tell you again how happy that would make me for I would like all my shy intrusions on the world of letters to be thru N.D.

Thanks for the poems. They are very simple and direct and in the case of "Avalanche"—particularly forceful. I liked that one best—perhaps the "implacable girl" disturbed the misogynist in me but I found directly relating to her less moving than the mountain ones.

There is an almost terrifying candor here and there—more than I would dare. But which I respect highly. I think you have a story to tell that is bigger than you can put into short-lined lyrics. How about a short novel with the lodge as a background and the girl and the avalanche and the same but expanded frankness?

Tennessee

« • »

"Avalanche": This poem was published in the volume of JL's poetry, *Some Natural Things* (ND 1945).

35. TLS—2

Sunday [March 11, 1945] [Clayton]

JAY!

How silly of you to think I was letting you down about the *Menagerie* publication!

I didn't answer your letter because Audrey wrote me that "everything was settled" and you were putting the book in print, that is, getting the type set up in preparation—so I assumed it was all ironed out. She did say, however, that Cerf had turned down your hundred and that nothing could be done till after the opening—that is, definitely.

I know I should have gotten the final script off to you by now. I enquired a couple of times for a copy but the script girl put me off saying there was only one which she needed—I have none at all. And Dowling's drunk scene still only exists in his voice-box: he destroys paper copies for some reason. Can Audrey give you a script or must you get one through me, and how soon? I guess we must get legally disentangled from Cerf before actual printing can start, but I have every intention—if your printers can give you a reasonable date on it—of taking any action necessary to get clear of Cerf. I want no part of any commercial publishers now or ever! Not as long as I am eating without them. Once you get tied up with one you become, for better or worse, a professional writer which shouldn't happen to anyone!

I have let other things slip lately because I've been amusing and torturing myself with a group of somewhat surrealist poems, loosely connected under the general title of "Electric Avenue," mostly with a southern background: might fit in with "The Couple" which I sent you last Spring. My main aggravation is inability to break from the five beat line or slight variations of it: it has become a fixation, monotonous and inescapable. In this connection I have been studying St. Jean Perse as he has the most flexible cadences of all. Crane is not really good at cadence, though he is powerful enough not to need it. He usually has either five beats or machine-gun bursts that only he can get away with. Except in the prose-poems like "Eternity" and "Havana Rose" in which I think he reached his pinnacle of style, or form.

I left *Menagerie* in a state of chassis. Pandemonium back-stage! Intrigues, counter-intrigues, rages, smashed door panes,—quelle menagerie! I was in the dog-house with nearly everybody—with the backer because I wrote a Sunday paper column on business-men and gamblers in the theatre which he took as a personal affront. With Tony and Laurette because Tony has developed an alcoholic persecution-complex and has convinced Laurette of God knows what imaginary offenses of mine! Things are so tense all the time you never know when the whole company will just blow up and vanish! Actors are just not believable—so fantastic! especially the good ones like Laurette and Tony.

I am sorry about the disappointment in N.Y. though I might have told you, for I have been through it continually. A thing like that is so firmly rooted in one time or place, in one set of circumstances, that try as you will you can't breathe life into it the second occasion. But why should you want to, as it is not <u>duration</u> that gives it <u>value</u> really.

The evils of promiscuity are exaggerated. Somebody said it has at least the advantage of making you take more baths. But I think one picks a rose from each person, each of a somewhat different scent and color. Each affair can make some new disclosure, and whether it builds or reduces your range of feeling and understanding depends pretty much on yourself. Of course you pay for it with something—perhaps a cumulative distrust of what is called "real love."

As for hurting people who love you—nothing is less avoidable! I have been home for a week—every night this week some feeling of compulsion sent me out of the house from about five in the afternoon till after two in the morning—any excuse just to get away and escape talk and questioning! Though I knew I was insulting and hurting them. Tonight I came in at ten—the earliest—and was greeted with a flood of tears and reproaches—and how could I explain or excuse myself except by saying—Yes, it's true, I can't stand it here, not even one night out of one week out of one year!

I will be in New York about or on the 24th. If Audrey permits, let's call on Cerf together and have it out with him.—Have been reading the 1942 Annual—many thanks—the stuff by Alvin Levin has brilliant patches—I can't follow Goodman, he is so abstruse or intricately intellectual—I like the W.C.W. play to read but I question its plasticity, its stage values—but I haven't finished it yet.

Returning to Chicago tomorrow evening.

A riverdici [sic]

10

« • »

"everything was settled": refers to a memo from Audrey Wood to TW of February 9, 1945.

nothing could be done till after the opening: *The Glass Menagerie* opened on Broadway, March 31, 1945.

"Electric Avenue": An early title for the poem "Jockeys at Hialeah."

"The Couple": A TW poem published in *Androgyne, Mon Amour* (1977).

St. Jean Perse: Saint-Jean Perse, pseudonym for Alexis Saint-Léger Léger (1887–1975), French poet and Nobel Prize winner for literature in 1960. ND published his *Selected Poems* in 1982.

state of chassis: a reference to a line in Sean O'Casey's *Juno and the Paycock* (1924).

Tony: The actor Tony Ross who played the role of the Gentleman Caller in the original production of *The Glass Menagerie*.

the 1942 Annual: See note following letter from TW to JL of 12/22/42 for the history of the *New Directions in Prose and Poetry* anthologies [*NDPP* hereafter].

Alvin Levin: American novelist published in *NDPP* 7 (1942). A compendium of his writing, *Love Is Like Park Avenue*, was published by ND in 2009.

W.C.W.: William Carlos Williams (1883–1963), American poet and physician. Along with Ezra Pound, WCW was the mainstay of ND when JL first began publishing. JL and WCW had a lifelong friendship, JL finding a mentor in WCW. The play referred to by TW is *Trial Horse No. 1 (Many Loves), an entertainment in three acts and six scenes*, published in *NDPP* 7 (1942) and later WCW's *Many Loves and Other Plays* (1961).

36. TLS—1

[Spring 1945] [New York]

DEAR JAY

Everybody is getting copies of *Battle* but me. Can I have a couple? The two that went to your office were promptly claimed by Audrey and Donnie respectively, I think they came out beautifully, though I haven't had a chance to read through one yet.

I have been so exhausted from all the goings-on here—infinitely worse than Chicago—that I have gotten right down sick. I am going in the hospital tomorrow for a fourth and I trust final eye operation and will rest up and be agreeably out of touch with the world for five days or so—then the critics dinner—which I have to wait for—then complete release and a long, long trip somewhere! Maybe Mexico, maybe New Mexico.

View has just written for passes to the play for their critic. Shall I allow them any? I gave a big cocktail party last week for my mother and Laurette and my 88-year-old grandfather. 112 guests at Sherry's! Cornell and James T. Farrell and lots of other famous people were there.

Send my copies of *Battle* c/o Audrey Wood, 551 Fifth Avenue but mark them for me personally so she won't confiscate those also. I still haven't given a script of the play to Cerf and he is fairly boiling with rage about it. Good for him!

Love,
Tenn.

≪ • ≫

Cornell and James T. Farrell: Katherine Cornell (1893–1974), American stage actress. James T. Farrell (1904–1979), American novelist best known for his *Studs Lonigan* trilogy (1932–1935).

37. TLS—2

June 4, 1945 [Mexico City]

DEAR JAY:

I just flew down here from Dallas where I had been visiting Margo and "The Project," which seems to be going great guns. Margo is hoping to put on *Battle* as the premiere production and with that in mind I've been re-vamping the script, prologue and epilogue are out, also Val's book and fire phobia and the second act congestion relieved by working some of its material into act three. It is too bad we printed the other version already, for this makes a better play of it. However, if it creates a sensation perhaps you can do it again in book form. Incidentally everyone raves about the *Pharos*, it is certainly the loveliest printing job—type and paper and format—that I've ever seen! Several friends of mine are binding it in tooled leather—over the covers—they are so pleased with it. *Town & Country* is going to carry a nice column about it by Mr. Bull, the editor. Of course I dread to see what some avant-garde critics are going to say about the play!

27 Wagons is out in Mayorga's anthology and I think it is my favorite writing of mine so I hope you will get a copy of it. I don't have one to send you. I think it would be the best item for your proposed *Spearhead* if you don't mind re-publishing from Dodd-Mead.

If you want to do *You Touched Me!* write to Audrey or Guthrie McClintic directly for the final draft of that play.

I think he's the only one [who] has the definitive script, including the preface "Homage to Ophelia" which I added to it. Edmund Gwenn and Catherine Willard are definite for the cast and we are likely to get Montgomery Clift for the boy. I have to return to N.Y. in early August for rehearsals. Sorry I had to leave before you arrived for the Brecht show, but Margo had to leave right away and I didn't want to take the long trip by myself. The two of us had a stateroom and kept the porter hopping with drinks and telegrams. I wired friends in

New York: "The Project has blown up and Margo Jones is now vitally interested in the problem of restoration."

You ask for a poem so I am sending you a long thing I started in Chicago and finished in Dallas, an impressionistic recollection of a boarding-house in Miami occupied mostly by Hialeah jockeys. It is too loose and sprawling like "The Couple." Of the latter poem I think perhaps you could submit the last part separately, that is—description of the couple on the street—only passages of it are interesting enough.

Best fun here so far has been a bull-fight yesterday and Friday hearing Chavez conducting Shostakovich's Fifth Symphony which I think gave me the biggest musical thrill of my life.

Not sure where I'm going but will give you an address soon as I am.

Tenn.

≪ • ≫

"The Project": Margo Jones's Federal Theater Project, Houston, Texas.

Mayorga's anthology: Dodd Mead's *Best One-Act Plays* series, edited by Margaret Mayorga. *27 Wagons Full of Cotton* was first published in 1945 in *Best One-Act Plays of 1944*.

Spearhead: *Spearhead: 10 Years' Experimental Writing in America*, edited by James Laughlin (1947).

Guthrie McClintic: American stage director and producer, married to actress Katherine Cornell.

Edmund Gwenn and Catherine Willard: The actors who played the parents in the Broadway production of *You Touched Me!*

Montgomery Clift: (1920–1966), American film star. Clift appeared on Broadway as the young man in *You Touched Me!* and later in Gore Vidal's screen adaptation of TW's *Suddenly Last Summer*.

You ask for a poem: "The Jockeys at Hialeah" was dedicated "for J." when it was published in *In the Winter of Cities* (ND 1956). See the next letter.

Chavez: Carlos Antonio de Padua Chávez y Ramírez (1899–1978), Mexican conductor and composer.

38. TLS—1

Sunday 11/4/45 [New York]

DEAR JAY:

In my ivory tower over an emerald pool I have been immured for weeks, with only nocturnal emissions—I mean excursions—to draw me forth, while banging away at a play.

You wrote me a letter about *You Touched Me!* which I answered but did not mail. The gist of it was that I understood and agreed.

Much has happened and is about to happen. I have received two invitations to read verse, one at Harvard, some Gray Fund, and the other at YMHA Poetry Center, dates respectively being November 14th and December 1st. And I have indicated an acceptance of both. Since talking to the students of Hunter College about the drama I have decided that I can face any audience with anything, and the novelty of the experience is fascinating. So I would like to get together with you and decide upon a program. That is, if you approve of my doing such a thing. I know it is rash! AND presumptuous.

I would like to include some things that haven't appeared in the volume. Here are two new things, one a sort of verbal abstraction but which <u>does</u> have a meaning, the other pretty conventional but musical. And I want to read the long one I brought you from Mexico, "Camino Real." You have the only copy of it. When can I see you? Have supper with me some evening, early, go over the poems and then to the theatre. Are you in town? I don't have your office phone number.

Tenn.

≪ • ≫

Gray Fund: A poetry reading series at Harvard University established by Morris Gray in 1929.

YMHA Poetry Center: The Unterberg Poetry Center at the 92nd Street Y in New York City.

I would like to include: Presumably TW is talking here about his poems that were included in the upcoming ND Annual: *NDPP 9* (1946), "The Jockeys at Hialeah," "Recuerdo," and "Lady, Anemone."

"Camino Real": This poem is a precursor to TW's one-act play *Ten Blocks on the Camino Real* (Dramatists Play Service, 1948) and the full-length play *Camino Real* (1953).

39. ALS—3

Wed. 3:30 AM [November 14, 1945] [Boston]

DEAR JAY—

I'd hoped we'd have more time and less company last night. There's a lot I <u>wanted</u> to talk over with you, mainly my work. I have a childish need, right now, for reassurance about it—more than usual—and that is why I started reading things to you. It was not out of vanity but out of self-distrust. I have become suspicious of myself and what I've been doing—perhaps because of the vast alteration (improvement???) in my manner of living.

<u>You</u> are my literary <u>conscience</u>—the only one outside of myself—so I am over-awed by you and it isn't easy to talk to you.

I am disturbed by your apparently real dissatisfaction with your own life. I would be glad to have you tell me more about it if you think I am able to advise or help in any way.

We should have had 2 or 3 bottles of champagne last night and talked a lot more. So let me know when you have another evening in New York.

Ever,
Tennessee

(The reading has not <u>yet</u> occurred. <u>I</u> have a <u>room</u>—Oliver is prowling the streets.)

≪ • ≫

my manner of living: After years of struggling financially, TW initially found his sudden and much larger income problematic both socially and artistically. See the 1947 essay for the opening of *A Streetcar Named Desire*, "The Catastrophe of Success," later published with *The Glass Menagerie* and in *New Selected Essays: Where I Live*.

Oliver: Professor Oliver Evans, a lifelong cruising and drinking buddy of TW's.

40. ALS—2

[November 1945] [Norfolk]

DEAR TENNESSEE—

I'm off—most unexpectedly to Utah but hope to be back the first week in December and perhaps in a happier frame of mind.

Write another story as good as "One Arm" while I'm gone!

What would you think of a photo of yourself—George P[latt] L[ynes]'s—as frontispiece in 27 *Wagons*? If you approve, will you take a print of it to Bob Lowry at the office, telling him I asked for it and explaining what it's for. Tell him to advise Rittenhouse to print it on glass stock and tip it in facing title. And to have Rau make the cut. The caption should acknowledge GPL if his is used.

If you don't like the idea just forget it.

Auver

Jay

≪ • ≫

I'm off—most unexpectedly: Margaret Keyser Laughlin's father died suddenly in November 1945.

Bob Lowry: Robert Lowry (1919–1994), American fiction writer. Lowry's story "Layover in El Paso" was published in *NDPP 9* (1946) and his novel *Casualty* was also published in 1946 by ND. In late 1945, JL hired Lowry to run production at ND.

Auver: Given that JL is going to Utah for a funeral, and with his mordant frame of mind, it is conceivable that his intended close was *Au ver*, "to the maggot"—a play on his usual "Ever."

41. TLS—2

<Dear Jay, wrote this in N.Y.—just found it among my papers.>

Monday—[November/December 1945]

DEAR JAY:

Your letter meant a lot to me! Immediately I felt a resurgence of vitality and went back to work on the play with such vigor that I worked out a brand new climax and ending which I think makes it definitely a solid thing in my hands.

The work on "One Arm" was so long-drawn-out and tormented by my inability to fuse matter with style and the sensational with the valid, that I was unable to read it myself with a clear perception, but what you say about it—if you are not just being kind—indicates that I have done the second thing at least acceptably. That gives me a wonderful feeling! All of my good things, the few of them, have emerged through this sort of torture going over and over—*Battle, Menagerie,* the few good stories. *You Touched Me!* is an example of one that <u>didn't</u> work out, not with any amount of struggle, though it was (the labor) pretty terrific. But always when I look back on the incredible messiness of original trials I am amazed that it comes out as clean as it does.

In one way the reading went off pretty well. I was not scared of the <Boston reading> audience as I thought I would be and they all said that I read so everybody could hear me. But I made the terrible mistake of trying to read *Dos Ranchos.* It went all to pieces while I was reading it. It began to sound like shit. My voice became loud and expressionless and I kept going on, hoping to find a passage suitable to close with. I really murdered it! As I did not give them a synopsis to begin with or select in advance the parts that could be offered out of context. However I closed with a couple of very bawdy folk-poems which at least put them back in a fairly pleasant humor. I kept looking at poor Mr. Matthiessen on the front row. He was squirming in his seat the whole time and looked much more unhappy than I was, like a school-boy about to suffer some awful punishment. However he was wonderfully nice about it and I like him best of anyone there. Oliver says that he is the most erudite man in America! There was an English faculty tea preceding the reading. I had told Mr. Spencer that it would be necessary for me to have a stiff drink on the platform just to give me moral support, even if I didn't drink it. But he demurred over this, said he didn't think there was [sic] any opaque glasses and if I drank anything on the platform it would have to be something that looked like water, such as straight gin or vodka. All I had with me was a pint of yellow brandy, so I poured a stiff shot of it in my tea at the faculty thing, and I think they were all shocked and apprehensive over it, though very polite. All except a professor named Sterling Lanier. I told him that my middle name was Lanier and that we must be related and he raised his eyebrows and said, "The ramifications of the Lanier family are immense and appalling!"

I was just drunk enough (I was cold sober soon as I got on the platform) to be just as saucy as he was and engaged in a verbal tilt over our tea, in which I, having the stronger tea, did not come out unimpressively.

The next day I made some recordings. They said the records could be offered for public distribution provided they were subsidized so I gave them a cheque for $142 to subsidize them. If they are all sold I will get back royalties amounting almost to that sum. Anyway it seemed to please them a great deal, as it was the first time a poet had done such a thing.

Ought to make them suspicious of the poetry!

See you Wednesday.

Tenn

《 • 》

Mr. Matthiessen: Francis Otto Matthiessen (1902–1950), preeminent American scholar of his generation, best known for his book *American Renaissance: Art and Expression in the Age of Emerson and Whitman.*

Mr. Spencer: Theodore Spencer, a Harvard professor and a lifelong friend of JL's.

Lanier family: TW was a descendent of the nineteenth-century American poet Sidney Lanier (1842–1881).

SECTION IV

PF: Well, at the same time that *Menagerie* is on Broadway, he's sending you the short story of "Night of the Iguana" and other things that didn't come to fruition for years like the first sketches for *Camino Real*.

JL: Yes, he did that. You know he wanted some encouragement of what he was looking ahead to do and I was always glad to give it. I thought it was just wonderful.

PF: You seem to have started making carbons about 1947, so then we have your letters and one of the things that's amusing . . .

JL: He wrote me a terribly funny letter from New Orleans about a lady, asking me to come down and get her off his hands. It was so funny. He had such wit.

≪ • ≫

42. TLS—1

January 4, 1946 [New Orleans]

DEAR JAY:

Do with this what you will!

It is wonderful to be back in the Quarter. And this time with money, which does make a difference.

I am purring with gratitude.

Please add Windham to the list of those to receive Isherwood's book, and bill me for it. He sent me a lovely Japanese wind instrument to hang in my apartment.

I can't tell you my delight in the Henry Miller, first thing of his I've really enjoyed much. It should be read aloud to Kate Smith immediately before and after each broadcast, and she should be compelled to chant passages from it on Sunday evening networks!

I have hardly found a single statement in it I disagree with, that is—pertaining to places and ways of American life.

I am getting a lot of work done here, as the conditions are excellent.

Let me hear from you.

Tenn

<Come down here when you want a change. It is heavenly.>

≪ • ≫

Do with this what you will!: TW had sent JL a blurb for the new Isherwood book, *The Berlin Stories*, which ND published in 1945: "If I were called upon to name, out of this century's English letters, five works nearest to my heart, *Goodbye to Berlin* would be one." Tenn. Williams

the Henry Miller [book]: *The Air-Conditioned Nightmare* (1946).

Kate Smith: Kathryn Elizabeth Smith (1907–1986), American singer with a long radio and television career, called "The Songbird of the South" and famous for her rendering of "God Bless America."

43. TLS—2

Jan 25, 1946 [in transit]

DEAR JAY:

We are passing through Hattiesburg Mississippi en route to Washington D.C. for the "command performance" of *Menagerie*. I had decided not to go up for it as I have so fallen in love with N.O. LA that I was unwilling to part with it for even a weekend, but a young lady friend of mine thought differently and bought my ticket and poured me on the train more or less forcibly. She is along too and that may be why she was firm about it. In fact I am going through quite an experience with this young lady. She is one of these people with a passion for lost causes, is beautiful enough to have anybody she wanted but is apparently attracted only by the line of most resistance. So she came down here from New York and so far the most complete and graphic candor on my part has not convinced her that propinquity will not conquer all. I have always been more or less overlooked by good looking women and once upon a time I sometimes suffered acutely from the fact, so the novelty of the situation makes it all the more impossible to cope with. I dare say you have had infinitely more experience in the matter and at any rate are infinitely more resourceful, so let us exchange fatherly advices. No, I don't want to be "saved," I don't think anyone has ever been happier with his external circumstances than I have learned how to be, and as for my internal circumstances, only I can affect them. So is there anything to be gained from the complicating entrance of a lady? I would like to arrange for you to meet her, for she is a delectable article for anyone on the market. Or are you still engaged by the dark lady of the sonnets in New York? I do hope you will come to New Orleans with her, and if Sylvia—yes, that is her name—is still down here—she threatens to get a job here—something very interesting might develop for you. At any rate you will love New Orleans and it is a grand place to take anybody you are in love with as it rains so much but always clears up after awhile.—Your poem about the girl and her lost husband—like the one about Baudelaire—has a richness of texture that you don't always indulge in. Incidentally I received a letter of lavish praise from Bigelow about your book of poems. I hope I have saved it for you. Bigelow is my brightest friend, too. He is a fascinating personality that I hope you may get to know. A bit like Isherwood's Mr. Norris,—that is, in the mysteries of his origin Etc.—but much deeper and warmer I think. I think he is a bit supernatural, a sort of very wonderful witch!

I got all the books and am delighted with 27 *Wagons*, it is perfectly gotten out. Bob's jacket is a dream! I hope the critics don't make you suffer for it. Some of the characters are a bit peculiar and the author does not come thru as a terribly wholesome individual. I wrote Audrey at once about W.C.W.'s play—I hope she will feel inclined to do something about it. She will if it appears at all marketable.

In spite of what you say about my prose I think it is pretty awkward and I think I can get my best effects, with good directors and actors, on the stage when there is so much besides verbal values to work with—except when there is a subject like "One Arm" that you can't put on the stage as it now exists.—If you have a chance to—see a picture with the awful name of *Fallen Angel*. I think it's extraordinary in some respects. It could almost be happening, the characters come as close to life as any the screen has ever touched and some of the scenes—the psychological suggestions, perhaps undeliberate—are really haunting.

I hope that this new girl will continue to give you interest if not happiness in New York or Vermont.

Ever,
Tenn.

P.S. I am so shy with this girl Sylvia that I suffer acutely when alone in a room with her. Have you ever felt that way with anyone? I have told her I feel that way—she makes it worse by enquiring every few minutes "Am I making you uncomfortable? Do you want me to go out now? Is it all right if I sit here? Don't talk to me unless you want to, Etc." Then she sits there with her brilliant eyes taking in every embarrassed change of expression as if she were conducting some marvelous experiment in a lab so that I don't know where to look, let alone what to say. Exactly like Lillian Gish or at best Harold Lloyd in an old silent film. What are women made of?!

<In a week or so I am going to send you a 30 or 35 p. Ms. of a "work for the Plastic Theatre" with a Mexican background and characters that include Oliver Winemiller, Baron de Charlus, and Don Quixote! I want it produced on a program with *Dos Ranchos*.>

≪ • ≫

"*command performance*": *The Glass Menagerie* was honored by the National Theatre with a command performance on January 27, 1946, in commemoration of the Roosevelt birthday celebration. It was billed as a "Drama Critics Circle Award Command Performance, starring 'Helen MacKellar in America's Greatest Play.'"

the dark lady of the sonnets in New York: Gertrude Huston (1919–1998) was a young war widow whom JL met at a Halloween dance party in 1945. They began an affair that continued intermittently through both of JL's earlier marriages until Gertrude became his third wife on December 5, 1990. Gertrude trained at the Pratt Institute of Art and designed many books for New Directions from the late forties to the late seventies.

Sylvia—yes, that is her name: Sylvia has yet to be identified.

poems about the girl and her lost husband: A reference to "The Summons," which talks of making love under the picture of a husband lost at sea, a picture JL saw in Gertrude Huston's apartment. It would appear in JL's second book of verse, *A Small Book of Poems* (1948).

Bigelow: TW's friend and traveling companion, Paul Bigelow (1905–1988).

Bob's jacket: Robert Lowry created the original jacket design for *27 Wagons Full of Cotton and Other Plays* (ND 1945).

Fallen Angel: A 1945 suspense thriller starring Alice Faye and Dana Andrews.

a 30 to 35 p. Ms.: *The Rich and Eventful Death of Oliver Winemiller* (an early draft of *Camino Real*).

44. TLS—2

April 23, 1946 [Blytheville, Arkansas]

DEAR JAY:

Here is one of two stories which I have recently finished. The other one, called "The Night of the Iguana," I have sent to Audrey to have typed up, requesting that she send you copy of it. I didn't dare send her this one. The other one will shock her but this one would give her fits. I wish you would have this one typed up for me, billing me for the cost or deducting it from my royalties which may be coming in from the one-acts. Return a copy of it to me when I have acquired a mailing address. Right now I am on the road between New Orleans and Saint Louis. I have bought a super-jalopy, a 1937 model Packard convertible roadster. It is still beautiful in spite of its age, the motor is O.K., but all four tires blew out on the road and the radiator developed a leak which I am now having mended while I wait here in the middle of Arkansas, sharing a room with a stranger who works on the levee.

I might have stayed in New Orleans for the summer but trouble with the landlord forced me to give up my lovely apartment and I couldn't find another that was suitable. So I am going home for about a week. Then I will probably drive out West, to Taos for at least a while.

I worked all the while I was in New Orleans but only two or three short items were finished to my satisfaction, or anything near it. Two long plays are still a good way from completion. I hope I'll get one of them done this summer.

I don't know if I thanked you for the reviews you sent me. I know I wrote but may not have mailed the letter. The review in the *Times* was painful but I guess it contained some good pointers. I know the editor of their *Book Review* so I wrote him to enquire why he gave the book to this obviously unfriendly person. He answered that the person came to him highly recommended as a student of poetry and the theatre. Invited me to write an answer but I thought I'd better not. Author's defense of own works is always foolish. And it is not to be argued that my imagination is peopled with peculiar types. Trouble is I don't run into any other types, or if I do I don't seem to have anything to say about them. Bad fix!

Creekmore's publishers sent me his novel in proofs. I was agreeably surprised by his writing. Parts of it have a very powerful simplicity and much more seriousness than his good looks and easy manner would lead you to expect. I liked it all but the ending.

Tennessee

≪ • ≫

this one would give her fits: Probably the story "Desire and the Black Masseur."

Two long plays: Most likely *Summer and Smoke* and *A Streetcar Named Desire*.

this obviously unfriendly person: Weldon Kees unsympathetically reviewed *FYAP* (1944) for the *New York Times*, June 17, 1945.

Creekmore's publishers: Hubert Creekmore (1907–1966), American poet and novelist, worked for JL in the 1940s. *Fingers of the Night* was published in 1946, *The Welcome* (Appleton-Century-Crofts) in 1948.

45. TLS—2

[circa June 1946] [Nantucket, Massachusetts]

DEAR JAY:

It is good to know that you still think of me. I have been having a bad time of it and have felt disassociated from almost everything else. The physical machine in a state of collapse and what may politely be called the spiritual element, crouching in the corner with both hands clapped to its eyes.

I was on my way to New Mexico in an ancient Packard convertible which I bought in New Orleans when I took suddenly and without any warning quite ill. Had to have an emergency operation in Taos, performed by an almost amateur doctor and some nervous Nuns. They thought it was acute appendix but it turned out to be an acute "Meccles diverticulum" which they say is a section of the small intestine. It was cut out and I have been in a prolonged state of shock ever since. The day after the operation one of the good Sisters of the Holy Cross came into my room and advised me to make my peace with the Lord as whatever improvement I showed would only be temporary. Ever since then, and despite the assurance of the doctors, I have been expecting to die, which is something I have never really looked forward to at all. So I gave up my plan of remaining in Taos for the summer and rushed East and took a house on Nantucket—and tried to forget my apprehensions in hard work on a long play. But it is not so easy. I had x-ray pictures taken last week which they told me did not show anything wrong but even if this is quite true, I will probably remain in a state of morbid alertness for a long time. Consequences of having nerves!— "Oh, for a robust conscience and the Viking spirit of life!"

I am interested to hear you are going to Europe. I am planning (if I don't die!) to go to Spain next year. And Constantinople, Greece, and Russia. My Mexican friend, Pancho, is still with me and wants to go to Europe, too. Perhaps we can make a party of it.

I got the typed story. The Masseur does not eat the bones. It is clearly stated that he puts them in a sack which he drops in the lake at the end of the car-line. So the story is all right on the realistic level.

I am sending two more. Have the "Saint" one typed for me, it's the original only copy. The long one gets a bit too preachy toward the end as I started thinking of it as a one-act or two-act play. It would be good theatre if one could get it produced, I think.

Audrey read this long one and showed it to my kid brother, just out of the CBI air-force, when he visited New York while I was out West. She asked him if she ought to show it to anybody and he said "Yes." But right afterwards wrote me a letter saying I was going to come to an end like Edgar Allan Poe, if not worse. On the whole, a sympathetic letter, however. He is a bright kid, though not at all like me. Has a law-degree. I want him to practice law in New York so he could take a hand in my affairs (theatrical). I think they have been bungled. The *Menagerie* has not been sold to the movies and it is slowly dying at the box-office—should have been sold in the very beginning when it was hot! But I am kept in the dark about such matters and never really know how things stand. Not even what I have in the bank!

Have you read Carson McCullers's new book? I think it's superb.

Ever,

Tenn

P.S. I wrote this some time ago. Just discovered I hadn't mailed it. Damned gloomy letter! Ought to tear it up as I am feeling more cheerful now. Carson McCullers is here, visiting me as the result of a brief correspondence. The minute I met her she seemed like one of my oldest and best friends! We are planning to collaborate on a dramatization of her last book soon as I get my present play finished. I think this play will be last effort to write for Broadway. From now on I shall write for a nonexistent art-theatre.

I am enclosing the two "myths" which belong with the one about the "Masseur." Will you have these typed for me, as you did with the other? Either send me a bill for them or deduct the typing cost from royalties. And send me copies. I read them to Carson and she seemed very pleased with them.—Tell Lowry I think his story in *ND 9* is magnificent!

≪ • ≫

"Oh, for a robust conscience and the Viking spirit of life!": The paraphrasing of a sentiment from Henrik Ibsen's *The Master Builder* (1892).

My Mexican friend, Pancho: Amado "Pancho" Rodríguez y González (1920–1993), TW's boyfriend from 1945 to 1947.

CBI air-force: Dakin served in the Army Air Corps (the predecessor of the U.S. Air Force) in the China and Southeast Asian (or India-Burma) Theater, commonly called the China Burma India (CBI) Theater by the Allies. U.S. forces were overseen by General Joseph Stilwell.

Carson McCullers's new book: (1917–1967), American novelist. McCullers's novel *The Member of the Wedding* was published in 1946.

my present play: *Summer and Smoke*.

two "myths": Most likely the short stories "One Arm" and "The Malediction."

"Masseur": The main character in the short story "Desire and the Black Masseur."

46. ALS—4

[after December 7, 1946] [New York]

DEAR JAY—

I have been in the final throes of work on the long play [*Summer and Smoke*] so have neglected correspondence. Tonight, having finished, I am going around the used car lots to pick out a serviceable jalopy that will take me down the Gulf coast for a much-needed rest and change.

Isn't it awful about Laurette? The *Times* gave me 12 hours' notice (before deadline) to do an article on her. I'm afraid it was sloppy. Hard to write anything at all adequate about her.

I will try to send you a few more stories though I am feeling sort of witless, like a land-bird, a cuckoo, that has been blown way out to sea.

I wind up every day at the club which has a natural salt water pool. It revives me. Pancho is with me, working in a department store.

I am so anxious to get a copy of *Huis Clos*, Giraudoux or Camus— Do you have them?

I will ask Audrey to give you a copy of my new play [*Summer and Smoke*]. I mail her the final draft tomorrow. It is intensely romantic— what else I don't know.

Thanks for the three books—Isherwood's is definitely the best. My response to Dylan Thomas is admiring but passive.

Bernarda Alba is the best thing I've had lately.

Ever,

Tennessee

《 • 》

Isn't it awful about Laurette?: Actress Laurette Taylor died during the Broadway run of *The Glass Menagerie* on December 7, 1946.

Huis Clos: The English title of the existentialist play by Jean-Paul Sartre is *No Exit*.

Giraudoux: Jean Giraudoux (1882–1844), French novelist and playwright.

Dylan Thomas: (1914–1953), Welsh poet. ND was the first and remains the only American publisher of Thomas's volumes of poetry and prose.

Bernarda Alba: García Lorca's play *The House of Bernarda Alba*.

47. TLS—2

December 20th [1946] [Alta]

Dear Tenn—

Was so pleased to get your letter, and look forward to seeing the new play when Audrey gets it typed.

Anytime that you have the bunch of stories ready we can get started on that. I sent Audrey all the ones I had—at her request—because she wanted to make copies or something.

About the French books. *Huis Clos* is almost impossible to find. I couldn't find one in Paris or London. In time there is to be an English translation in London.

The Camus and Giraudoux I have but alas they are up at Norfolk and there is nobody up there this winter to dig them out for you. But I'll get them for you when I go up in the Spring.

Have just been down in Los Angeles but it wasn't much fun as I got sulpha poisoning and was sick all the time. Had one nice walk with Christopher [Isherwood] along the sands near where you used to live. He seems fine. Very peaceful and giving off a kind of aura of content. He has mapped out the rough for three big novels, he tells me.

I saw Henry Miller up at Big Sur. His Polish wife is just the most wonderful thing for him in the world. They have a little baby girl and Henry spends all his time dandling—I believe that's the word—her. What a change. Imagine his falling into young love domesticity at his age, and in his career. It's a world.

I have had no luck getting my English one over here and am more or less reconciled to a stolid dull winter trying to get a lot of work done. There's plenty to do if I can just get my mind onto it.

Lots of luck,

J

« • »

His Polish wife: Miller was married to Janina Martha Lepska from 1944 to 1952. The baby girl was their daughter Valentine.

my English one: JL had been in London in late November 1946 and is probably referring to an English girlfriend.

SECTION V

⌒

PF: Tennessee seems to have liked the way the plays looked—the physical look of the plays was very important to him.

JL: Oh, he did, and we always had him see sketches by Alvin [Lustig] or other jacket people and he took a great interest in them. And then there was the event with *Streetcar*—the cover had first a crimson, a strong red background, or was it the other way around, then he scotched that or was it the lavender?

PF: He didn't like the lavender. That's in here.

JL: So we used the stronger color. He was very much interested in that. Well, he was very difficult about establishing a text. He never really knew what the final text was going to be, and he kept on changing it, changing it through rehearsals, and in the end I think we tried to get hold of the director's script or the prompter's script.

≪ • ≫

48. TLS—2

April 9, 1947 [New Orleans]

DEAR JAY:

I was afraid you had decided that I was "Derriere garde" and crossed me off your list.

The heat and dampness are descending on New Orleans and it is like a Turkish bath only not as socially inspiring. So I am wondering whether to go East or West. From the looks of things generally, one would do well to get clear out of the country and stay out for at least the opening stages of "The American Century." I have a feeling that if we survive the next ten years, there will be a great purgation, and this country will once more have the cleanest air on earth, but right now there seems to be an unspeakable foulness. All the people at the controls are opportunists or gangsters. The sweetness of reason died out of our public life with FDR. There doesn't even seem to be a normal intelligence at work in the affairs of the nation. Aren't you frightened by it?!

I have done a lot of work, finished two long plays. One of them, laid in New Orleans, *A Streetcar Called Desire*, turned out quite well. It is a strong play, closer to *Battle of Angels* than any of my other work, but is not what critics call "pleasant." In fact, it is pretty unpleas-ant. But Audrey is enthusiastic about it and we already have a pro-ducer "in the bag." A lady named Irene Selznick (estranged wife of David Selznick and a daughter of Louis B. Mayer). Her chief appar-ent advantage is that she seems to have millions. Audrey says that she also has good taste. Of course I am skeptical. But I am going halfway to meet her. She is flying down to Charleston and I up and we are to have a meeting-conference tomorrow evening at the Hotel Fort Sumter. This is all Audrey's idea. I recognize the danger of working with a Female Moneybags from Hollywood but Audrey claims the woman is "safe" and will give an "all-out" production, which is what the play requires to put it over. Unfortunately we have fallen out with Dowling and the main problem is to find a really strong but fastidious director. (And a good female star.)

The other play [*Summer and Smoke*], which I worked on all last summer, intended for Miss Cornell, was a disappointment and a pretty bad one. In fact, I was so depressed over it that I am surprised that I was able to go on working. Margo doesn't feel that way about it and she is planning to try it out this summer in Dallas. Eventually something might work out of it. The basic conception was very pure and different from anything else I have tried. It was built around an argument over the existence of a "human soul" but that got pretty thoroughly lost in a narrative that somehow slipped to the level of magazine fiction. Or worse.

Donnie [Windham] sent me a group of his short stories and I am happy to report that they are excellent, especially a long one called "The Starless Air" which I want you to read. I think it is the finest portrait I have seen of middle-class southern society. It makes KAP seem "cute." I am to write a foreword before Donnie submits them to publishers. It is a difficult job as the qualities I like in the stories are so difficult to define. Except in such vague and cliche terms as "organic" "pure" "honest" Etc. But then I could never write criticism anyhow.

I am becoming infected with your passion for Kafka, since reading "The Burrow." It is so like our State Department, or any neurotic personality. Except that of course the little animal in the burrow devoured the "smaller fry" for much more sympathetic motives, and his apprehension was more sensible.

[. . .]

Ever,
Tennessee

《 • 》

Irene Selznick: Irene Mayer Selznick (1907–1990) was the Broadway producer who optioned *A Streetcar Named Desire*. The daughter of MGM mogul Louis B. Mayer and the wife of film director David O. Selznick, she was considered a tyro when it came to the theater.

49. TL—2

April 23rd '47 [San Francisco, California]

DEAR TENNESSEE—

It was swell to get your long letter and learn that your writing was moving along well. I wish I could say the same. Several months devoted almost entirely to putting on ski races for handsome but dumb young men, followed by intensive weeks in seclusion down here catching up on correspondence has not done much to get me in the way of composing. Have had to abandon the idea of having a preface in *Spearhead* because it all sounds like a pedantic joke.

But there is a sort of satisfaction, of a kind that is much less perilous than "risking" a story, in sitting here in this pleasant city, with a fine view out over the slums and shipyards, not to mention the bridge, from which a veteran just leaped and survived, not to mention the man in the gas chamber who wishes to contribute his body to science for the revivification experiments . . . well I was saying: to turn out a lot of letters to a lot of people at least keeps you pleasantly stultified. This is still a good city. Hills are a fine thing—look at Rome—and it gets even better when to these you can add water and fogs. Also Chinese food. And Rexroth, one of the unique minds alive today, a constant reservoir of information on every subject, and very funny stories, which grow with the years, and each year you hear it more has been added till it takes on the quality of myth.

I enclose a copy of my letters to Audrey about the stories. I want to get started on them soon. We still lack scripts of a couple of them that you list in your list, and I hope she can find these. Of the bunch that she sent me that you didn't list I find that I like one called "Sand"—about an old couple—and one called "The Vine"—about an ageing actor out of work—rather better than I like "Silently, Invisibly"—about the wife, pregnant, whose actor husband is leaving her. What do you think? Let me know.

Yes, I agree with you that the world is going to hell in a hack, but fast, and we'll probably be at the Russians' throats any day now, or at least protecting Iguanas from the Red Menace. I have gotten to the point of not thinking about it, because what can you do about it? Ten years ago I used to believe Social Credit would save the situation, and I still think it would help a lot, but I never was able to convert anyone then, and they're more skeptical now, so . . . let's go to Tibet!

I'm very anxious to see your new play—*Streetcar.* Can you loan me a copy of the script? I'll get it right back. I'd also like to see Donnie's stories. I'll send him a card to that effect, but I'm vague about his address, unless Lincoln will forward to him, so maybe you might mention it if you write him.

I haven't turned up anything new that seems much good. I guess most all of the young writers are just hell bent for success, copying books that have "succeeded" rather than trying to get down what their souls whisper to them in the black of their despair. Mostly I've been re-reading old books that we are reprinting—Celine, who is better than Miller, and Faulkner's *Light in August*, which moved me very much in spite of one or two little patches that are rather pompous in their attempt to be "poetic" or "meaningful"—still and all he can write, and he makes you believe that what he tells is so. I liked Paul Bowles's stories that were published in magazines this winter, and I like J. F. Powers' stories.

I'll probably be here in San Francisco for several more weeks. It's a good atmosphere for me, perhaps as New Orleans is for you. I get away from interference here, and from that hypocritical home atmosphere which pretends to respect my ND work but actually hates it and is always trying to undermine it and get my attention to other things.

In October I'm moving back to Europe for a good long time. It becomes essential—because of the fantastic inflation of printing costs here—to do two things: find sources of cheap printing in Italy, and build up English and continental sales. I'll keep on the main sales office in New York—and they are running pretty efficiently now—but try to print over there, shipping the books here and to England and Paris for sale. A complicated maneuver, but it will be nice, as you say, to be away from this country during its period of moral goiter.

You better come over sometime. I think you would like Rapallo a great deal. Dylan Thomas is there now, no doubt a waterfront character all right. But Pound got the inhabitants used to poets and they probably won't toss him in the buggyhouse, but just leave him lay in the street for the sun to waken.

Best wishes,

[James Laughlin]

≪ • ≫

Rexroth: Kenneth Rexroth (1905–1982), American poet and translator. ND first published Rexroth's poems in 1940 and continues to publish his works.

Social Credit: A philosophy of economic distribution developed by British engineer C. H. Douglas (1879–1952) and championed by Ezra Pound.

Celine: Louis Ferdinand Céline (1894–1961), French novelist and physician. Céline's novel *Journey to the End of Night* has been published by ND since 1949.

Paul Bowles: (1910–1999), American novelist, husband of American novelist Jane Bowles (1917–1973). Bowles's first novel, *The Sheltering Sky*, was published by ND in 1949. The Bowleses became expatriates, settling in Morocco and Tangier where they regularly hosted American writers.

J. F. Powers: (1917–1999), American novelist.

complicated maneuver: With the exception of several limited editions published in Italy, JL's scheme was never realized.

50. TLS—1

[late May 1947] [New York]

DEAR JAY:

I'm writing half a dozen letters this evening so I got to be brief. We're leaving early tomorrow morning for Provincetown where I hope I can spend a relatively peaceful summer. I shall have to go to Dallas in July to see Margo's production of *Summer and Smoke* and there will be excursions in and out of New York and possibly even to California in reference to casting the other long play. It's almost more trouble than it's worth, having a show put on. I hope after this one I can retire from the whole bloody business, buy a hacienda in Cuba or Mexico and let the "inner man" rule the roost for the remainder of my time on earth.

I am hoping that I can give a good deal of time to short prose writing this summer, so wouldn't it be a good idea to hold off the volume until early Fall, so that it can include whatever I may turn out that is good this summer? There are only two or three in the present bunch that have much distinction, I am afraid. Maybe none. I have had so little time for the stories.

<Later—I am in P-town, address Gen. Del. one or two new stories will be ready for you shortly. Also I will ask Audrey to send you a copy of *Streetcar*. Hope you can visit us here—have plenty of room>

—Tenn.

≪ • ≫

Margo's production of Summer and Smoke: Margo Jones directed the premiere of *Summer and Smoke* with Theatre '47 at the Gulf Oil Playhouse, Dallas, Texas, on July 8, 1947.

51. TPS—1

[Postmarked July 3, 1947] [Albuquerque, New Mexico]

<JAY—>

Westward bound for casting! Very anxious to have "Desire and the Black Masseur" in annual but Audrey claims she has no copy of it. Creekmore had it typed for me. Didn't he keep a copy? Mine is in New Orleans. In trunk in store-room. See if you can't dig up copy at N.D. Let me know. What other stories are missing? *Streetcar* is a big gamble: needs brilliant actress. Ou est Laurette d'antan!

Love—10

≪ • ≫

Westward bound for casting!: Director Elia Kazan, producer Irene Mayer Selznick, and TW went to Los Angeles to see an actress for the role of Blanche. Actor Hume Cronyn had produced TW's one-act *Portrait of a Madonna*, with his wife, Jessica Tandy, in the leading role for their consideration.

52. TLS—1

August 10th [1947] [Norfolk]

DEAR TENN—

The reports that have been coming up from Dallas have been extremely encouraging. I am terribly glad for Margo's sake that she got off to a good start, and very happy for yours too that *Summer and Smoke* seems to be both a good play and appreciated. I still haven't seen a copy but it sounds to be in your best vein and to be very touching and moving. I hope I can see it soon.

Probably you got my letter in which I told you that I was very anxious to do the book of the play. I hope this can be worked out and that we can start on it soon. When will you have a definitive text?

I really feel the need of a lift like that. Look at the new list (enclosed) it is much too European and reprint. But I just haven't found young US writers that I thought were good enough. So I do terribly much want to do this new play of yours, for this, as well as for many other reasons.

Do try hard to swing it for me with Audrey. She sounded pretty favorable in her last letter to me.

It still takes time to get a book out so I'd like to start soon, to have the books ready when the play opens in NYC.

Margaret and I are just off for a week in Nantucket. We will be at Charles & Henry Boathouse on Old North Wharf and hope to get to all the different beaches and get really soaked in the ocean.

Best wishes,

J

« • »

Dear Tenn: TW sent his copy of JL's letter to Audrey Wood with this handwritten note: <Dear Audrey—Send Jay the play and make contract with him for publication please. Tenn.>

53. ALS—2

[November 1947] [New Haven, Connecticut]

DEAR JAY—

There have been some important changes in the play [*A Streetcar Named Desire*] which I think you would probably want to put in the book. If you will contact Joanna Albus (who holds the book) she will bring you up to date. I have the proofs and will go over them at earliest chance. The heroine's last name has been changed from "Bois-seau" to "DuBois." That may not require change in book. I will also tell Joanna to contact you and maintain communications while we are on the road. The show looks good.

Love,

Tennessee

Why don't you come to New Haven? Opens Thursday.

54. TN—1

December 4, 1947 [New York]

[TO JL:]

Streetcar opened last night to tumultuous approval. Never witnessed such an exciting evening. So much better than New Haven you wdn't believe it; N.H. was just a reading of the play. Much more warmth, range, intelligence, interpretation, etc.—a lot of it because of better details in direction, timing. Packed house, of the usual first-night decorations,—Cecil B'ton, Valentina, D. Parker, the Selznicks, the others and so on,—and with a slow warm-up for first act, and com-ments like "Well, of course, it isn't a play," the second act (it's in 3 now) sent the audience zowing to mad heights, and the final one left them—and me—wilted, gasping, weak, befoozled, drained (see reviews for more words) and then an uproar of applause which went on and on. Almost no one rose from a seat till many curtains went up on whole cast, the 4 principals, then Tandy, who was greeted by a great howl of "Bravo!" from truly all over the house. Then repeat of the whole curtain schedule to Tandy again and finally. . . . . 10 Wms crept on stage, after calls of Author! and took bows with Tandy. All was great, great, GREAT! As you can see by the reviews enclosed. Will send from evening papers tomorrow. 20th-Century Fox has already called for a copy. I want to go to [the] play again! Beilenson is printing it this minute and shd be bound and ready next week. E says that [there] are many many orders already, and with the success, we think we shd bind all 5000. What do you think? Pauper will hold type for re-print if necessary, but cdn't possibly know now. [. . .]

≪ • ≫

This memo was written to James Laughlin, who was away in Europe at the time, about the opening night of Streetcar *on Broadway, December 3, 1947, by someone who worked in the New Directions office, most likely Hubert Creekmore. It has often been misattributed to Tennessee Williams, who would not have known of the details about orders, printing, and binding, etc. in the letter, and who rarely referred to himself in the third person, outside of his journals.*

55. TLS—1

December 29, 1947 [New York]

DEAR JAY:

I sail tomorrow afternoon on the *America*, and I will go directly to Paris where I am stopping at the hotel GEORGE V. I don't know anybody there, I just have a bunch of letters to people, so I do hope you will [be] in Paris now and then. I will probably travel around a bit, to Italy wherever it is warm and there is some swimming.

My first reaction to the book cover was adverse. I think it was the color more than the design. It's a sort of shocking pink which reminds me of a violet scented lozenge. However, everything else about the book is very fine and I have only myself to blame for not paying more attention when it was being planned. I don't need to tell you what a deep satisfaction it is to have you bring it out, so forget about the cover. The design was original and striking. I hope you will like *Summer and Smoke*, when it is ready to be seen well enough to bring it out too.

I'm glad you liked the article. You bet I meant every word of it, and you of all people should know that. Get in touch with me when I arrive. I will be lonesome as hell I expect. Poor Carson McCullers is over here half paralyzed due to nervous shock over a lousy dramatization of her book, but she is slowly recovering. I will arrive about January 7th. Warmest regards.

As ever,
Ten

P.S. I am nervous over the advertising on *One Arm*. I don't think the book should be publicized and sold through the usual channels. We agreed to have it sold on a subscription basis. This is mostly because of consideration for my family, and because only a few of us will understand and like it, and it is bound to be violently attacked by the rest.

« • »

the book cover: The color of the dust jacket for the first printing of *A Streetcar Named Desire* was a dusty lavender with a matte finish. JL was not only inclined to work with an author and a designer to come to an amicable solution under such circumstances, but he was colorblind as well and relied on his designers for precise color identification.

the article: "The Catastrophe of Success," published in the *New York Times*, November 30, 1947.

dramatization of her book: Possibly *The Member of the Wedding*.

SECTION VI

PF: I think it was 1948 that the volume of stories *One Arm* came out. What kind of critical reaction did they have? I can check this, of course, but "One Arm" is a very strong, hard-hitting story, very graphic about . . .

JL: About the prisoner.

PF: About the prisoner and about the fact that he was forced by his injury into male prostitution, and I would think that in the late forties this would have been rather shocking.

JL: Well, you see the problem was, you may run across this in these letters, Tennessee was afraid of his mother, and he didn't want those books—he wanted them done in expensive limited editions and not many review copies sent out.

≪ • ≫

volume of stories One Arm: The volume *One Arm and Other Stories*, published by ND in 1948, included "Desire and the Black Masseur," "One Arm," and "The Angel in the Alcove," among other stories that were sexually graphic to such an extent that TW did not want his family to see them.

56. TLS—3

January 7, 1948 [Paris]

DEAR JAY:

Your letter came up with my breakfast and was distinctly the better of the two items. No, this hotel is not for me and I am wondering if Paris will suit me either. It has changed terribly since I was here at sixteen. Of course everything has changed since then, remarkably. The lights are so dim and murky at night. I remember the streets as having a marvelous galactic whiteness but that is all gone, and it rains, rains continually. I am not satisfied with the French producer or Agent who met me here. He claims that I only have about eighty thousand francs from the *Menagerie* which ran here for a pretty long time. He is Adolf Rothschild. Have you ever heard of him? I want to make other arrangements for *Streetcar*, with the best producer around and perhaps you can advise me. Last night, my first night here, I explored the town by myself and was nearly murdered, not by Frenchmen but by a bunch of drunken GI's who "did not like my looks." I got in the wrong place, apparently, and there was some real excitement, but I escaped unscathed, although it did little to make me feel at home here.

The idea of snow in Switzerland does not attract me however. I cannot ski and New York was buried in snow when I left. I feel more inclined to the Mediterranean, or perhaps Rome where I know an art student or Tangiers where Paul Bowles is staying. He seems to love it, and our tastes are not dissimilar, I believe.

It is strange to be traveling by myself again after being with Pancho for a couple of years. He reacted very badly to the life in New York, it brought out the worst elements in his nature, so it was necessary to separate. It is both good and bad to be alone again, principally good I suppose, for it makes me more dependent and consequently more aware of other people and I feel close to my old friends again.

However there are moments of acute insecurity, especially when I have just made some drastic move such as this.

So Bill Smith is married! I had not heard of that nor did I expect to. Give him my felicitations both on that and the book of verse he sent me without any return address last summer, and also my affectionate greetings. He is an awfully nice boy and I hope the girl is good for him.

I am on a scientific kick right now. I took with me a little library on physics, mostly atomic and astronomic, some thrilling stuff. I am so stupid I have to read each page twice and sometimes twice again to latch on to the abstractions but it is worth it. Sir James Jeans, Einstein, Selig & Hecht [sic], DuNouys [sic]. Relativity and the Quanta [sic] theory are still somewhat beyond my comprehension but I am getting at least a poetic concept. They seem to feel, at present, that the universe is just an abstraction in the mind of a pure mathematician. I find it difficult to reconcile this with my personal experiences.

This is a little Swiss typewriter called Hermes Baby which Margo gave me as a parting gift. It is a machine of infinite and capricious complexity although the size of a schoolbook. Each little gadget seems to have a dual purpose, usually full of surprises!

I don't have to come back to the States before late summer or early Fall when *Summer and Smoke* gets started. We must get together somewhere before then and I shall try to avoid people who don't like my looks and cholera and the blue devils. Watch those ski jumps! And remember what I asked you about sort of keeping *One Arm* under the counter. After the first edition of *Streetcar*, could we change the color to something primary like red or blue: no more lavenders, please!—With love.

10.

≪ • ≫

since I was here at sixteen: TW traveled in Europe July 6 through September 12, 1928, with Grandfather Dakin's church group.

Bill Smith: William Jay Smith (1917–2015), American poet and translator. Smith, Clark Mills McBurney, and TW met at Washington University and called themselves "The Literary Factory," sharing the poems, stories, and one-acts they wrote with one another, and submitting to every contest and journal they could find. Smith later wrote a memoir about TW: *Tom: My Friend the Poet/Playwright Tennessee Williams*. Smith was married to the poet Barbara Howes from 1947 to 1963, and to Sonja Haussman from 1964 until his death.

Sir James Jeans: (1877–1946), British physicist and mathematician, proposed the continuous creation of matter.

Selig & Hecht: One and the same person, Selig Hecht (1892–1847), American physiologist, whose *Explaining the Atom* was aimed at the layman.

DuNouys: Pierre Lecomte du Noüy (1883–1947), French physicist and inventor of the tensiometer to measure the surface tension of liquids.

57. TLS—2

2/3/48 [Rome]

DEAR JAY:

This is more like it—Roma! I like it even better than Mexico City and the Italians are like especially good Mexicans. Were you here? If so how could you stand to leave it? In Paris I was depressed and ill but this city makes up for it.

The list of stories is okay [for *One Arm*]. It does not include "The Angel of the Alcove" which is one of the rather queer stories, of which perhaps we already have a sufficient representation. Be sure to use the version of "Bobo" that was published in *Town & Country*—under title "The Yellow Bird" probably a better title for it. If I ever get a piece of good paper and a soft pencil I will draw the chair for you. If I don't—the picture should be just the chair with crude label—"The Hot Seat—Ha-HAAA!**!"—A tack in the middle and another label and arrow that says "Tack in middle. Ha-haaa!***!?"—wires & plugs and a visor with label that says "Fits over puss!." However I shall make an effort to reproduce this great primitive myself.

Flying to Sicily Saturday to watch filming of *The Earth Shall Tremble*, a great picture being made there with natural setting and native performers under direction of man who directed *Zoo di Vetro* here on the stage. But my address remains American Express in Rome, as I shall return and probably keep this my base until I leave for the States some indefinite time hence.

In the volume, as a counter-irritant, it might be well to include a perfectly normal and rather poignant tale such as "Something About Him" which appeared in *Mademoiselle* or "The Important Thing" published a couple of years ago in *Story*. Get these from Audrey. They will leaven the book. If I were in New Orleans I could dig up some others but these will be enough anyhow.

Now be careful on those snow-shoes! I liked your friend McDowell in Paris. I think he will make a good worker on N.D. though you should perhaps have Charles Henri Ford to maintain a sort of equilibrium. One must remember that ultra violet is the most intense ray of the spectrum, one piece of information that I have gleaned from my studies of physics.

Ever,

Tennessee

≪ • ≫

If I don't—the picture should be just the chair with crude label—"The Hot Seat": TW's sketch of the "hot seat" in the published version of the story.

The Earth Shall Tremble: The Italian title of the film is *La Terra Trema*.

the man who directed Zoo di Vetro: Luchino Visconti (1906–1976).

your friend McDowell: When Hubert Creekmore left ND in 1948 to teach at the University of Iowa, JL replaced him with David McDowell (1918–1985), who had been representing ND in Europe where TW met him. As "sales and promotion manager," McDowell was able to secure favorable notices for Paul Bowles's *The Sheltering Sky* when it was published in 1949, helping to guarantee its success. But a modest print run of 3500 copies meant that orders could not be filled and the book lost momentum until a reprint of 45,000 copies could be rushed through. McDowell jumped ship to the hated Random House at the end of 1949, taking with him not only Bowles's second book but also ND mainstay author William Carlos Williams. While JL in time repaired his relationship with Bowles, and WCW returned to ND by 1960, he never forgave McDowell and remained suspicious of charming young literary men with their own agendas.

58. TLS—1

[1948 in Italy]

DEAR JAY:

Yes, I would like very much to see proofs of the stories. One of them, "Night of the Iguana," particularly needs cutting and a little rewriting of the didactic discourse by the older writer which breaks the mood of the story. My copy of the story was left at St. Paul de Vence with a young lady who seems to be too angry with me to write or forward my manuscripts so I am helpless to make these revisions until I get proofs from the printer.

I have taken an apartment in a strange pensione, operated by six or a dozen crazy women whose continual services and ministrations are driving me to distraction. They flutter about me like doves, emptying ash-trays, all kinds of little services, and I can't exclude them for none of the locks work. They have one redeeming virtue. They make excellent coffee which they serve in big steaming white cups and they fetch it almost before the order is given. This is of immense value when you are working as I now am. I am still repairing *Summer and Smoke* and making tentative excursions into a new one which is still quite amorphous. I love the Italians more every day, and even more every night. They are better than Mexicans! I wonder if I will ever live in America again.

[. . .]

How about putting the "E Chair" on the jacket? (In the red & blue crayon.) I think it would be striking.

Ever,

10

59. TLS—2

May 18, 1948 [Rome]

DEAR JAY:

These days the melancholy task of collecting the wildly scat-
tered papers, letters, manuscripts begun and abandoned, sorting
out, throwing away or packing: the sad and exhausting business that
always puts a long-drawn period to my stay in a place: wondering if
anything is worth keeping except a few letters from friends but not
quite daring to obey the impulse to make a bonfire of it all. This stay
in Rome has been relatively felicitous. Sunny. Peaceful. I have made
some good friends here such as Frederic Prokosch and that unhappy
young egotist Gore Vidal who is now in Paris and a great number
of ephemeral bird-like Italians, sweet but immaterial, like cotton-
candy: I shall remember all of them like one person who was very
pleasant, sometimes even delightful, but like a figure met in a dream,
insubstantial, not even leaving behind the memory of a conversation:
the intimacies somehow less enduring than the memory of a conversation, at least seeming that way now, but possibly later invested with
mere reality: ghosts in the present: afterward putting on flesh, unlike
the usual way. Anyhow, Italy has been a real experience, a psychic
adventure of a rather profound sort which I shall be able to define
in retrospect only. [a line and a half is then crossed out]. (A sentence
that doesn't say what I mean.) I also have a feeling it is a real caesura:
pause: parenthesis in my life: that it marks a division between two
very different parts which I leave behind me with trepidation. The
old continuity seems broken off now, by more than just travel and
time. I have an insecure feeling more acute than usual. It is certainly
not a good point at which to return to Broadway, but that is what I
must do after a brief period in London for the Helen Hayes production of *Menagerie*. Right after that, in July, I must return to New York
for rehearsals of *Summer and Smoke*, which is an uncertain quantity.

How right you are about the prizes! They mean nothing to me except that they make the play more profitable. Even so I shall probably not make much out of it. All I made out of *Menagerie*—after taxes and living expenses—was $30,000. If *Streetcar* had not been a success I would have been broke again in two years. It is evident that I have not been well-managed financially, but there is nothing that I can do about it without devoting my life to personal care of my earnings. It bothers me mostly because there are people I want to help and am not able to as much as I should.—Oh! While I'm on the subject of *Streetcar*—I thought the first format was infinitely preferable to the second: would it be possible to revert to it if there is another edition? All that I didn't like about the first was the color. The design was quite wonderful. The present is the worst I've ever seen on a New Directions book! I am afraid there must have been a total misunderstanding between Audrey and Creekmore. Unfortunately I was too busy at the time to make my own reactions clear to him.

[. . .]

I suggest that you send me the proofs [of *One Arm*] c/o Hugh Beaumont, H.M. Tennant Ltd., London. (Address is Globe Theatre, I believe.) I am afraid they might not reach me here before I start north in my Jeep with Margo who is arriving on the twenty-sixth. I may even start before she arrives and have her meet me in Paris or London. There is to be a congress of Gypsies near Arles on the 24th of May and I should very much like to see it, as well as the town where Van Gogh wrote and painted the fiercest expressions ever made of this world's terrible glory. I wish that God would allow me to write a play like one of his pictures, but that is asking too much. I am too diffuse, too "morbido"—that wonderful Italian word for soft!

You must get Carson's "Ballad" for your anthology, but I do not quite know how to get the manuscript for you immediately. Joshua Logan who was to direct her play borrowed it and promised to return it by mail from Florence. As yet he has not done so. Surely there are other copies! It was published twice, first in *Harper's Bazaar* and again in a collection of stories selected by authors as the story they would like to have written. Kay Boyle selected Carson's. If you want to use one of mine, use "Desire & The Black Masseur" which is probably the best. Carson and I exchange letters continually and we talk about making a home together. I doubt however that we could agree upon a location. She likes places near New York: I could not live anywhere that close to Broadway and continue to function as anything loosely resembling an artist.

Windham's novel [*The Dog Star*] is the finest thing, in some respects, that I have read in American letters: the quality is totally original. I wish that you were in a position to make him the necessary advance: he would need about a thousand dollars: for it is a book which only New Directions should publish, no one else. It is literature of the first order, the order of angels! However Audrey is sending around to publishers like Dodd-Mead who have no idea what it is worth artistically, now and to be. I am afraid he will settle with them simply because he needs money. I am lending him some but naturally he is reluctant to take it and anything of that sort is deleterious to a friendship. I am afraid of the book being mutilated by uncomprehending suggestions and demands from a commercial house. I have never quite understood your lack of excitement over Don as a writer. (apparent.) I do understand the difficulty of advancing money, however, when one is not a commercial publisher. That I do understand thoroughly. I am one of those who feel that New Directions has been a notably altruistic concern, the only one that exists. I also feel, however, that Windham's novel would be a sound investment financially as well as artistically if it is handled by an understanding house. Windham is now in Rome: perhaps you will see him here or elsewhere in Europe.

Ever,—10.

≪ • ≫

Frederic Prokosch: (1906–1989), American novelist.

Gore Vidal: (1925–2012), American novelist, essayist, historian, playwright, and screenwriter. The friendship between TW and Vidal was often strained and competitive, though after TW's death Vidal became a champion of his work and wrote the introduction to TW's *Collected Stories* (1985).

the Helen Hayes production: Actor John Gielgud (1904–2000) directed the London premiere of *The Glass Menagerie*, starring American actress Helen Hayes as Amanda.

Carson's "Ballad": McCullers's *The Ballad of the Sad Café* was published as a novella in 1951 by Houghton Mifflin.

Joshua Logan: (1908–1988), American stage and film director.

Kay Boyle: (1902–1992), American novelist and political activist. ND first published Boyle's poetry volume *A Glad Day* in 1938 and then two more books in the 1940s and 1950s. It reissued five more volumes of her novels and short stories in the 1980s.

Windham's novel: JL rejected *The Dog Star*, which was published by Doubleday in 1950.

60. TLS—5

7/9/48 *[London]*

DEAR JAY:

The little blue book is with me and I think it contains your very loveliest poem which is the one called "Generations": close to it is the one about the men tattooed Baudelaire. The level of work is higher, I think, than in *Some Natural Things*.

Jay, the book is too little, too hard to keep hold of for anything but cocktail recipes. It is characteristic of your humility about your own work that you do not trouble to bring it out properly but in a small apologetic way like this. Yes, it is a charming little book but in this case the contents deserve a more impressive or permanent-looking enclosure. Make this only a preliminary edition: add some more and bring them out yourself in a book that will fit on a shelf. When I think how many bad, pretentious volumes come out from bad, pretentious people! When a thing is true and good but unpretentious one is deeply moved by it. I am.

I am deeply sorry that Audrey caused so much disturbance about the volume [*Streetcar*] when all that need to be said was, Please bring out the next edition in a different color! Try to understand her. She is like an old mother hen and apparently she is afraid of other influences in my life which she feels less capable of managing. Back of it is love as there is often back of disturbing manifestations of various sorts. I was too busy to know or take part in the trouble. Let us revert to the old cover soon as these green horrors are sold out! And in the next books, put anything on them you please, just so it is not any shade of lavender and for God's sake tell Lustig that I <u>loved</u> his design, as I did.

England is a great and indefinable horror like a sickness that has not been diagnosed but drains the life from you. The upper classes are hypocritical, cold and heartless. They still eat off gold plates and dress for dinner. They entertain you lavishly for the weekend. On Monday you get a little note enquiring if you stole a book from them. The people on the street are cheerless and apathetic: everybody is rude: the theatre stale and unimaginative.

The living thing here is Sartre's new play *Mains Sales*, which is called *Crime Passions*. In fact Sartre seems the only living thing among European artists—except on the scale Rossolini [sic] and Anna Magnani are living things too. Italy is a very living thing in its heart, very warm and living. I would rather live there than anywhere else if it remains possible to.

[. . .]

Hayes promises to be very good in spite of Gielgud's sissified direction but my distaste for the country makes it hard to feel interest in the production.

Olivier's *Hamlet* is about as far as you can go in the vulgarization of Shakespeare. Isherwood was here: continually drunk so impossible to really communicate with.

I have a very difficult problem on my hands with Carson expecting us to live together when I return to the States and me knowing that as much as I like her I can't live with anybody I'm not in love with and even then it is almost impossible for me. However she seems to be working again and perhaps that is all she really needs. I guess that is all that any of us really need. Have you any influence with the automobile people? I must have a convertible car when I return to the States to make it bearable. So I can run to Nyack and places like that for weekends. I will be back around the 30th of August.

I sold my Jeep when I left Rome.

Ever,

Tenn

≪ • ≫

little blue book: JL's *A Small Book of Poems* (ND 1948).

the men tattooed Baudelaire: JL's poem, "The Man in the Subway."

Some Natural Things: A book of poems by JL (ND 1945).

Rossolini: Roberto Gastone Zeffiro Rossellini (1906–1977), Italian film director and screenwriter, husband of actress Ingrid Bergman.

Anna Magnani: (1908–1973). Fiery Italian actress of stage and film, Magnani won an Academy Award for her portrayal of Serafina in the film version of *The Rose Tattoo*, 1955.

Olivier's Hamlet: Laurence Olivier (1907–1989). Olivier directed the London premiere of *Streetcar* starring his wife, Vivienne Leigh, as Blanche DuBois.

61. TLS—1

October 27, 1948 [New York]

DEAR JAY:

Please remember not to let *One Arm* be displayed for sale in bookstores. When I heard that Miss Steloff had ordered 200 copies, I became alarmed with visions of you and I pinned up like our one-armed hero. I hope that the book will be distributed as we planned, entirely by subscription. Let me know how you plan to distribute it. It is the most beautiful book you have yet made, and I am crazy about it.

Call me as soon as you can.

Sincerely,

T. Williams

« • »

Miss Steloff: Frances Steloff (1888–1989), founder and longtime owner of the Gotham Book Mart in New York City.

62. TL—1

November 29, 1948 [New York]

DEAR TEN:

I have a lot of things to talk to you about, and I hope you will be sure to see me before you plunge off into the African Velt, or sandstorm. But there is one thing that I want to write a letter about, so that I will be sure not to forget it.

When I was in Boston the other day, I went in to see the Houghton Mifflin people, and they gladly gave me permission to reprint Carson's book, *Reflections in a Golden Eye* in a New Classics Series, and they will lend me the plates to do it.

Now what I was wondering was, whether when you got over there in Africa, you would find the time and inclination to write a special introduction for our edition. I know how you feel about Carson, and all I can tell you is that your name is very hot at the moment, as you know, and that it would help to sell the book a great deal, and get it the kind of notice which it deserves.

Isn't it an awful commentary on our culture that a writer as great as Carson should have to have any help at all in getting her work to the public. But that's the way it is, and all we can do is just get in there, and kick and scratch the best we can.

Are you going on December 2nd, or will the strike hold you back? I'm going to Utah on the 5th, so be sure to call me when you get back from St. Louis, so we can get together. There are a lot of things to talk about.

As ever,
James Laughlin

SECTION VII

PF: When did Tennessee and Frankie get together? Do you remember? Sometime in the late forties I guess.

JL: There again, could you pick up anything out of the diaries? I remember Frankie vividly, how he was.

PF: Tell me about it. Tell me about him.

JL: Well, he was a little man, a Sicilian from Newark. Very conversational. He annoyed a lot of us because he would answer for Tennessee you know, and I'd ask Tennessee a question and Frankie would say, Tennessee thinks this or that, which it might not have been. Frankie was a vulgar little man—he'd been a sailor—he was very small. I once asked Tennessee, I said, "Tennessee, why do you love Frankie?" and Tennessee sort of smiled and said, "He has the most beautiful skin."

≪ • ≫

Frankie: Frank Philip Merlo (1922–1963). Sicilian born Merlo and TW met in Provincetown, Massachusetts, during the summer of 1947. They ran into one another in Manhattan the following year and remained a couple, lovers and partners, until just about a year before Merlo's death from cancer. Enduring nearly fifteen years, their relationship lasted longer than any TW had before or after.

63. TL—3

December 18, 1948 [Alta, Utah]

DEAR TEN:

I hope that you had a good trip over and have been having fun in Spain, and that this letter will eventually reach you. I didn't know any other address where to send it, except in care of Paul [Bowles].

This will be mailed to you from the office in New York, but I am dictating from out in Utah, where I have been for ten days, getting the ski place started up for the winter. We already have about eight feet of snow on the ground, and the atmosphere is about as removed from that of New York as anything could be, which I rather welcome. On the other hand, it doesn't begin to have the peasant village kind of charm that I found in Switzerland last winter, and I'm very home-sick for those places where I was last year.

Maria was in the office the other day, asking for copies of all your books, and I'll see that she gets them when I get back. I must say that situation has me pretty well buffaloed. I like her, and would like to do something to help her out, but I just couldn't possibly give her the job that she wanted in the office, because there is absolutely nothing in our line that she is qualified to do. She can't even type. Even if I put her at something like filing addresses, I'm afraid that that terrific voltage of Russian emotion, which she gives off all the time, would set the place half on its ear. However, I'm sure that she knows that I am always good for a meal, if she gets hungry, and maybe something will break for her unexpectedly on the stage.

I have read the scripts which you left with me, and wanted to let you know what I thought about them.

First of all, the little play about the two old dollies in a restaurant in St. Louis during the Legion Convention [*A Perfect Analysis Given by a Parrot*]. These are good characterizations, I think, and the tone rings very true, but I don't feel that there is enough dramatic development to make a play of it. It seems to me that it is just a sketch in its present form, and that you ought to hang on to it, and perhaps work it into something else later. I don't think it is up to the level of the other ones in the 27 *Wagons* volume.

As for the play about the death of D. H. Lawrence [*I Rise in Flame, Cried the Phoenix*], I think that is simply beautiful and terribly convincing. I have read a good many books about Lawrence, mostly by that horde of women who chased after him, and I think that your interpretation ranks with that of Knud Merrild for supposedly human veracity. I say supposedly, because I never knew Lawrence, and only have my own idea of what he must have been like, but your picture fits in with mine and is credible. It's a terribly moving thing. Did you write this after you had been in Taos with Frieda, and what does she think about it. To the uninitiated, it might seem a bit rough on her, and I suppose you ought to get her permission before you publish it. For that reason, I daresay, we ought to wait, and not try to get it into the new edition of 27 *Wagons* right now. We have to hurry with that printing because the stores are clamoring for books. So I think we will go ahead with the same contents of 27 *Wagons* this time, just adding the little essay that appeared in *The Star*, which I liked.

But I do definitely think that the Lawrence play ought to be published, and I want to suggest that you let it be done in a small special edition, printed by those boys who do that gorgeous hand printing up at the Cummington Press in Massachusetts. Do you know their work? It is about the best hand printing being done in the United States today. I have an enormous admiration for those two guys. They live together up there in the hills of Massachusetts, under the most primitive conditions, cutting their own fire wood, and sometimes almost starving, and doing this beautiful printing unassisted by modern technical means. I would love to throw a thing like this their way, because I know it would sell well, and help them to make a little money, and they certainly desperately need it. And I know that you would be absolutely delighted with the beautiful piece of printing which they would make out of it. As they run by hand on a dampened sheet, they would only print 200 or 300 copies, I think, which would sell at a fairly high price. After these were gone, we could then include the play in the next printing of 27 *Wagons*, or, we could photo-offset it for a little book by itself. Will you let me know how this strikes you, and perhaps drop a word to Audrey about it, and then I will follow the thing along. I think also that we ought to show it to Frieda, and get her okay in written form.

Now about the story, "The Kingdom of Earth," I must confess that I like this a great deal. This is something to which I would apply my phrase of "clean dirt." To me, there is salacious sex, such as you find in magazines like *The Ladies Home Journal*, and there is good, clean honest sex, such as you find in Henry Miller and Lawrence in a story like that one. I think it is well done, and makes a terrific impact, and is honest and clean. Of course, however, there's absolutely no possibility of printing that in this country. If you wanted to have it appear, it could be arranged to do it in Paris with the man who publishes Henry Miller there. I suppose, however, that Audrey would have a fit over such a project, and possibly she is right from her point of view. Anyway, there is no hurry to do anything about it as far as I can see.

[. . .]

As ever,
[James Laughlin]

≪ • ≫

Maria: Maria Britneva (1921–1994) was a British would-be actress and ballerina of Russian extraction who met TW at a party given by John Gielgud after the opening of the London production of *The Glass Menagerie*. JL first met her when she came to New York in the fall of 1948. JL and Britneva were briefly engaged in 1954, but JL decamped to India, breaking the engagement. In 1956, shortly following JL's marriage to Ann Resor, Maria married Lord Peter St. Just, but she remained friends with both JL and TW.

the little play about the two old dollies: The two women from *A Perfect Analysis Given by a Parrot* later appeared as the two floozies in *Rose Tattoo*. The final version of *Perfect Analysis* was published in *Esquire* magazine in October 1958, later collected in *Dragon Country* (ND 1970).

play about the death of D. H. Lawrence: *I Rise in Flame, Cried the Phoenix*, originally published in a limited edition (ND 1951) and printed at the Cummington Press.

Knud Merrild: (1894–1954), Danish painter known for his cubism and abstract surrealism; he influenced Man Ray, Jackson Pollock, and others.

the little essay that appeared in The Star: TW's "On the Art of Being a True Nonconformist" was originally published in the *New York Star* in 1948 and later titled "Something Wild . . ." when it was published in the paperback edition, *27 Wagons Full of Cotton and Other Plays* (ND 1953).

those boys [. . .] *Cummington Press*: Beginning in the late 1940s, the young couple, Harry Duncan and Paul Wightman Williams, ran a highly successful letterpress printing company in Cummington, and later Rowe, Massachusetts, until Williams was killed in a 1956 car crash.

the man who publishes Henry Miller there: JL is referring to Maurice Girodias, the son of Jack Kahane, who published Henry Miller (and other innovative writers such as James Joyce and Lawrence Durrell) at his Obelisk Press in Paris in the 1930s. Kahane died in 1939, but Girodias (who had assumed his mother's non-Jewish surname during World War II) revived his father's operation as the Olympia Press in 1953.

64. TLS—1

4/10/49 [Rome]

DEAR JAY:

I had quite a hard time writing this introduction [for Carson McCullers's *Reflections in a Golden Eye*] since I didn't quite know what I was supposed to do with it, that is, what purpose it should serve, since Carson and her work are already so well-known and established. I may have taken altogether the wrong slant on it, particularly in the personal anecdotes and the stuff about her influence on a writer that will certainly be recognized as Capote. Please use your own judgment in trimming this down and editing it as much as you deem necessary or discreet and it might be a good idea to let Carson see it first, since it is her book. I honestly could not think of any other way of dealing with it. It was a good hard exercise but I don't want to try it again any time soon!

I have gotten the two reprints of *Menagerie* and *Wagons* and find them stunningly well done. After a disturbing period of apathy last winter, I am plowing ahead once more and completed a first draft of a play [which became *The Rose Tattoo*] and of a long story [which became *The Roman Spring of Mrs. Stone*] so if I come home next Fall it won't be empty-handed. We, Frankie and I, are going to London the end of this month for a conference with the Oliviers, and after that we will spend some time in Paris which I found very stimulating last year, but we are keeping the little apartment in Rome to return to when it is time to relax again. The days are one long blue and gold ribbon always unwinding and giving you an illusion of permanence of at least a physical kind, which is no small bargain. Vidal has not yet returned to Europe but Capote is now on Ischia with a new redheaded lover that he dotes on. They have radioactive springs on that volcanic island, which are supposed to create enormous sexual vitality so perhaps Truman will have to leave Italy with a board nailed over his ass, which is the way a red-headed sailor once said a Mardi Gras visitor would have to leave New Orleans! How is Carson? I haven't heard from her in a good while. Donnie's book [*The Dog Star*] is being rejected by all the big houses which is discouraging to him and mystifying to me. Maria is said to be on her way back to England in a few days and is arranging to be surprised by a big bon-voyage party and "shower."

Ever,
Tenn

<Lustig cover's a dream!>

≪ • ≫

two reprints: This was the first publication of *The Glass Menagerie* by New Directions. The jacket was designed by Alvin Lustig and the small clothbound volume appeared as part of ND's New Classics series.

Capote: Truman Capote (1923–1984), American novelist, short-story writer, playwright, and screenwriter. As with Gore Vidal, TW had a strained friendship with Capote and yet there was always a sympathetic feeling between them.

Lustig's cover's a dream!: Alvin Lustig's original drawing for the 1949 edition of *Menagerie* is still used on the ND paperback.

65. TL—2

April 14, 1949 [New York]

DEAR TENNESSEE:

Today I have just been doing some accounting for Audrey, and I thought it would interest you to know what your books earned for you during the past year, that is, during the calendar year of 1948.

Here are the figures. *One Arm* brought in $1478.25; *Streetcar* earned you $5574.93; *Summer and Smoke* brought in $1263.17; and 27 *Wagons* brought in $368.30.

Then, in addition, according to my records, I never paid you for *Battle of Angels* which earned you $104.40.

So, all of that adds up to a rather tidy little sum of past $7500, which is being held in the bank for you until such time as it is good business for you to take it from the tax point of view.

I'm off tonight for Utah, where I have a lot of work to do on my ski business out there. Naturally I expect to get in a little mountain climbing and skiing on the side, but I'll only be gone for three weeks, and then will be back here in New York.

I don't think there is anything else to report on this end, though I have a scheme cooking with George Braziller which may amount to something, and if it does, I'll write for your views and approval. He is the fellow who runs the Book Find Club. It has suddenly dawned on them that they have been neglecting the contemporary drama all this time, and that they ought to do something about it. They have a readership of about 30,000 which isn't exactly to be sneezed at. I'm trying to get across to him the idea that he should present you in the round, with a volume made up of plays, stories, poems and a couple of essays. But more of this later if it actually comes to anything practical.

With best wishes,
James Laughlin

≪ • ≫

George Braziller: (1916–), American bookseller and publisher who founded the publishing company George Braziller, Inc., in 1955.

66. TL—2

May 2, 1949 [New York]

DEAR TENNESSEE:

This is just a hasty note to let you know that the second draft of the introduction of Carson's book [*Reflections in a Golden Eye*] has arrived and I am very well pleased with it indeed. I shall write to Carson at once and see whether she would like to look at it or whether she would prefer to be surprised when it comes out.

I think this introduction will help the sale of the book enormously. It is very charming and engaging, and yet it gives you a good picture of the author, not to mention a rather good one of the introducer himself. Possibly Truman may object a little to what is said about Carson's influence on his work, but it may do him a little good, too.

I was glad to note that you mention our hoped-for publication of *The Ballad of the Sad Cafe*. In that connection I wonder if you could help me a little bit with the artist. His name is Guttusu, and he is very famous and lives there in Rome and I am sure you have met him, or know people who know him. I have written to him several times about arranging to do the illustrations for this story, but haven't had any answer. I wonder whether you could see him and find out whether the reason is that he doesn't want to do business with me because he is a communist and I am not, or just because he is a little perplexed because he doesn't read English. Vittorini is going to use that story in his anthology of American stories and he will make an Italian translation which the artist could then read in order to make his illustrations. I would really be awfully grateful if you could get me some word on this rather ticklish situation. Possibly if you are busy, you could prevail on Frankie to run out and see him. He lives at a very attractive studio out in Villa something or other, whose name I can't remember, but I'm pretty certain that he's in the telephone book.

[. . .]

Have fun in London if you go and if you see John Lehmann, give him my best regards.

With best wishes,
James Laughlin

≪ • ≫

The Ballad of the Sad Cafe: Carson McCullers's novella was eventually published by Houghton Mifflin in 1951.

Guttusu: Renato Guttusu (1911–1987), Sicilian painter who also designed for the theater and did illustrations for books. A committed communist, his art was robustly realistic.

Vittorini: Elio Vittorini (1908–1966), Italian novelist. ND published four titles by Vittorini, one of them, *In Sicily* (1949), introduced by Ernest Hemingway.

John Lehmann: The London publisher of TW's work from the 1940s through the 1970s.

SECTION VIII

⌒

PF: What do you remember about *The Roman Spring of Mrs. Stone*, which was the novella? It seems to have grown out of a real person. Tennessee sent you a story? Eyre de . . .

JL: Eyre de Lanux. She was a leader of the expatriate literary colony in Rome. She had that beautiful apartment at the top of the Spanish Steps, and she, I think, liked Tennessee and had him around when she could, and he just used her as he often did use people, to be a character in a play or story.

PF: There's a letter where you say, "Oh, I'm surprised that she's forty-five years old, I thought from this story that she was much younger." She apparently had a much younger Italian boyfriend named Paolo who took terrible advantage of her.

JL: I don't think I met her more than once. She was attractive and bright. She had money and she dressed well. She gave a nice party. But I don't have any strong impression of her.

≪ • ≫

Eyre de Lanux: Elizabeth Eyre de Lanux (1894–1996), American artist and art deco designer. She was the inspiration for the character of Karen Stone in TW's novel *The Roman Spring of Mrs. Stone*.

67. TL—2

DEAR TENNESSEE:

This is just to say that, at her request, I showed your introduction for the Carson McCullers book [*Reflections in a Golden Eye*] to Audrey, and she made the request that we should change the reference to the talented young writer who has imitated Carson to read in the plural so that it would not be such a direct slap at Truman Capote. It now reads: "Imitation is a strong word to use concerning the work of some very talented young writers who have been influenced too strongly by the work of a predecessor."

I told Audrey that I would make this change, but subject to your approval. So please let me know if you would prefer to have it exactly as you wrote it. In any case, I shall try to see that proofs are sent to you before the book goes to press, so that you can make any final changes that you want to.

I was personally a little bit worried about the phrase on page 2 which refers to the famous house in Brooklyn where the poets and tourists lived as "vaguely similar" to the inferred house of prostitution mentioned above. It occurred to me that this might catch the eye of some ambulance chasing lawyer, who would bring it to the attention of Gypsy Rose Lee and get her to try to bring suit for libel. Therefore, I have taken the liberty of changing this to read as follows: "in Brooklyn where she became enmeshed in an extraordinary menage whose personnel ranged from W. H. Auden to Gypsy Rose Lee." I hope you will approve of this change in the interests of caution.

Here, everything seems to be going along well, though the book business in general has been dropping off rather badly.

Did I ever thank you for sending over the charming little story by Eyre de Lanux? It is a fragile thing and not terribly substantial, but what there is of it is excellent, and I would be glad to run it in the next number of *New Directions*, where we will also have the story about his aunt by that young Italian whom you kindly sent us. Is "Eyre" a boy's name or a girl's name? I can't make out from the letter which came with the script, and thought I had better ask you about this before writing an answer. The handwriting looks like a girl's, and the general feel of the piece seems to be that of a girl, but I thought I'd better make sure.

Have you had a chance to look at the ending of the play about D. H. Lawrence [*I Rise in Flame, Cried the Phoenix*]? The two boys up in Massachusetts at the hand press have gotten very steamed up about the possibilities of making something beautiful out of this, and they would like to start on it this summer if possible. The one of them who is an artist will make abstract line designs which fit right into the printed text. If this idea worries you at all, I could send over one of their earlier books where this technique has been used for your approval. But I think you will like it, as the treatment is very severe and restrained.

Before going ahead with the Lawrence play, we would also want to clear it with Frieda down in Taos, I can't see why she or Brett would make any objection, but we ought to have releases from them in the files just to be on the safe side.

I hope you had some fun in England and write when you get a chance.

> With best wishes,
> James Laughlin

≪ • ≫

the famous house in Brooklyn: A brownstone known as "February House," 7 Middagh Street in Brooklyn, was the location for an experiment in communal living during World War II, whose participants included poet W. H. Auden, Carson McCullers, Jane and Paul Bowles, stripper Gypsy Rose Lee, composer Benjamin Britten, and editor George Davis.

Brett: Dorothy Brett (1883–1977), British painter who was associated with the Bloomsbury Group but later moved to Taos, New Mexico, to be near her friends Mabel Dodge Luhan, and Frieda and D. H. Lawrence.

68. TLS—2

6/3/49 [Rome]

DEAR JAY:

Many, many thanks for your letters. I am relieved that you are satisfied with the introduction to Carson's book [*Reflections in a Golden Eye*]. I had misgivings about it, and I still hope that you will let me have a look at the proofs before it goes into print. I was afraid, for one thing, that I might have written too much of a personal nature, and of course I was also a bit worried about the unavoidable comments on "imitators." I don't want to incur the wrath of Truman, which is probably worse than the wrath of God. I have not heard directly from Carson in a long time, not for about two months, but I have heard through Audrey that she has been in the South, is well, and that her play has been sold to the producers of *Medea*. I can't rejoice in that last bit of news for I am afraid that it may only bring her worry and grief, unless they pay her a good-sized advance to compensate for it.

Myself I have been terribly happy over some wonderful news about my sister. She is now out of the asylum for three days a week in the custody of an elderly couple in a pleasant country town in Missouri and Mother sent me five letters she had written expressing her great joy in the liberation. The letters were quite normal except that in one of them she sent her love to her offspring, of which of course she has none, but that seems a fairly harmless and comfortable delusion compared to the ones she used to suffer.

The story I mentioned has grown to the length of a novella [*The Roman Spring of Mrs. Stone*], about 75 pages, and is still expanding, so I have neglected the play [*The Rose Tattoo*]. This may turn out to be foolish of me but I don't seem to have any choice in the matter.

I cannot make up my mind about the Book Find deal of selected writings. Sounds more like something to be done in the hypothetical future, but I would love very much to have a little volume of verse brought out that is all my own, with maybe a couple of stories for ballast. Is there any way we could print "Kingdom of Earth" or get it typed up? I am afraid the only copy may get lost. Do what you like about the Lawrence play [*I Rise in Flame, Cried the Phoenix*]. Perhaps it could be reserved to go with the eventual selection of poems and the stories: but dispose of it exactly as you think best.

Warners sent a very stupid, commercial director over here to discuss the filming of *Menagerie* which they are now casting and will start filming next Fall. The movie-script is a real abomination and I am raising hell about it, but perhaps quite helplessly as I have no legal control. The characters are all vulgarized, there is a ridiculous happy ending, and the director has no taste or distinction, but they have rounded up a stunning array of actors, probably headed by Bette Davis and Jane Wyman, who recently won an Academy Award. Would you like to read a copy of the film-script just to see how awful they can be? Audrey could provide you with one. And do you think, since the play is really a dramatized memoir, I might sue them for libel if the characters are made too disgusting? The Mother, for instance, steals some money to bet on a race-horse! It is really worse than the proposed changes by Louis J. Singer. The director, Irving Rapper, is coming to see me for another conference at five o'clock, and the feathers will fly!

Paul and Jane Bowles are in Tangier. Lehmann in London is very happy over advance reactions to Paul's novel and I suspect it will make a real impression there. He now has the manuscript of Windham's novel, which has been rejected by most of the big commercial publishers in the States.

Eyre de Lanux is woman who was a <u>great</u> beauty, is now about 45 and I think she has recently had her face lifted while she was mysteriously away in Paris. She has a young Italian lover, a boy of 25, startlingly beautiful and the only real rascal that I have met in Italy. Her blind adoration of him is shocking! But quite understandable.

I have not yet located the painter (engraver?) you mentioned but I am sure I shall find him if he is still in Rome. The city is now at its loveliest, dangerously lovely for a person who should sit at home working all afternoon if he hopes to continue to get anywhere with his work.

Yours ever,

10.

Eyre's boyfriend, Paolo, recently brought her a two-year-old infant that he claims to be his bastard child and wants her to take care of it for him. It has no resemblance to him, it is obviously a trick of some kind. She has written a story about their "menage" as if it were being observed through the eyes of their cat. It is not yet good enough to send you, but perhaps the second draft will be.

≪ • ≫

my sister: Rose Isabel Williams (1909–1996). Rose Williams and her brother were inseparable as children and continued to be extremely close into young adulthood; however, Rose, who had always been outgoing and personable, began to retreat mentally, eventually showing signs of a psychotic break in her late twenties. In 1943 her parents, presumably her mother, authorized one of the first prefrontal lobotomies in the United States to be performed on Rose. It left her calmed but in a childlike state for the rest of her life. After 1945 Williams assumed the total responsibility of care for his sister, making sure that she always lived in comfortable circumstances and was visited regularly by friends and family.

Warners [. . .] stupid, commercial director: Irving Rapper directed the first film version of *The Glass Menagerie* (1950) for Warner Brothers.

Bette Davis and Jane Wyman: Davis would have been cast as Amanda, but the role was played in the 1950 film by Gertrude Lawrence. Wyman ended up playing Laura in the film.

Louis J. Singer: The original stage producer of *The Glass Menagerie*.

a young Italian lover: Eyre de Lanux's lover, Paolo Casagrande.

69. TL—4

June 9, 1949 [New York]

DEAR TENN:

Thanks ever so much for your fine letter of June 3rd. A letter from you is always a breath of fresh air in this terrible New York, and you don't know how I look forward to them. The atmosphere of this place is gradually getting me down, as exemplified especially this week by a really dastardly attack on Eliot and Pound by that old swine, Robert Hillyer, up at Harvard. He has gotten in cahoots with the editors of *The Saturday Review* and put on a really disgusting show. Where will the jealousy and resentment of anything first rate in those little pigs and pills stop?

[. . .]

The introduction for Carson's book [*Reflections in a Golden Eye*] has gone to the printer, and I will be sure to let you see proofs when they come back from him so that you can make a final check on them. Audrey and I are both very anxious that your swipe at Truman should be so concealed that it won't make him lose face and turn him into a dangerous and spiteful enemy for you and for all of us. You can check on the wording when you see the proofs, but I think we have it fixed now so that he will privately get the message but he will not think other people know it is about him, so he won't be prompted to take revenge on you.

That is good news about your novella [*Roman Spring*]. I hope you are making a carbon of it so that I can see it just as soon as possible. I am very curious to find out whether you are able to maintain the intensity of the short stories when the work spreads itself out to a greater length. I have always admired the ease and grace of your prose style and felt that you had enormous possibilities as a fiction writer if you once put your mind to it. It sounds as though the thing has now gotten to a length where it could stand as a little book by itself, or possibly with one or two short stories to reinforce it.

We can talk about the Book Find project the next time I see you. Meanwhile, the idea of a little book of verse has definite appeal for me. The only real problem is to get ahold of all the material. In addition to what was in the *Five Poets* anthology, I have quite a number of your things in my file, but I'm not at all sure that I have all of them because you have a way of dashing them off and then hiding them away. Do you have most of your scripts with you, or are they stored over here somewhere, and if so, could anyone get access to them and hunt out the poetry. A book of verse doesn't take very long to print and maybe we could get one ready to put out this fall if it were possible to locate the manuscripts now. Then the novella with a couple of short stories added to it, if it needs it, would follow along in the following Spring if you and I are both satisfied with the way it turns out.

[. . .]

There will be no trouble at all about getting the "Kingdom of Earth" printed for you the next time that I get over to Europe. I have several printer friends there who can do it up very tidily. I don't think, however, that we ought to offer it for sale even in the limited way which we did the *One Arm* stories. It would be much better just to do a couple of hundred copies and give them to a selected list of friends. Meanwhile, I will have some copies of the typescript made so that there won't be any danger of the single copy getting lost. I'll send one over to you there and keep one in my safe at Norfolk, and one here in the office.

I can well imagine the awful mess which Hollywood would make out of something so delicate and subtle as *The Glass Menagerie*. I guess you'll just have to get used to that. By the way, Tom Merton had the guts to tell Hollywood to go to hell. They wanted to make a movie of *The Seven Storey Mountain*, starring Don Ameche, and you can imagine what a hash Hollywood would have made out of life in the monastery. Of course, it's a lot easier for Tom to turn down a big chunk of money because [of] where he is living, he can't even spend a dime. Nevertheless the Order needs the money badly, and I think it showed a lot of good sense on the part of the Abbot in the monastery to refuse it. It seems to me that the only thing you can do to protect yourself is to write an article tearing the movie to pieces, and release it about the time when the movie goes into the Broadway houses. Then the next time that Audrey makes a sale to Hollywood, have her insist that certain provisions are put in that you must approve the shooting script before they can go ahead with it.

I'm glad that people in London are so enthusiastic about Paul's novel [*The Sheltering Sky*]. I have a hunch that we may be able to do something with it here too, but I'm keeping my fingers crossed. London is a much better environment than New York for something of that kind. I will probably print the novel here after all, instead of doubling up on the production with Lehmann because I am having a row with him. It turns out that he has been systematically overcharging me for the work he has done for me in England, and now that I have caught him out in it, he has withdrawn into the Englishman's traditional huff of hurt pride. I had always thought Lehmann as a brilliant editor, and never realized that he was also a very astute and hard driving businessman. However, those are the qualities which a publisher needs to stay afloat these days. I'm afraid that I am much too soft and easy going.

I'm amazed to learn that Eyre de Lanux is 45 years old. The little story had given me the impression of having been written by someone with the dew still fresh on her cheeks. The story about her menage sounds very funny. Do by all means let me have a look at it if she gets it whipped into shape.

The painter whom I had in mind for illustrating Carson's *Ballad of the Sad Cafe* is named Guttusu. I think you ought to be able to find him pretty easily because he was in the telephone book and besides, he is extremely well known. I'll be most grateful if you could find out what his attitude is about illustrating the book for me, when we locate a French or an Italian translation so that he can read it easily. Get him to show you the illustrations that he did for the Milan edition of Faulkner's *Sanctuary*. I think they are quite remarkable. The guy has never been in America, let alone in the South, and yet he seemed able to catch that chronic sag which Southerners have as they stand about in the streets of little Southern towns.

I don't know as there's much news to report here on the literary front. We have run onto a kid named John Hawkes up at Cambridge who seems pretty promising, and I'll send along his first little book [*The Cannibal*] as soon as we publish it. It is a bit in the vein of Djuna Barnes, but he claims that he had never read her at the time when he wrote it.

I've managed to dash off a few little poems in the past few weeks, but they haven't seasoned enough yet for me to know whether they're any good. They usually drop out of nowhere when I am riding on a commuting train and their coming is a great comfort in a life which is not otherwise exactly what I would like it to be. I was certainly never cut out to be businessman and yet, more and more, I find myself being cornered into doing that and almost nothing else. I surely envy you being over there in Rome.

With best wishes, as always,

James Laughlin

≪ • ≫

Robert Hillyer: (1895–1961), American poet, critic, and academic. After Ezra Pound was awarded the Bollingen Prize for the best volume of poetry by an American in 1949 for *The Pisan Cantos* (ND 1948), Hillyer wrote two highly critical articles on Pound (and T. S. Eliot) for *The Saturday Review of Literature*. The ensuing literary donnybrook ultimately led Congress to remove the awarding of the Bollingen from the Library of Congress; the Bollingen Foundation continued the Prize as administered by Yale University.

Tom Merton: Thomas Merton (1915–1968). Trappist monk and most widely known American religious writer of the fifties and sixties, Merton was also a poet whose work was introduced to JL by Mark van Doren who had been Merton's professor at Columbia. ND published Merton's poetry in its "Poet of the Month/Year" series in 1944—the same year that ND published TW. JL delighted in visiting Merton at the Abbey of Gethsemani in Kentucky and considered him one of his best friends and confidants. ND published Merton's poetry and many other works not directly related to Catholic doctrine. JL was named one of the original trustees of the Thomas Merton Legacy Trust, which was created as a "fail-safe" before Merton left for his trip to Asia in 1968; after his death, the trust oversaw, and continues to oversee, publication of any Merton papers and letters not published in his lifetime.

The Seven Storey Mountain: Thomas Merton's spiritual autobiography, published in 1948, became that year's nonfiction best seller (over 600,000 hardcover sales). While JL had thought he had first refusal on the manuscript, Merton had sent the manuscript to his agent, Naomi Burton, apparently without mentioning his commitment to JL; she posted it to Robert Giroux then at Harcourt, Brace, who immediately signed it up. The book is credited with inspiring a large number of monastic and priestly vocations in the late forties and early fifties.

Don Ameche: (1908–1993), American film actor.

the Order: The Abbey of Gethsemani is a monastery in the Order of the Cistercians of the Strict Observance.

the Abbot: Dom James Fox (1896–1987), Abbot of the Abbey of Gethsemani from 1948 to 1968. He was frequently at odds with his most celebrated monk, Thomas Merton, and was reluctant to allow any project that would give Merton any higher visibility than his books already brought him.

Paul's novel: At TW's recommendation, JL published Bowles's first novel, *The Sheltering Sky*, in 1949.

John Hawkes: (1925–1998), American novelist. His first book with New Directions was *The Cannibal* (1949). ND published fourteen more titles by Hawkes.

Djuna Barnes: (1892–1982), American writer and artist whose most famous novel, *Nightwood*, was reissued by ND in 1946 and remains in print.

70. TLS—1

6/21/49 [Rome]

DEAR JAY:

[. . .]

Maria Britneva is here and sends you her love. Arthur Miller is also in town and Kazan said to be approaching. Oliver Evans lands in Naples today. He and I are taking to the lakes and hills in the Buick for a couple of weeks, but my address remains American Express in Rome.

Ever,
Tenn

<Dear J. love from Maria>

≪ • ≫

Arthur Miller: (1915–2006). TW and Miller shared mutual respect and a cordial professional friendship as fellow American playwrights, though they did not socialize with one another.

Kazan: Elia Kazan, born Elias Kazantzoglou (1909–2003), Turkish-born, Greek-American stage director, producer, film director, and author. A member of the original Group Theatre and a founder of the Actors Studio, Kazan was the most influential American stage director of the twentieth century. His professional relationship and friendship with TW was long and loyal: Kazan directed the premieres of *A Streetcar Named Desire, Camino Real, Cat on a Hot Tin Roof,* and *Sweet Bird of Youth* and the films *A Streetcar Named Desire* and *Baby Doll.*

71. TL—2

June 23, 1949 [New York]

DEAR TENNESSEE:

Enclosed please find a set of proofs of your introduction to Carson's *Reflections in a Golden Eye*.

I hope you will approve of the changes which Audrey and I have made in the matter of the affair of Truman and also the reference to Gypsy Rose Lee, which she might not have liked.

The little scrawl in pencil at the left of the second page is Carson's. She would like very much to point out that her age was different than you have noted it down.

[...]

We recently acquired a very interesting electric typewriting machine to speed up our office procedures. With this machine, it is possible to make 8 or 10 copies at a time, and so I am having that number made of your story "The Kingdom of Earth." I will send six of them along to you in due course, and keep the two others filed away here in safe and confidential places.

Audrey said that there was a possibility that you might be coming back here soon to go out to Hollywood to work on the script of *Menagerie*. I can't imagine anything more gruesome for you, but I suppose you really ought to do it. She says that they are making a genuine effort to keep the thing artistic, and if they really mean to, I suppose you ought to help them out.

I'm just setting out for Aspen, Colorado, for two weeks to take part in the Goethe Festival out there, but I'll be back in New York after that, and if you do come through, I hope you will let me know ahead so that we can have a good get-together. If you felt like coming up to the country for a few days, Margaret and I would certainly love to have you. There isn't much excitement up there, but the swimming isn't bad in the local lake. We would guard you carefully from the local cocktail set, unless you would find it amusing to have a look at them and see how dreadful they are.

Have you had a chance to look at the ending of the little play about Lawrence [*I Rise in Flame*]? Audrey and I are both keen to get ahead with the production of that, but she agrees with me that you ought to look at the ending and see if it is just the way you want it to go through.

Please also keep in mind that you are going to look about for copies of old poems that I might want to see with a view to making up that book of your poetry. I hope your work is going along well. I'm keen to have a look at that short novel [*Roman Spring*], or long story, or whatever it is.

With best wishes,
James Laughlin

≪ • ≫

72. TL—1

August 1, 1949 [New York]

DEAR TENNESSEE:

[. . .]

I am back in the East now after a wonderful month out at Aspen, Colorado, where I was working on the Goethe Festival. The Goethe gathering turned out very well. The musical program wasn't exceptional, but many of the lectures were quite wonderful. They had brought the great Goethe scholars from all over the world, and some of those old boys really know their stuff. Stephen Spender was there for a while, and we had a good time together. He gave a fine talk, comparing *Hamlet* with *Faust*, and the way Shakespeare and Goethe handled their characters. I'll remind you to take a look at his paper when it is published, because I think you would be interested in the points he made. Surprisingly enough, about the best talk, at least the most dramatic and moving one, was given by Thornton Wilder. Did you ever run into him? He is a strange and curious and fascinating character. Something of an old maid and rather affected in that sense, but a real humanist when you get beneath it. I got quite fond of him out there in Aspen. One evening he recited his new play [*The Emporium*] to us aloud, and it is an absolute howl. As he himself frankly admits, it is all made up out of Kafka, the setting being in Philadelphia, where a giant department store corresponds to Kafka's *Castle*. He borrows very liberally, but at the same time, the detail of the characters is his own, and very funny. He also seems to enjoy writing things with his tongue in his cheek. Everything that he does is very artificed, but when it is good, I think it has wit and style of a kind. Did you read his book about Julius Caesar [*The Ides of March*, 1948]? If you didn't, I think it would amuse you living there in Rome.

Well, enough for now. I have an enormous stack of work piled up after the long visit in Colorado. I hope your work is going well and let me know if I can do anything for you over here at any time.

Best wishes, as always,

James Laughlin

≪ • ≫

Stephen Spender: (1909–1995), English poet and novelist.

Thornton Wilder: (1897–1975), American novelist and playwright who won Pulitzer Prizes for both fiction and drama.

73. TLS—2

8/17/49 [Rome]

DEAR JAY:

Whatever decision you and Carson reach about the two prefaces [for *Reflections in a Golden Eye*] is O.K. with me. My feeling was, when I read over the first version, that I appeared in that version to be talking too much about myself. If you revert to that original version I hope that you will preserve the cuts that I have made in it, particularly the long portion about "imitators." I believe that I scratched out (in the returned proofs) all but about two sentences of that material which was provoked mainly by a personal antagonism for Truman which I think should not be indulged in this place. I also wish you would compare the two versions very carefully, again, and perhaps something from the second, which I still believe had a great deal more dignity in keeping with the novel, could be appended or worked into the other.

I received yesterday a long letter from Carson, most depressing. "Health has failed steadily—can't walk more than half a block—neuritis has set in—damaged nerves constantly spastic—dreadful headache—nausea, prostration—a gland went wrong in the neck—prolonged suffering—a sort of convulsion at dawn . . ." It sounds almost fantastic! Surely she has not been given any really intelligent diagnosis or therapy. I think she should be hospitalized for several months and exhaustively examined from every angle, physiological, emotional, Etc. Of course there needs to be a special branch of medicine for the understanding and treatment of such hypersensitive artists, but since they practically never have any money, they are simply condemned. I dread the play production that she is now facing as her emotional involvement is certain to be great. Clurman is a fine director for it, but when I last saw the script it was far from being in a state to produce.

I am sailing out of Naples on the twentieth, the crossing takes ten days, and must go directly to Hollywood when I land. My work on the movie script is practically complete but they are not yet satisfied with the ending and I think I shall have a fight with them about that. They say they don't want a fairy-tale ending but there is evidence of double-talk. At least I should learn something more about the technique of film-making which I can use creatively on some other assignment perhaps over here. I am on excellent terms with Rossellini and De Sica and Visconti and would enjoy working with any one of them. Last week had supper with Ingrid Bergman and Rossellini. Their "Fuck you" attitude toward the outraged women's clubs and sob-columnists is very beautiful and should have salutary effect on discrediting these infantile moralists that make it so hard for anyone to do honest work and live honestly in the States. If Bergman has the moral courage she appears to have, it will be a triumph.

Several weeks ago I sent you two long poems, "The Soft City" and "Counsel," which you haven't mentioned receiving. If you hate them, for God's sake Jay, don't hesitate to say so! I depend so much on your critical opinion as there are times when my own seems to fail me. I lose objectivity about my work, as everyone does at times, but you know that I am not morbidly sensitive to adverse opinion, but on the contrary, I am grateful for it. I showed Kazan and his wife a long synopsis of the play I had been working on. They both wrote me from London of their disappointment in it quite frankly and while I felt that the synopsis had not conveyed a true idea of the play as it existed in my conception, their criticism will be helpful when I go back to work on it, if I do. Whatever I do badly (even if it is everything!) I want to know, I want to be told! Honesty about failure is the only help for it.

I am enclosing two versions, first and second drafts of another poem. I don't know which is better or worse. Also, the other ending to the Lawrence play [*I Rise in Flame*]. I wonder if it would not be better to change Brett's name in the play to something like Brady, since the incident is fictitious and she might object. I don't believe Frieda would.

It is dreadful to leave here, but I have thrown a coin in the Fountain of Trevi.

Ever,

10

≪ • ≫

Clurman: Harold Clurman (1901–1980). American stage director and founding member of the Group Theatre, Clurman directed McCullers's stage adaptation of her novel, *The Member of the Wedding* (ND 1951), and the original production of TW's *Orpheus Descending* on Broadway in 1957.

De Sica: Vittorio De Sica (1901–1974), Italian director and actor.

Ingrid Bergman: (1915–1982). In 1949, while working on the film *Stromboli* for the Italian director Roberto Rossellini, Bergman and Rossellini fell in love and she became pregnant. Though she later divorced her husband and married Rossellini, American public opinion was slow to forgive the Swedish-born actress who had played Saint Joan as well as Ilsa in *Casablanca*. She and Rossellini remained in Italy for several years until the "scandal" subsided. TW's attitude is evident.

Kazan and his wife: Molly Day Thacher Kazan (1905–1963) happened to be the reader at the Group Theatre who singled out TW's group of one-acts, "American Blues," for an honorable mention in 1939, which led him to New York and to his longtime agent, Audrey Wood.

74. ALS—3

December 9, 1949 [Key West]

DEAR JAY,

Theseus came today and it is resting beside my bed, the proper place for any good work of art. We have a snow white rooster next door to us who flaps his wings and crows every half hour or so. I always wake up and continue my reading.

Life here is as dull as paradise must be. Consequently I do more work. I have, at long last, finished a first complete draft of a new play called *The Starry Blue Robe of Our Lady* [which became *The Rose Tattoo*]. It may be weeks before I dare to read it. Am also working on another novella. Audrey wrote me that you were interested in publishing *Moon of Pause* [which became *Roman Spring*]. That was not my impression. I did a little more work on it. I would really like to publish it, first in a magazine such as *Harper's Bazaar*. I think it is a good study of the malignant power-drive but how effective it is otherwise I still don't know; Carson sent me an enthusiastic wire about it. Evidently Bigelow had showed it to her, as he is retyping it.

I may come to the Philadelphia opening of Carson's play Xmas week, in which case I'd spend a few days in N.Y. Isherwood's friend, Bill Caskey, is having dinner with us one night.

À bientot. 10.

« • »

Theseus: An essay on the Theseus myth by André Gide was published by ND in 1949 (in a translation from the French by John Russell) in a limited edition of two hundred copies, hand printed by master printer Giovanni Mardersteig at the Officina Bodoni in Verona. JL loved fine printing and Mardersteig was a favorite printer for special projects.

Carson's play: *The Member of the Wedding* (ND 1951) opened on Broadway January 5, 1950. During their time spent together on Nantucket in the summer of 1948, TW greatly helped McCullers to shape the play and, though he took no credit, McCullers was always keen to thank him for his help.

Bill Caskey: William Caskey was a photographer with whom Isherwood lived and collaborated.

75. TL—2

December 16, 1949 [Cambridge, Massachusetts]

DEAR TENNESSEE,

Thanks ever so much for your good letter of December 9th, which reached me up in Cambridge, where I am busy with my duties as a member of the Visiting Committee for the English Department. It is very funny to go around from class to class and observe the students and the funny old professors objectively. Re-visiting these scenes of a good many follies of youth certainly gives me a feeling of old age. But there is no question but life becomes less troublesome as you get older. The senses seem to get dulled so that you no longer get into the emotional agonies that certain situations produced when you were eighteen years old. On the other hand, a lot of the excitement is gone too.

I'm glad to hear that Key West is turning out to be a success and that you're getting a lot of work done. Audrey told me you were doing some revision on the novella [*Roman Spring*], and I think that is fine. I do definitely want to publish it when you get it in such shape that it satisfies your own feeling about it. I just didn't want to push you into publishing it until you yourself are ready. I was trying to lean over backward lest I should have to accuse myself of a commercial motivation. Obviously, the thing will sell pretty well, and that sets up a kind of pressure in a publisher which has to be guarded against by a strict examination of conscience. When you get it in a shape that satisfies you, let's go ahead with it, with the idea that it will first appear in one of the magazines, and then later on be done as a book, perhaps with a few short stories added to it to fill out the book. Audrey also said something about your starting of another one, which might pair up with it. But we can work out the details of that later on.

That's fine that you have blocked out the new play [*The Rose Tattoo*]. Is there any chance of getting a look at it? I am always sort of fascinated to know what you are going to do next.

[. . .]

> With best wishes as always,
> James Laughlin

≪ • ≫

76. TL—2

December 22, 1949 [New York]

DEAR TENN,

Thanks ever so much for sending along the poems. My favorite is the "Old Men With Sticks" and I believe that is the right one to send first to *Partisan Review*. I shall pass these on to Audrey with the request that she make copies of them, in case you didn't keep copies, and then put them out to the magazines. She has tactfully hinted in the past that it confuses her records if I send things out independently from this office. But I will advise her as to where to send the things, as I don't think she knows too much about poetry channels.

Mulling over these poems, it occurs to me that you are achieving a consistent vein, which might well be labeled a sort of "new romanticism." Possibly if I ever get ambitious to be a critic again I'll write an essay about you under that title. To my way of thinking it is a very good force to have around. The academic poets of the neo-metaphysical school have gotten far too dry. They are afraid to let their gussets out, as it were. I hope you will keep on with your poetry because I really think you can accomplish a lot with it. Your approach to any given subject is so different from the average that there is never any danger of your falling into the commonplace, no matter how far you let yourself go with explicit feeling. And don't forget that I would like to get out a little book of your poems when you think you have enough gathered together that you like.

The big news up here these days is that we are having a bit of luck again after a rather dry late summer and fall. The Bowles [*The Sheltering Sky*] is going along great guns. It has had the most flamboyant kind of reviews in all the provincial papers, as well as good ones here in New York, except for rather contrary ones in *The New Yorker* and *The Saturday Review*. We have gotten what I call a "green light" on it in the way of large orders from the jobbers which supply little neighborhood shops in the suburbs and lending library chains, and so I am throwing a lot of money into advertising to try to make a big thing out of it.

The Firbank [*Five Novels*] and the Vittorini [*In Sicily*, introduction by Ernest Hemingway] are also doing well, and the latter has been taken by the Book Find Club for March.

Carson has invited me to the opening of her play [*The Member of the Wedding*] and I am looking forward to that very much. *Reflections in a Golden Eye* has been printed and ought to get through the bindery next month. I'll send you down some copies for you to give around to friends.

Well, I guess that's all for the moment, so will close with a Merry Christmas and all that.

As ever,

James Laughlin

[. . .]

« • »

Firbank: Ronald Firbank (1886–1926), English novelist. ND published six titles by Firbank.

SECTION IX

—⁓—

PF: In 1950 Tennessee was writing to you about completing *The Rose Tattoo*, and you wrote him a long letter about Serafina, her character and how vibrant she was and it just seems to me that you were, in a way, much more important to him than you probably realized because he needed this kind of validation coming from "above."

JL: Yes, I was a sounding board for him. That was the Anna Magnani play.

PF: Right.

JL: He wanted to talk to somebody. I think he knew he couldn't trust those sycophants who were around him and didn't know anything about anything, just vagabonds. He needed somebody to talk to and in the early days he talked to, what's the agent's name?

PF: Audrey Wood.

JL: Audrey Wood. And then they began to tense up and work themselves into quarrels for some reason, I never knew why. I never understood why because she certainly devoted herself to

pushing Tennessee's plays, pushing them around, but some—
I wish I could remember things better—he got some grudge
against her.

PF: This is one reason I said maybe it was good that you had
professional distance from him, because over time he got very
paranoid about the people he was with constantly and saw on
a daily basis. He got paranoid about Audrey and thought she
was trying to do him in.

≪ • ≫

77. TL—2

January 26, 1950 [New York]

DEAR TENNESSEE:

Last night I went to see the opening of the T. S. Eliot play, *The Cocktail Party*, and found it absolutely delicious. In parts the dialogue seemed to me almost as good as Oscar Wilde. Of course, the religious message is a bit murky, but Eliot has pulled himself together and attained a degree of professional showmanship which I had never thought him capable of. There are all kinds of very clever stage tricks which build up suspense and create animation in the acting. I daresay the critics will all hop on the play for being long winded and too wordy, but I certainly enjoyed it very much, and I hope you will get a chance to see it before it closes, which probably won't be very long. Obviously, Eliot isn't any more of a dramatist really than Carson is, though they are quite different, but it certainly is a fine evening.

Audrey kindly sent the revised version of the novella [*Roman Spring*] and I wanted you to know right away how pleased I was with the changes you have made. I think it is enormously improved. Adding that additional bit of background makes all the difference in giving the main character the necessary three-dimensionalism. I don't believe that you need to have any further hesitations about publishing it now. It is integrated, creates a successful atmosphere, and has a lot of impact.

So I have told Audrey that we would like very much to go ahead and publish if that suits your plans. Paul Bigelow, with whom I talked at length about the script, feels that it would be a mistake to add another novella or additional stories to it. He would prefer to see it printed in such a way that it would make a little book by itself. This is entirely possible from the technical point of view. After all, this is just as long as *Reflections in a Golden Eye*. So think about this a little, and let me know what you'd like to do. If you want to put it in one of the magazines first, that would be quite all right with me. It would be nice if we could publish the book next fall, as naturally it would be a strong addition to our list and give us something to base on.

Frieda Lawrence sent in her preface for the little play [*I Rise in Flame, Cried the Phoenix*], and if it is typed out by the time I sign this letter, I'll enclose a copy for you. Her preface doesn't seem to me quite as strong as what she put in her first letter, but it serves the purpose, and I'm sure you will agree that it helps to have it in the book. Mr. Colton has volunteered to draw up releases for Frieda and Brett to sign. That is just a routine precaution. Then we will be able to swing into action and probably the boys will be able to get it printed in their beautiful way in the next year.

Paul's book [*The Sheltering Sky*] continues to do very well. It is hovering around 10th place on the *Times* Bestseller List. We are keeping up the advertising on it, and hope to keep it at that level, or drive it a little bit higher.

He has now arrived in Ceylon and seems to like it very much. The accounts in his letters are fascinating. If you want to write to him over there, his address is care of The Chartered Bank of India in Colombo, Ceylon. He says he has started thinking about a new novel, and that is encouraging. Of course, we will do his short stories next fall.

With best wishes,
James Laughlin

P.S. Your brother came in the other day and we had a nice talk. He wanted some advice about the manuscript which he has written on his war experiences and his Catholicism. I tried to help him on it, but I don't know whether I succeeded too well. It isn't exactly my dish, if you know what I mean. I suggested to him that he try to get Audrey to [do] some work on it.

« • »

the little play: ND published TW's play, *I Rise in Flame, Cried the Phoenix*, hand-printed at the Cummington Press, in 1951.

Mr. Colton: ND lawyer at the time.

78. TLS—1

1/30/50 [Key West]

DEAR JAY:

I am delighted that you want to publish the novella separately in the fall and that you think I've improved it. I am still making little revisions, from time to time; it might be helpful if you would go through it, sometime, very carefully and make a note of all those points at which the writing falls down. I may be doing this myself but of course I can't altogether rely on my own perception. Since it is such a short thing it should be possible to get it completely polished. Audrey and Bigelow were displeased with my original title, *Moon of Pause*, but I like it much better than the one they prefer, *The Roman Spring of Mrs. Stone*, which I think is comparatively banal and much less pertinent but I have thought of another, *Debris of Giant Palms*, which derives from a passage of Perse's "Anabasis." I think I would prefer either that or the one I had first. Which do you like?

I have completed the long play *The Rose Tattoo* and had it typed up by Audrey. She has been rather cagey about it and my own feelings about it are tentative and mixed, I am afraid to read it over. Yesterday I wired her that I must have some comment, however brief and devastating that might be, and she wired back that [she] was "very optimistic and thought it had the making of a great commercial vehicle." I am not sure that I feel very pleased about this reaction. So far I have never aimed at a commercial vehicle and I hope that I will never be willing to settle for that. I now have $113,000 in govt. bonds which is enough to live on in Sicily or Africa for the rest of my life without bothering about making money in the theatre. What I want, of course, is to continue to write honest works with poetic feeling but am haunted by the fear that I am repeating myself, now, have totally exploited my area of sensibility and ought to retire, at least publicly, from the field. The work on this play, begun last January in Rome, has exhausted me physically and nervously. I have suffocating spells in my sleep. Sometimes they wake me up but sometimes they are woven into my dreams, such as last night when I dreamed that I was trying desperately to crawl down a long corridor of a house in the vacuum of a tornado.

Vidal arrived here about two weeks ago and since coming has written a really excellent short story, the best thing he has ever done in my opinion. I want you to see it, and so does he. Of course I also liked his story about "the street" ("Some Desperate Adventure") which you didn't care for. I thought it was not well written but that it was the most honest expression of Vidal that he has yet offered. I am encouraging him to do it as a play. It could be terrifying as a study of the modern jungle. Vidal is not likable, at least not in any familiar way, but he and Bowles are the two most honest savages I have met. Of course Bowles is still the superior artist, but I wonder if any other living writer is going to keep at it as ferociously, unremittingly as Vidal! If only he will learn that people are not going to give a hoot for his manufactured pieces like *Search for a King*, Etc.! He has a mania for bringing out one book a year! They are now stacked up like planes over an airport, waiting for the runway.

Audrey suggests that I come to New York but I am waiting for news that at least one swimming pool has reopened. Since coming here I took off fifteen pounds by diet and swimming and I don't want to put it back on in one week of Manhattan high life.

Ever—

10.

≪ • ≫

79. TL—2

February 7, 1950 [New York]

DEAR TENNESSEE,

Thanks a lot for your letter of the 30th, but I was very sorry to hear that you hadn't been sleeping well down there. My opinion, of course, is worth absolutely nothing, but I would like to make the suggestion that there might be some simple physical cause for all this, and that it shouldn't be attributed to your feelings about your work. Up until two years ago I used to have the most terrible nightmares myself. I also used to have about six colds every winter. Then all of a sudden I put on twenty pounds, and the nightmares and the colds almost disappeared. Something or other had happened to the metabolism, or whatever you want to call it, in my body, and with the change the nocturnal anxiety disappeared. I'm not suggesting that you should try to get fat, but maybe a change of diet or something of that kind would be helpful.

I think that is a lot of bunk about your having exploited your area of sensibility. I think the new novella disproves that, and certainly the poems and stories do. I have heard people criticize the similarities in some of the plays, but they haven't read the poems and the stories. Of course, everything that you write has something personal out of yourself in it. But there's nothing wrong with that. Some writers externalize and others don't. For me, the personal quality in your work is part of the poetic impulse. However, I didn't start out to deliver a lecture on literature, but here's a thought: don't think of yourself as a literary figure, and try to see what others see in you. Just go on living your life by your own standards, which are the right ones for you, and write what comes.

I'm glad that we can go ahead with the novella by itself for next fall. I talked to Audrey on the telephone and she says fine, and will send along the contracts. Do you want to see it again or can we go ahead and start composition next month? Whoever typed it up at Audrey's the last time misspelled a lot of the Italian words, but I fixed those. I like the new title—*Debris of Giant Palms*—the best. Audrey still likes *The Roman Spring of Mrs. Stone* best. Well, I guess we can fight that out with her.

I am off for a bit of skiing in the West, so write to me at the Hotel Jerome in Aspen, Colorado, if you have the time. I'm eager to have a look at the new play. When will it be visible? I don't like to nag Audrey to see it, but I'm very curious.

As ever,
James Laughlin

≪ • ≫

80. TL—3

March 7, 1950 [New York]

DEAR TENNESSEE,

I was sorry to miss you when you were up in New York, but I was out in Colorado and Utah. The skiing was absolutely marvelous, and the weather was terrific. Lots of snow on the ground, but sun all day long and almost as warm as spring.

I have been back in New York now for a few days, working madly, and tomorrow—Sunday—I take off for Switzerland. I hadn't thought I would be able to get over there this year, but all of a sudden the Swiss government came through with a very nice invitation to make the trip, in return for a couple of ski articles, and so I am off. It will probably take me about three weeks to do the ski writing work, and then I hope to drop down to Rome and Sicily for a week each. But I'll be back in New York on April 11th, and hope to see you again soon.

I had a very pleasant session with Audrey today in her office, and we worked out details for the contract on the little novel [*Roman Spring*]. She suggested that we put in as part of the contract a provision about the amount of money to be spent on advertising, and that is quite acceptable to me. I think a lot can be done with the book, and am quite willing to give it the "big treatment." I believe we can do even better with this than we did with Paul's book [*Sheltering Sky*], which is now hovering around the 20,000 mark. We have spent about $7,000 advertising him so far.

[. . .]

I am sending my copy of the novel out to Lustig in California now, so that he can start working up a jacket, which will include, I am urging him, some good visual symbol which we can use in all the advertising to tie the promotion together.

Will it be all right for us to start setting the book very soon? I mean, have you finished working on it? The sooner we can get it into print, the more we can do in the way of long range advance publicity. Audrey feels, and I think it is a good idea, that we ought to try to get the book out in the last part of September. Then it would avoid the big mad rush of all the big novels that are always brought out in the fall season. However, I am not much worried about the competition. I think this piece is strong enough to hold its own and make its way in the world.

A new printing of *Streetcar* is now on press. For this, we are following the suggestions made by your friend [Paul Bigelow], in adopting the text to the actual playing script of the New York version. I trust that this meets with your approval. I think I asked you about it before, and you said to go ahead and do that.

[. . .]

Some time when you happen to feel like it would you jot down for me some phrases that I might use in the promotion for the little novel. I would rather gear my blurbs to your own idea about the book than risk getting off the bean on my own interpretation. By the way,

Audrey now thinks that the best title would simply be *Roman Spring*. Is that all right with you? I like it myself. I think it is a good title from a sales point of view, and while it isn't awfully poetic, it is apt and does the job smoothly.

Well, I must sign off now if I am going to get some work done and get off.

As ever,

James Laughlin

≪ • ≫

A new printing of Streetcar: In 1950 TW pursued a suggestion made by his friend Paul Bigelow and asked JL to publish an updated and accurate text of *Streetcar*, primarily taking out characters, stage directions, stage business, and lines that were dropped or that TW cut from the initial Broadway run. That revised edition of the play, which TW chose to have published as his definitive version, came out in 1950 and continues to be in print with ND.

81. TLS—1

3/16/50 [Key West]

DEAR JAY:

I don't suppose you'll get this till you return from Zurich in April. I will be in New York about May 1st and until May 20th when Frank and I sail back to Europe on the *Ile de France*. By that time all my revisions on *Mrs. Stone* will be completed and I can leave you the final draft of it. I don't like the title *Roman Spring* but would settle for *The Roman Spring of Mrs. Stone* if that makes everyone happy. I think "spring" is too hackneyed a word to be redeemed even by "Roman." Of the various titles I still prefer *Moon of Pause* but that seems to give really serious offense to Audrey and perhaps to other women it would have the same antipathy. I am now busy working on the last American version of *The Rose Tattoo* (my new play) and on the *Streetcar* film script which Kazan is going to shoot in July. I will give you a copy of the play before I sail. So far I have shown it only (prematurely) to Audrey and Kazan who seem interested but worried. I am less worried than I was, for my interest in it continues and I feel I will be able to work it out finally.

Bigelow is now a house-guest. He told me about the McDowell-Bowles affair and I must say I think David's conduct has been unprofessional. Knowing as well as I do your enormous enthusiasm for Bowles, his novel and stories, I am totally unable to credit the suggestion that you have failed in any way to push Bowles's book as well as you can without the high-pressure methods of the big commercial houses which you naturally don't wish to emulate. As for Bowles, I suppose he gets a little panicky about money, and that, too, is understandable and will call for some patience on your part. Do you think I should write him, or is it better for me to stay out of it? I think what he needs is a little reassurance, perhaps most suitably coming from you.

On a separate page, some "copy" for *Mrs. Stone.* Could I see the Lustig jacket-design when I get to New York? Awfully happy that he is doing it and you are publishing it!

Ever,

Tenn

≪ • ≫

McDowell-Bowles affair: See note to TW's letter to JL, February 3, 1948.

82. TLS—2

4/5/50 [Key West]

DEAR JAY:

By a very dramatic coincidence I got letters from you and Bowles in precisely the same mail. I agree with you that the agent is probably the real villain in this sad mix-up. If I were Paul's agent I would certainly never have permitted him (with my advice) to abandon the publisher who has launched him, even for a temporal advantage, however important that obviously is to a writer without independent means and a terrific lust for life and travel. Agents always consider it their duty to make the most strictly materialistic terms for a client. It's their duty, because I think very often their motives are conscientious. They think that is what they are for, to convert talent into dollars. What they are blind to—and this sometimes makes them a real hazard to an artist—is the immense value of the personal relationships involved. Bowles and Cerf are a marriage surely contrived in the nether regions. Poor Paul will soon come to see this. It is my guess that it will take perhaps three years before Paul will have another book comparable to *Sky* and that in the meantime he will have fallen out with several commercial publishers besides Cerf. If I were you I would maintain an Olympian (or Alpine) calm about the whole thing. You published easily the most distinguished book of the year and perhaps of the last ten years <except McCullers> by probably the most deserving artist. What more could be asked of you? I think Cerf's methods are really very poor business. Waiting for someone else to discover and bring out a great new talent and then bribe it at a grossly inflated figure. He is bound to lose money and he will get second-best books, lose interest and drop them while you do the creative and constructive work of finding the artists and introducing them with their best, freshest and most original things. After all the jackal only gets the picked-over quarry. Inspired taste and keen scent and intrepid stalking are not in his domain. The only serious loss, for you, is through becoming angry and bitter, which I think you can avoid by thinking very objectively about the predicament of a writer such as Paul. Paul knows he is not a quick or facile writer. He is not going to turn out a best-seller every season, and he is worried about bread and butter until the next really good book is ready and he probably knows that may not be for quite a while. How's he going to live until then? Cerf offers him a kind of subsidy. I'm sure Paul in his heart would rather stick with you and that he must feel a certain *devoir* about it. The agent and his own anxiety pull him the other way. In this letter, for instance, he says he can't get any of his 1950 royalties until March 1951. Of course how Paul lives, and travels, has always been a mystery to me. He "talks a poor mouth" and yet I notice he not only manages to travel all around himself but to maintain Jane in the style to which she is accustomed (humble as that may be!) in some separate (usually) part of the world! I have not yet written Paul, but I shall answer this letter of his and try to present a more bi-lateral view.

[...]

A couple of weeks ago a middle-aged man was clubbed to death by a sailor, and in reprisal for this terrible offense on the part of the civilian, the police are booking all the New Bohemians in town on vagrancy charges, fining them heavily and giving them twelve hours to get off the Keys. The overseas highway is jammed with convertibles North-bound. So far we have not been bothered, perhaps the advantage of having a grandfather with a round collar or a house on the outskirts of town. But we are planning to leave sooner than we had planned, probably about the fifteenth of this month—and sail the 20th for Europe after three or four glamorous weeks at the Sherry-Netherland (which Bigelow has booked us into).

Ever,
Tenn

« • »

83. ALS—2

[1950] [New York]

DEAR JAY—

I am really <u>enchanted</u> by Lustig's jacket design which Audrey just gave me. I <u>don't</u> want a <u>thing</u> changed on it. I also like the title *Cold Sun* (without "a" or "the") but how about *Bird of Prey*—which seems to fit even better? And it would go perfectly with the jacket design, also. The design is the best I have seen by Lustig and should greatly enhance the book.

I forgot my typewriter, Frank is bringing it in the car— Grandfather and I came ahead by plane.

New York is upsetting as ever, especially since I feel that a clash is imminent with Audrey. She wants to tell me exactly what to do with the new play in spite of my suspicion that she is not really interested in it. I want Irene to have it—she hates Irene—will call Carson now—Ever

Tenn

≪ • ≫

84. TL—2

May 5, 1950 [New York]

DEAR TENN,

I thought you might like to see a copy of this first release that went out about *Mrs. Stone*. I notice that it was picked up almost immediately by the Book Section of the *New York Times* daily. We will be getting out three or four more general publicity releases about the book before it comes out, so if you have any good ideas for story angles on it, be sure to let me know. Otherwise I will think up some myself, but you might have some angles which wouldn't occur to me. Publicity, as you know, snaps at all kinds of flies. For example, you said, I think, that you were friends with Ingrid Bergman, and if somebody could take a snapshot of you and Ingrid sitting at a cafe table in Rome poring over the proofs of *Mrs. Stone*, that would be an absolute knock-out for advance publicity, since the story is about an American actress in Rome, even though it has nothing to do with Ingrid. I know that you have more important things to think about than nonsense of that kind, but possibly we could deputize Frank as a special kind of publicity man who could keep me posted of anything of this kind that came up.

[. . .]

We are scheduling a full page ad in the Summer announcement number of *Publishers Weekly* which hits the bookstores on May 27th. This announces books which are going to be published up through September, and it's good for the stores to begin thinking about the book right away. We have also sent out a letter about it to all of them, requesting that they send in their orders for the special copies immediately. Then the salesmen will begin hitting them, with actual books to show, on their trips in July. So it's important to get the proofs read in a hurry in order to have finished books for the salesmen to take with them on their trips. While in Washington and Princeton this past week, I called on several booksellers, and found that there is a great deal of enthusiasm about the novel. They are all eager to see it, and I believe that it will go very well.

Let's get together again before you go. I asked Carson if she would like to come up to the country and she said she would, but she isn't just sure when it can be because of her trips to the hospital for this new treatment. When I hear something definite from her, I'll give you a ring and see if you can work it in.

See you soon,

James Laughlin

≪ • ≫

85. TLS—1

[mid-July 1950] [Rome]

DEAR JAY:

I am delighted with the appearance of the book [*Roman Spring*]. Reading over the text was not as bad an experience as I had anticipated. I wish that I had taken more time over one or two passages, or had had a little more power, but all in all, I feel that Mrs. Stone comes through with a fairly vivid reality, and that is the main thing. Is there any indication of what the reviewers will do with it? I suppose there will be some violent squawks of "decadence," "wet rot," Etc., from people like Orville Prescott and the charge that I can only deal with neurotic women. If the book is properly publicized, I think it can over-ride this sort of criticism. I hope you will wait on laudatory notices, as Doubleday did with Windham's novel, but advertise extensively in <u>advance</u> of the notices.

I returned the colophon sheets several days ago, all signed by my own little hand.

There has been an unprecedented heat-wave here: the hottest in one hundred years! To escape it, I am leaving Tuesday for Vienna and will stay there till Frank notifies me that Rome has cooled off a bit. Have felt quite stupefied, which is unfortunate since I have a lot of work to do. I have never finished a satisfactory draft of the new play [*The Rose Tattoo*] and am still making radical changes in it. I am hoping that I will have a resurgence of energy in Austria. It has been so long since I have traveled alone, without Frank, that I am rather alarmed at the prospect.

I would love to have "Hard Candy" in the anthology, but would you please let Delmore Schwartz see it, too? Before I left New York he called to ask me if I had a new story and I mentioned that one. I had promised to bring it to him, at his house, but I hope you will explain to him that my last few weeks in the States were all but annihilating.—Here are two more poems. In a later letter I will suggest a selection of my verse to bring out in a new volume. I think it should certainly include a number of those in the *Five Young American Poets*—the best ones such as "Summer Belvedere" and "Angels of Fructification." And the long poems that came out in ND annuals, especially the one called "Camino Real." Incidentally, the play *Ten Blocks on the Camino Real* has been greatly revised since its publication by Barrett Clark and you might like to include it with the poems in a volume. It is the most experimental poetic play I have done, in its present form. I don't know if Audrey has had it typed up to include all the changes.—Eyre de Lanux (inspiration for Mrs. Stone) is still around but her Paolo has married a young girl. She says they are unhappily married and she still sees him. She has not yet seen the novella. I don't think she would recognize herself in it, but Paolo is fairly close.

Ever,

Tenn.

<Wonderful to know you and Bowles have made up!>

≪ • ≫

Orville Prescott: (1906–1996). For twenty-four years, he was the head book reviewer for the *New York Times*.

I returned the colophon sheets: Five hundred specially bound copies of the first edition of *The Roman Spring of Mrs. Stone* were signed by the author.

Barrett Clark: Then editor of Dramatists Play Service, he published the "acting editions" of TW's plays.

86. TL—1

October 15, 1950 [New York]

DEAR JAY,

I deeply appreciate the long account you have given me of your promotion plans for *The Roman Spring*. I know that this particular aspect of the publishing world is not what attracted you to it, any more than it is the aspect of writing that is attractive to me. I must admit, though, that I am deeply concerned about the distribution of this book, and its reception, because it comes at a point in my life when I have a need for some confirmation or reassurance about my work's value. I certainly didn't get any from the notices the book has received in New York. I was startled and hurt not only by the harsh opinions but much more by the apparent lack of interest, as if the book (and my work in general) did not seem even to merit a little attention. For instance, the fact that the *Herald Tribune* has ignored it completely, both in the daily and Sunday book-review sections, is the worst sort of slap in the face, not only to this one book, but also, I feel to all the work I have done to my whole—position is not the word I want to use! But you know what I mean. I feel that I have worked very hard and very seriously over a considerable period, that I have not done anything cheap or meretricious, that regardless of my known limitations as a writer, I have shown taste and courage and do have honesty: and, consequently, have a right to receive from journals that have literary criticism, such as *The Herald Tribune*, *The New Yorker*, Etc., the minimal courtesy of some space within two or three weeks of the publication date, a courtesy which I am sure they have extended time and again to writers who make far less effort than I to explore the world and experience of our time with some truth and significance. If other writers such as Edith Sitwell, Christopher Isherwood, Carson McCullers, and Rosamund Lehmann have expressed an admiration for the book which I know must be sincere, surely there is something in it that merits a token of interest from the various book-page editors, even though the book may not at all accord with their personal tastes.

(FIRST PARAGRAPH OF A LETTER TO JAMES LAUGHLIN)

Tennessee Williams

≪ • ≫

Edith Sitwell: (1887–1964), English poet and the most famous of the three Sitwell siblings.

Rosamund Lehmann: (1901–1990), British novelist.

FIRST PARAGRAPH: This is a partial draft letter. There is no evidence that it was ever sent.

87. TL—2

November 3, 1950 [New York]

DEAR TENNESSEE,

These first sample pages have come through from the boys up in Cummington who are doing your little Lawrence play [*I Rise in Flame, Cried the Phoenix*] on the hand press, and I would be grateful if you would look them over and see if you like the general style they have worked out. Everything, as you know, is being done by hand, and they will print on dampened paper.

I like the spacious size of the book, don't you? And I think that is a very lovely type.

As the plan now shapes up, they will print 300 copies, and in addition, they will print 10 very special copies on extra superb paper, probably with hand coloring, and an extra special binding.

On the basis of their advance estimates, the books will cost us about $7 each to make, so that it will be necessary to sell them for

$15, since we have to give the stores their usual discount. However, I am convinced that we will find a ready market for them at that price. Naturally we will want you to sign them, and they will be numbered.

I think the boys up there are going to give us a really magnificent book, which will be a collector's treasure, and a real work of art. Please shoot the proofs back to me at the office, and telephone me your comments. I probably will be up in the country on Monday, but I ought to be down by Tuesday or Wednesday.

I feel very excited about this book. As you know, I am nuts on hand printing, and it is very rare nowadays when I get the opportunity to do something like this, working with people who have the real old fashioned standards of craftsmanship.

As ever,

James Laughlin

≪ • ≫

88. TL—2

November 3 [1950] [New York]

Dear Tenn—

I have finished reading the play [*The Rose Tattoo*] now and am very impressed with it in certain ways. It packs a real wallop and I think it will be very strong on the stage. It strikes me as being written with the requirements of the stage constantly in mind. The character development and the narrative are telescoped and condensed in deference to the needs of the stage in a way that you would not do it if you were writing a novel about the same theme.

Yet the remarkable thing is that the characters are so alive that I can accept them and believe in them as real and credible people even though they move like veritable express trains through events more dramatic than those in plain and ordinary lives. They are souped up, so to speak, in their pace of living, and yet they are still real and alive. It is quite a triumph of stage writing technique, I think.

There are fewer of those beautiful poetic lines in this work. You probably know that. You probably intended it. More is done with motion and less with revery. The wonderful dreaming quality of *Menagerie* is not here. But there is no reason that it should be. A creative artist need not repeat himself. You are breaking here into new ground. Serafina takes a bad beating but she ends up on the rise. Her problem is solved for her—in a very unique way, to be sure.

This work must be judged in the proper historical perspective. This is in the romantic, not the classical tradition. This grows out of the Elizabethan plays of violence and comes up through the tradition of the Romantic movement where passion rules and not reason. The elements here are movement, bright color and symbolism—the dummies are excellent, and so are the tattoos themselves. The goat and the witch are all in place here.

It is my own inner feeling that your work is going ultimately to develop along another line—do you remember *The Purification?*—but that is not to say that you have not turned out a powerful piece in this vein, and one with which you can be very well pleased. It would be my guess that this might be even more popular than *Streetcar.* Much, of course, will depend on the acting and the direction. The girl who plays Serafina has got to have terrific fires in her. This is a big part for a big actress, or rather, one who has bigness in her waiting for such a part to bring it out.

About the Italian lines. This is effectively used, I think. Nothing is said in Italian so complicated that its meaning will not come through, aided by the attendant action, and it will give a lot of atmosphere. With a few exceptions, I think the phrases are right and idiomatic. I'd be glad to consult with Frank about these things, except that I imagine you will have a much more reliable source of advice in some of the Italian actors you will have in the cast. I suggest that you let them say what comes natural to them in the situations. Then you will get the authentic intonation. Once they get it stabilized I'll be glad to sit in on a rehearsal and take down how it is and see about getting it spelled right for the book version. The spelling as it is now strikes me as being pretty wild. But this may be Sicilian spelling. The Italian I know is mostly Tuscan. But I do know that Venetian spells quite differently and the same may be true of Sicilian. In any case once the text is established I can locate a literate Sicilian down in the village and check the spelling with him.

Is it all right for me to send this script to Lustig so that he can get started on some designs to show you? I'll caution him against showing the script to anyone, and to get it right back to me as soon as he has read it.

Knowing how you like to change things in rehearsal it's probably best to hold up on the composition for a while. If there is to be a month's run in Chicago that should give us time to get a playing script and then get the book out for the opening here.

[. . .]

Is Paul [Bowles] going to come back to do the music?

Well, the thing packs a wallop, and you must not have misgivings about it. It is a work for the stage and must be judged on that basis. If you were telling the same story in a novel you would have done all sorts of things differently, having more freedom of time and place to work with. The great thing is that Serafina's passion comes through as believable human glory and suffering. The stuff is there. Now it's up to director and actors to project it.

Let's get together soon again, when you have the chance.

Best to Frank,

[James Laughlin]

« • »

Is Paul [. . .] the music?: While Paul Bowles did compose music for *The Glass Menagerie* (1945) as well as incidental music for *A Streetcar Named Desire* (1947) and *Summer and Smoke* (1948), he remained in Tangier at this time and did not provide music for *The Rose Tattoo*.

89. TLS—1

November 7, 1950 [New York]

DEAR JAY:

Many, many thanks for your letter about the play [*The Rose Tattoo*]. Please do send your copy of it to Lustig. If he comes up quickly enough with a striking design I feel sure that Cheryl would be delighted to use it for playbills, advertisements, Etc. The values of the play being less literary than usual, I feel that it will be more impressive on the stage than it is in manuscript, at least, I <u>hope</u> so. The director, Danny Mann, is no fool, in fact he is a real New York intellectual but has humor and vitality to compensate for that defect. He says that "mood" is "doom" spelt backwards which probably means that I shall have to put up a fight for the plastic-poetic elements in the production. We shall see. If casting is completed by November 15th I can take a couple of weeks in Key West to train for the contest. The girl, Maureen Stapleton, is a God-send and the rest of the cast is being slowly and very carefully put together.

I am sorry you were mistaken about the novel [*The Roman Spring of Mrs. Stone*] moving up to ninth place on the best-seller list. In fact it moved quite strongly in the other direction. I doubt that there is any hope of resuscitating sales by further advertising. Do you think so? Perhaps it would be better to contribute the sum I was planning for the "Ad" to the Authors League to be given to the Patchens. I have gotten another letter from Miriam saying that their situation has deteriorated still further. The letter is quite touching and while I have never liked Patchen's work very much I am sure that he deserves aid and perhaps I can make a tax-deductible contribution to them through the League. Would you check on that with Louise M. Sillcox? If she approves, I can make out a check on my book royalties, ear-marked for Patchen.

I am enclosing a short-story by Oliver Evans which I think has a great deal of charm. He wanted you to see it for possible inclusion in the annual.

Will call you this week, if I don't hear from you, about the contribution to League. Audrey can also advise you about it.

Ever,

Tenn

≪ • ≫

Cheryl: Cheryl Crawford (1902–1986), American stage director and producer and cofounder of the Group Theatre, produced the premieres of *The Rose Tattoo* and *Sweet Bird of Youth*.

Danny Mann: Daniel Mann (1912–1991), American stage, film, and television director, directed the Broadway premiere of *The Rose Tattoo*.

Maureen Stapleton: (1925–2006). The lead female roles in *The Rose Tattoo* and *Orpheus Descending* are Italian characters written for Italian actress Anna Magnani, but Magnani never felt her English was strong enough for a stage performance and it turned out that Maureen Stapleton, an American actress of Irish descent, originated both roles. She was also a longtime friend of TW's.

the Patchens: Kenneth Patchen (1911–1972), American poet and novelist, and his wife Miriam Patchen (1914–2000) were facing financial difficulties due to Kenneth's ill health, so JL wrote to various writers asking them to chip into a fund for the Patchens. Kenneth was one of the early ND authors (first published in 1939) and, by the time of JL's death in 1997, ND had published sixteen of his titles. In addition he and Miriam had worked as the "office staff" of ND and lived in a cottage belonging to JL's aunt Leila when the fledgling firm was run from Norfolk, Connecticut.

Louise M. Sillcox: Executive secretary for the Authors League and Dramatists Guild. TW was in touch with her about establishing authors' grants for writers in need.

90. TLS—1

Dec. 2, 1950 [Chicago]

DEAR JAY:

I have just mailed my final revisions of the play and am now commencing the vacant interval between big pieces of work when I don't know what to do with myself except drink more than I should and run around too much at night.

The state of the world makes every other state seem very temporary. I was happy over the *Compass* notice which you sent me. Wish it could have been quoted somewhere. Did you use the Isherwood quote? I've been looking for it in the Sunday sections but it hasn't appeared in them.

I am reading old Ezra Pound's letters, a very tragic cycle from the trumpet notes before the first world war to the querulous incoherencies at the end, trying to find just where the failure of adjustment crept in, if it is not simply the natural declension of time. He was rather hard on "Bill" Williams, huh? I have never been able to get excited over Williams's work although I see its humanity and simplicity. Why did he go to Random House?—*Saturday Review* has sent me Bowles's stories to review which is the toughest reviewing job I've ever undertaken, as I can't help feeling that the best of the stories, except for "Distant Episode," should have been published <u>privately</u>— the sado-masochistic elements!—and there are least five more stories than should have been printed. But the good stories are <u>marvelous</u>.

Ever,

10.

« • »

old Ezra Pound's letters: *The Letters of Ezra Pound, 1907–1941* (ed. D. D. Paige) was originally published in 1950 by Harcourt, Brace. It was reissued in paper as *Selected Letters, 1907–1941* by ND in 1971.

Bill Williams: In 1950, William Carlos Williams (1883–1963), whom JL considered (along with Ezra Pound) the bedrock of the New Directions list, wrote to JL that he was taking all of his prose works to Random House under David McDowell who had recently left ND for the larger publisher. Although both WCW and Paul Bowles had some reason for dissatisfaction with JL's at times cavalier management style, Laughlin had sincerely tried to respond to their criticisms. What JL did not know at the time was that the ambitious McDowell had criticized ND's sales management to both authors and had told Bennett Cerf at Random House, before he was hired, that he could bring a few ND authors with him. (See also note to TW's letter to JL of 3/11/45.)

Bowles stories to review: "The Human Psyche—Alone," TW's review of Paul Bowles, *The Delicate Prey and Other Stories*, was first published in the *Saturday Review of Literature*, December 23, 1950.

91. TL—4

January 15, 1951 [New York]

DEAR TENNESSEE,

I hope that things are going well out there, and that you are now satisfied about the ending [of *The Rose Tattoo*] and the new character playing the priest.

I had a very pleasant session with Audrey the other night, and I think we have the front matter worked out exactly the way you and she want it.

Enclosed is a proof of the flaps for the jacket. Will you kindly approve this, adding anything you care to, and rush it back to me by airmail? Please be sure to get it off a few hours after you receive it, so that we can get the jackets ready for the salesmen on their trips. I enclose a stamped return envelope so that you can pop it right back.

Now I would like to give you a report on the session last evening with the three little Italian princesses over the Italian speeches in the play. It was most successful. They got very interested, liked the play, and really worked their little heads off getting everything grammatical and correct. They are most anxious to meet you, and sometime when you get back, we must all try to get together. Meanwhile, I am going to make arrangements for them all to see the show, because they worked so hard on it.

As I had anticipated, there were a great many wrong spellings. There were also one or two places where the grammar was a bit off. However, it is now fixed just the way it should be for simple Italian or Sicilian peasants. [. . .]

> With best wishes and many
> thanks,
> James Laughlin

≪ • ≫

92. Telegram—1

[January 16, 1951] Western Union

NEW ENDING GOES IN TODAY. PAUL SENDING FINAL GALLEYS IN NEXT TWO DAYS. BUSINESS EXCELLENT.

TENNESSEE

≪ • ≫

Paul: TW's friend Paul Bigelow worked for him doing secretarial work during the rehearsal period and out-of-town tryouts for *The Rose Tattoo*. (See also note to letter of 1/25/46.)

93. TL—2

February 23, 1951 [Norfolk]

DEAR TENNESSEE,

I hope that you and Frank are having a good time down there. The weather around here has been pretty miserable. I am getting off for some skiing at Alta next week, and will probably be away for about a month. But everything is organized here to do a good job on the new book. You can write me at Alta Lodge, Sandy, Utah, if anything comes up.

I have figured out your book earnings for the past year, and they seem pretty good. I am enclosing carbons of all the reports and the summary, the originals of which have gone to Audrey, and also a copy of my letter to her, which explains certain details.

[. . .]

The last time I was up at your apartment, you asked me about what you ought to do with your investments. Your government bond holdings are, of course, perfectly safe, but there is this factor to be considered, what with the continued inflation, the dollar is falling in purchasing power, and bonds do not appreciate comparatively the way good common stocks do.

Right now is no time to buy common stock, as the market is now at new peaks, but I think you ought seriously to consider putting part of your portfolio into "blue chip" common stocks at some time in the future when there is a substantial break in the market.

[. . .]

Everyone I have seen around town is talking about *The Rose Tattoo*, and 90% of it is extremely favorable. I should think you ought to have a very good and long run with that.

Best wishes to you both,
James Laughlin

《 • 》

you asked me [. . .] investments: On his tax returns, JL listed his occupation as "investor."

94. TLS—1

4/1/51 [Key West]

Dear Jay:

Although I came here, ostensibly, for a rest I have been busier than usual working my way into another play. The initial stages are always the most strenuous, perhaps even worse than the final. I have been very nervous. Hypertensive. Bigelow took me to a fashionable doctor in New York who gave me some pills that are supposed to make my face flush and my ears buzz as they open the capillaries—distend the blood vessels, Etc. I took just one and felt far more hypertensive than usual so have put them on the shelf. I drink too much. About eight drinks a day at carefully spaced intervals. I am trying to work down to six. Perhaps I ought to stop working. But then I would explode from sheer ennui.

I hate to make any derogatory remarks about the Cummington boy's design. Strictly *entre nous*, it does look a bit like *pigeon en casserole*. But I sense that he feels very strongly about designing something for the book and it might be mean of us to frustrate him. The typography and paper are so beautiful. I do wish that Lustig was doing the front cover, however. I am charmed with the rose cover of the book of *Tattoo*. The only other person I know who likes it is Donald Windham, but I like it very much indeed. I also love the ad, copy of which you sent me.

Thank you so much for the very detailed financial statements and I was agreeably surprised by the amount of funds. I hope sometime later in the Spring, when my own economic picture acquires more clarity, to make a new contribution to the Authors League fund, earmarked for Oliver Evans. He is having an operation for his deafness and I would like to be able to help him with it. I may draw on my account with you for this purpose, perhaps about $1500. He is in a desperate mental or nervous state, a great deal of which, I think, may be attributable to his affliction. Took eight sleeping pills one evening, fell down on the street and broke two ribs! Only quarts of black coffee saved him. On my birthday, while I was in New York, I took him to see *Romeo and Juliet* and when Miss De Havilland was delivering a soliloquy on the apron of the stage, Oliver, in the fourth row, suddenly cried out "Nothing can kill the beauty of the lines!" and tore out of the theatre. Later that night he called up an old lady who had formerly befriended him, a dowager who is the ranking member of the Cabot clan, and told her she was "just an old bitch and not even her heirs could stand her!" I think he deserves an endowment for life! Even if this intransigent behavior persists.

Frank, Grandfather, and I are still in Key West. Until the end of April. We sail the middle of May for Europe, again.

Ever,
Tenn.

Love to Gertrude.

≪ • ≫

Miss De Havilland: (1916–). Olivia de Havilland is a British-American film actress.
Gertrude: See note to TW's letter to JL of January 25, 1946.

95. TLS—5

April 20, 1951 [Alta]

DEAR TENNESSEE,

Many thanks for your letter of April 1st which has just reached me out in Alta. But I am extremely sorry to hear that you have not been feeling up to scratch. I wish I could offer some kind of advice on what you should do, but I am afraid that medical matters are all a mystery to me. At the risk of being thought a crank, however, I wonder whether you have ever tried anything along the line of osteopathy or massage. Maybe something of that kind might loosen you up a little bit and help that tense feeling. One way or another, I hope you find some way to lick it, as it must be terribly upsetting and aggravating.

That is good news that you are working on another play, though, as you know, I would probably rather see you writing poetry. I always enjoy the plays—they are wonderful—but I still feel that essentially you are a poet, and that in the end you will do your greatest work in that field. Before you go off to Europe again, won't you look through your things and get together as many poems for me as you can, because I would really like to bring out a book of verse next fall. I keep feeling that you must have a lot of them hidden away that I haven't seen yet.

[. . .]

I'm glad that you like the jacket for *The Rose Tattoo*. I do too, very much. I think it is extremely subtle and one of Lustig's best. However, it doesn't surprise me that other people don't like it. The real innovators are always ahead of the public taste.

I am glad that you agree with me that the phoenix which the boy up in Massachusetts drew is not suitable, and I have written to them that we definitely don't want to use it [for *I Rise in Flame*]. This book is going to have a kind of simple magnificence from the elegant typography, and I think it would definitely be a mistake to smear it up with something so fancy.

That is bad news about Oliver Evans. Do you think it would cheer him up any if I wrote to him and asked him for a group of poems for the next number of the annual? Let me know his address, and I will try it if you think it would help. Your idea of giving him a grant in aid also sounds like a very good one. Let me know what you want to do about this, and I will send the money to Audrey to give to the Authors League. I never knew Oliver very well, but always liked him very much.

[. . .]

Thinking about this question of helping authors who need help, and it becomes more difficult for the serious type of poet and writer every day, I want to make a suggestion to you which I hope you will ponder carefully. It is based on the possibility of exploiting the rather fabulous sums which can be earned from these 25¢ reprints.

I know that you don't think much of those reprints, and neither do I. They are pretty unattractive as bookmaking, and not very appetizing, but it is a fact that they sell enormously and pay big royalties. At various times in the past year or so each one of the big four in this field has approached me about the possibility of making a contract for 25¢ reprints of your books, both *Mrs. Stone* and the plays. I have always turned them down, telling them that you were not keen on this type of publication, but they keep coming back with ever larger offers and guarantees, and now the sum is so large that I think we ought to give the matter further consideration.

What I have in mind is this: that we should make a deal with the one who would offer the most, and then use the proceeds to help authors who need help. Young fellows in the situation of [Oliver] Evans or even Donnie Windham, whose books will not sell well enough to make their living expenses. I have not talked to Mr. Colton about the matter, but I could do so, and I am pretty sure that this thing could be set up in such a way that it would be tax deductible.

By playing one of these firms against the other, I think we could get an advance of as much as ten or fifteen thousand dollars against the 25¢ reprint rights for *Mrs. Stone* and three big plays. By the usual publishing practice, this sum would be divided between you and me, and we could then each use our share in the following way. Working through the Authors League, or through your own charitable foundation, which Mr. Colton could set up for you, you could give grants in aid from your share to young writers whom you thought worthy of encouragement and help. I, for my part, would use my share to finance and promote the publication of their books when they had written them, setting up a revolving fund, so that if any of them made a profit, the profits would then be used to finance other books of similar category.

In this way, we could really do an enormous amount of good for the state of American letters today, and both get a lot of satisfaction out of it. Of course, as you know, a great many of the books which I publish now are done on a similar basis, but with the continuing rise in costs and heavier taxes every year, I am severely limited in what I can do. A windfall of this kind would mean the possibility of doing three or four extra books each year which would not otherwise be possible for me on a business basis.

I have made inquiries among other publishers and they tell me that the sale of the 25¢ books does not materially interfere with the sale of the higher priced editions, providing that at least the year or two period elapses before the reprint is issued. I think also that it might be possible to make a stipulation in the contract with the reprint publisher that they should use jackets by Lustig instead of those dreadful chromo scenes of busty ladies that are the usual thing. In particular, I am thinking of Victor Weybright and the New American Library, who do the highest class of books in this field. He has done Donnie [Windham]'s book and Paul [Bowles]'s and a number of others that are first rate literature.

I hope you will think this over seriously and let me have your reactions when you have a moment. I also hope you will not feel that I am getting out of line in making such a suggestion. I realize that you would not be willing to sacrifice your principles about the quality of books and publishing simply for the money that is in it, but when the money is to be used to help other writers who need help, and whom you want to encourage, that puts quite a different light on it, I think.

I have not said anything about this idea to Audrey, but if you think it has merit I could take it up with her and Mr. Colton, and see what kind of thing could be set up for you.

I expect to be here in Alta for another couple of weeks, and then hope to get down to California, to see Christopher [Isherwood], Rexroth and Henry Miller, and a few others, before returning to New York early in June.

I get reports daily from the office, and I gather that things are going along well with the new book. Our new sales manager, Bob MacGregor, is really a crackerjack in his quiet unassuming way, and he has gotten a lot of fine window displays, and Barbara has also gotten some good publicity breaks. She is getting out a special wrap-around band to go on the books announcing the Perry Award, which was a fine thing, and I hope you get a couple of others before the season is over.

The new little Vittorini novel is out, and I will ask Betty to send you a copy at the same time as this letter. I think it is the most beautiful thing he has written.

You will remember John Hawkes, the boy up in Cambridge who wrote *The Cannibal*. His new novel has just come in and is terribly exciting. It is called *The Beetle Leg* and we will be bringing it out next fall. It has that same wonderful mixture of reality and unreality that was in the earlier book, and the same power of verbal poetry, and quite a bit more narrative flow. I think he is a comer and a boy to watch. We also have in the shop for next fall a very amusing little novel about life in Greenwich Village and the "hipsters."

I certainly envy you getting back to Europe again. I'm trying to work things out so that I will be able to get over on a business trip in the summer and possibly we can get together then.

Give my best to your grandfather. What a man! I hope I have as much beans as that when I am his age.

With best to you and Frank,

as ever,

J

≪ • ≫

Bob MacGregor: Robert Mercer MacGregor (1911–1974). Robert MacGregor was already the head of his own small publishing firm, Theatre Arts Books, when JL hired him to supervise the New York office and in effect be his second-in-command. A former foreign correspondent and decorated World War II veteran, MacGregor was intelligent, forthright, and an excellent manager. From the day he was hired, June 14, 1950, until New Directions was forced to move its offices from 333 Sixth Avenue to 80 Eighth Avenue in 1978, New Directions and Theatre Arts would share office space. MacGregor's partner at Theatre Arts, George Zournas, who ran the day-to-day operations, was also his life partner. As a gay man in the 1950s, MacGregor was particularly attuned to dealing with TW, his circle of friends, and the difficult dynamics of his life. JL was always adamant that any telling of the New Directions story should make clear MacGregor's great contribution to the whole enterprise. Ian MacNiven in his biography of JL, *"Literchoor Is My Beat": A Life of James Laughlin, Publisher of New Directions*, said of MacGregor: "Hiring him would turn out to be the most momentous personnel decision of J's publishing career."

new little Vittorini novel: *The Twilight of the Elephant* (ND 1951).

novel about [. . .]"hipsters": *Who Walk in Darkness* by Chandler Brossard (ND 1952).

SECTION X

―――― ⚬⚬ ――――

PF: You said you met Bob MacGregor in 1950?

JL: Yes, and when my job at Ford [Foundation] started in 1952, it was a godsend that he had taken on the work at ND. He knew my taste, he was a hard worker and straight. He's never had the credit that he should have had. I hope that when it's written [a proposed history of New Directions] it will give proper credit to Bob and to all of you who've done such superb work.

≪ • ≫

my job at Ford [Foundation]: When his marriage to Margaret Keyser Laughlin dissolved in 1951, JL accepted a salaried position with the Ford Foundation as head of Intercultural Publications. His job was to produce *Perspectives USA*, a magazine of his own creation to promote American culture and creative achievement. The final issue of *Perspectives* would be published in 1957. During this period, JL remained involved with everything going on at New Directions; however, he was frequently traveling, and the day-to-day running of the office was left in the capable hands of Robert MacGregor.

96. TL—2

July 25, 1951 [New York]

DEAR TENNESSEE,

What kind of a time have you been having over there? I've been hoping to hear from you, but I guess if you are working, you're probably too busy for letters. Anyway, I may get down to see you soon. By the time this reaches you, I will have arrived in Paris, then I have to do about three weeks' business in London, then I'll head South, and see you if you are visible. So drop me a card in England giving me your plans and dates. My address there will be c/o the Phyllis Court Club at Henley on Thames.

As you probably heard, everyone has been sick back here, but they seem to be making progress. Paul Bigelow had a very serious operation on his head over at the Manhattan General Hospital, and I haven't been able to see him, but I checked by phone with his nurse, and she reports that it was satisfactory and that he is making good progress.

Audrey also had quite a tough time in the hospital. I think it was more than just appendicitis. But she is on her feet again now, and seems all right though she looks very pale. She works much too hard, and ought to take it easier.

Do you happen to have any short thing around, either poetry or prose, that would be suitable for the next number of the Annual? I have gotten most of the book off to the printer before leaving, but there is still space, and it really wouldn't be the same without you. So if you have something, shoot it to me in England, and I'll pop it along to New Jersey to the printer. Of course, I have "Hard Candy" here in my files, but Audrey doesn't seem to like the idea of using it, so I guess we'd better let that lie for a while.

I hope you have been writing some more poetry. As I told you a good many times, I am very anxious to get together a group of your poems for a book soon, and I think this coming winter would be a good time, if you will only bestir yourself to search for them. I keep feeling you have others hidden around that I haven't seen.

Did you hear that Gore has become a manufacturer on the Hudson River? I haven't seen him, but I hear that his father has set him up some kind of a plant, which he is supposed to manage. That will be something.

I was awfully glad when I got the news from Audrey that you had changed your mind, at least temporarily, about 25¢ reprints. Not having heard back from you, I don't know whether my letter on this subject had anything to do with your decision or not, but anyway I was pleased. As you may have heard from Audrey, 25¢ rights on *Streetcar* have now been sold to Weybright of New American Library for a very handsome sum—$12,000 in fact, which is not chicken feed in any league, and surely the largest sum that has ever been paid for a play. But it nearly wasn't so good. Audrey was on the point of closing a deal with Bantam for only $3000 and I tipped her off that others were interested, and when she had to go to the hospital she turned the matter over to me, and by dint of playing one against another, they bid the advance up to the large figure.

I am particularly happy about getting this windfall, because my share of it will permit me to print two or three books by promising newcomers which I would not otherwise have been able to do, since business in general is lousy here now. I'll tell you more about it when I see you. I just hope you realize how very deeply I appreciate the enormous help you have given to New Directions.

Since getting back from the West, my life has been the usual rat race of trying to catch up with business in the office, though I did have several very pleasant days off at Nantucket. The weather was lovely up there and the ocean was fine. Of course, the place is getting much too crowded with tourists, but the architecture is still almost unspoiled, and you can get away on a bicycle or a car to those wonderful moors along the beaches.

Well, drop me a card to England, and I surely hope we can meet in Italy or the South of France later in the summer.

Best to you and Frank,

James Laughlin

Dictated by Mr. Laughlin
but signed in his absence
by the most wonderful, kind,
sweet, charming, brilliant,
trustworthy, fascinating [...]

≪ • ≫

but signed in his absence: ND book designer and future Mrs. Laughlin, Gertrude Huston typed this letter from JL's dictation.

97. TLS—1

7/24/52 [Hamburg, Germany]

DEAR JAY:

I've had you on my mind ever since I got to Europe but I just haven't had much chance to write a letter. We spent about a week in Paris with Maria and I have never seen her looking so well, the stay on the sea had done her a world of good, her vitality was such that I simply could not keep up with her. I left her in good hands. She had lunch with John Huston, José Ferrer and myself the day before I left Paris and from then on, I take it, they took up where I had left off and I think she is not quite sure which of them she prefers and gives me to understand that both are mad for her, which I do not find in the least inconceivable, do you? The Russians are mad!

I had a lot of work do and Rome was getting too hot for it so I left there after about two weeks and came up here to Hamburg which is very cool and invigorating. I thought I would be unknown up here. Quite the contrary! Had no sooner registered than reporters were calling and I had lots of pictures taken this afternoon. Alas, for the anonymous joys of the gay cabarets!—This hotel is so swanky that one cannot bring in friends at night, so don't be surprised if my next book of poems includes a lot of bucolics and eclogues and fauns and satyrs among the moonlit trees. Just so it doesn't also include the "polizei." Hamburg is really madder than the Russians.

Gadg is giving me many notes for revisions on *Camino* so I don't know just when I will get to work on the poems, but I will as soon as possible.

Affectionate greetings to Gertrude.

Yours ever,
Tenn

« • »

John Huston: (1906–1987), American film director who adapted *The Night of the Iguana* into a screenplay and directed the 1964 film version.

José Ferrer: (1912–1992), Puerto Rican–born actor and theater and film director, best known for his portrayal of Cyrano de Bergerac on both stage and screen.

Gadg: Elia Kazan's nickname, which stemmed from his skill at fixing things—pronounced like the first syllable of the word "gadget."

Camino: TW wanted the anglicized pronunciation of *Camino Real* used and asked that it be printed in every edition of the play: Cámino Réal [reel].

98. TL—2

March 26, 1953 [New York]

DEAR TENN:

I'm sorry that I didn't get a chance to see you before you went off to Key West to tell you how much I enjoyed the play [*Camino Real*]. I think I might be inclined to argue about some of the things that Kazan did with it, but certainly it is one of your finest works, and full of beautifully poetic passages. I think I have two main objections to the direction. First, it didn't make the actors speak the lines of poetry the way I think poetry should be spoken on the stage. They don't bring it out properly. They rush over it, either because they don't know how to speak it or because they don't realize how important it is. On the French stage, where there is a tradition of rhetorical theatre, this wouldn't happen. I hope that Barrault will do this play in Paris because I think he would really bring out what is in it. Kazan is just too Hollywood for my taste. He seems to think more of motion than emotion. He clutters up the line of the play with a continuous scurrying around of busyness on the stage so that the audience's attention is continually distracted from what is being said and meant. The real feelings of the play, its philosophical depth and tragic beauty, never managed to cut through all that scrambling around. He gets it now and then—in the love scene, for example, where he just lets the actors be quiet on the stage and do justice to the lines—but most of the time it is obscured.

Well, this is all water under the bridge—it's a lavish production—and I don't set myself up anyway to know anything about the theatre. But I keep feeling in the back of my mind that you will only be able to realize the full poetry that is in you when you forget about Broadway, with all its stereotypes and limitations, and look around for some small theatre somewhere which has an audience, and a management, that really cares about poetry and the imagination.

I hope you weren't letting yourself be upset by the silly things that the reviewers wrote about the play in the papers. Nothing better could be expected of that crew. They can only appreciate a thing if it fits within their own limited horizons. I'm convinced that you'll get a very different reaction on *Camino* when it gets to Europe.

The real quality of the play comes out in reading, so I'm glad that the book will be available. I hope you will let Bob [MacGregor] have the finished script as soon as possible so that we can get started.

I'm urging all my friends to pay no attention to the reviews but to go and see the play and judge it for themselves. Dr. Fischer, our German publisher who is here, is crazy about it—went twice—and wants to translate a scene for his magazine in Frankfurt, *Die Neue Rundschau*.

Well, let me hear from you when you have a moment, and I hope you and Frank have a wonderful time down there in Key West. I'll be writing soon about other matters, but wanted to get word to you about *Camino*. It's a wonderful play, and don't let anybody tell you different. This is real theatre, and what the American theatre desperately needs if it isn't going to become simply a bad copy of Hollywood.

As ever,

James Laughlin

≪ • ≫

Barrault: Jean-Louis Barrault (1910–1994), French actor and director.

the reviewers: The original production of *Camino Real* was almost unanimously attacked by the New York critics.

99. TLS—2

April 5, 1953 [Key West]

DEAR JAY:

I want to thank you for the never-failing appreciation you have for anything good in my work. Your letter meant a great deal to me, since I went through a pretty black period after those notices came out. I had suspected that we would be blasted by a quorum of the critics, ever since New Haven Gadg and I had expected or feared it pretty certainly, but even so there was a degree of militant incomprehension that seemed like an order to get out and stay out of the current theatre.

I'm glad that you felt poetry in the play [*Camino Real*]. I can't agree with you about Gadg. I don't think this play was nearly as easy for him as *Streetcar* or *Salesman*, it was a much harder and more complex job, and he was working with players at least half of which were dancers and had no previous speaking experience on the stage, an inadequate budget and far from adequate time in rehearsal and try-out on the road. Gadg is not as fond of verbal values as he should be, but of all Broadway directors he has the most natural love of poetry. Not a single critic seemed to have any sense of the abstract, formal beauty of the piece. They concentrated on what each thing might mean in a literal, logical sense, and I can't help thinking that there was a general feeling of ill-will among them at what seemed new and intransigent in the work. I have had a couple of letters from Atkinson, in London, expressing moral and chauvinistic indignation over the pessimism which he says "American audiences" will not accept, that they won't like it in Anouilh and Sartre and will not accept it from me. He repeated America and American several times as if the play was a violation of national respect. Nevertheless I think he, almost alone, did make an effort to divorce his personal repugnance from his professional appraisal, and was frank about the source of that repugnance. A couple or three nights ago I got a special delivery letter from Edith Sitwell, couched in the most extravagant heart-felt terms, for which I was rightly overcome with gratitude, and there has been a flood of letters from people known and unknown, more even than I got during the whole course of *Streetcar*, saying their love of the play and anger at its reception.

So although it is a great, almost overpowering, professional setback for me, I don't feel altogether hopeless about it.

Your advice is good. I have nothing more to expect from Broadway and if I go on writing plays, it must be with an absolute uncompromising fidelity to myself alone, that is, quite purely from now on. They say, on good authority, that the life-expectancy of an American literary talent is about 15 years and I have already long-exceeded that mark, since I got my first pay-check for writing at sixteen and have written every day since that I was able to punch the type-writer keys and very few days when I wasn't can be remembered. But I think the pressure of things to say is as great as ever, if not greater, but a lot of the native energy is depleted and the time has come to let up a little, shift gears, work under less steam. It would be a good thing if I could stop altogether for a while, but I find my daily existence almost unbearably tedious without beginning it at the typewriter. Frank and I plan to go abroad, this year, for a really extended stay, in fact we are planning to go all the way around the world, beginning in Italy, then Spain, then North Africa, then Greece and Istanbul, then Helsinki for a festival production of some plays of mine, then on from the near East to the Orient, to Ceylon and India and Japan. Thence back to America, when it will be necessary to start trying to "make a living" again, as I will have nothing left but my bonds by that time. Early next month I'm going to try my hand at directing a play. The play is Donald Windham's family-portrait called *The Starless Air*, structurally inept but very true and poetic, and there is a chance, if this Houston try-out goes well, I might return to the States to stage it for Broadway about Xmas time: it's about a family Christmas dinner in Georgia.

May I start sending you short-stories for the proposed collection? I have them with me and am getting them in shape. They will have to be typed at your end of the line, and I think they ought to be sold by subscription only, since I want to include some, such as "Two on a Party," that might precipitate an awful row in the present time of reaction.

Ever,

Tenn.

≪ • ≫

Atkinson: Brooks Atkinson (1894–1984), American theater critic for the *New York Times* from 1925 to 1960 and a generally positive advocate for TW.

Anouilh: Jean-Marie-Lucien-Pierre Anouilh (1910–1967), French playwright.

100. TL—1

April 11, 1953 [New York]

DEAR TENN:

Thanks for your very swell letter. I'm glad that you have been encouraged by lots of letters from people who liked *Camino*. They are right and the dopes are wrong. But it all takes time. You must just be patient. The world catches up with good things slowly. You've just got to develop a tough hide. I went through all this with New Directions. For years almost all the reviews of all the books were ridicule and scorn. You just have to sit tight and pay no attention and believe in yourself. It may be harder for you because you had a lot of success fairly early in the game. That makes you even more vulnerable for them because they really hate anybody who is truly creative. Most of these critics, I think, are thwarted writers anyway. But thousands of people want and need what only you can give them, so just you stick at it. Don't compromise. Just write what wants to come out of the heart of you.

By all means send along the stories as soon as you can. But I don't like the idea of a limited edition. No reason to keep the bulk of the stories from the wide public that would want them. Why not rather do a public volume and save the pieces that might cause trouble for a separate limited edition? Actually, I think that you may want to lengthen and extend "Two on a Party." I know Audrey doesn't like the piece, but I think it just makes her nervous. I think it is a terrific theme and you may want to develop it into a short novel, which could be the pièce de résistance of a limited edition which could also include "Hard Candy" and the one about the farmers in the South ["Kingdom of Earth"].

I hope you'll be keeping along on the poems, too. I like that idea of matching volumes of poems and stories.

And PLEASE rush us the final version of *Camino* so that we can get it set up. Everybody is talking about the play and it's a shame we don't have the book out right now. I know you've had problems, but do try to let us get started.

Re Gadg, nobody who really had a "natural love of poetry" could have behaved the way he did over his former Communist friends. There are limits. Gadg loves money and fame. I hope they make him miserable.

Directing Donnie's play sounds fine. I wish you would direct your own, so that people couldn't keep changing what is in them.

And going to India sounds fine. That was for me the great revelation of a lifetime. When you get ready to go there I'll make you up a list of places and things and people. Maybe you will settle down there. I could very easily, I think, except perhaps for the heat and the food problems.

Life moves along here like pieces of wood being pushed through a sawmill. This job is no bed of roses. I'm under constant pressure from reactionary Trustees who would like the magazine to be a kind of watered down *Atlantic Monthly*. I suppose they will knock my head off one of these days, but I'm giving them a battle. The reaction abroad is good, which is what counts for me.

Best to Frank,

[James Laughlin]

≪ • ≫

the dopes: He is referring to the New York critics who were nearly unanimous in their hostility toward *Camino Real*.

Re Gadg: Elia Kazan testified before the U.S. House Un-American Activities Committee (HUAC) where he identified former colleagues as Communists. In doing so, Kazan angered and alienated many people in the Hollywood and the theater communities for decades.

Donnie's play: *The Starless Air*, which TW directed in Houston that year.

India [. . .] revelation of a lifetime: In late 1952 JL went to India, taking Gertrude Huston as his secretary. Indian publishers had asked for Ford Foundation assistance in publishing Western books on a large scale, and JL went to assess the situation for the Foundation.

This job: During his tenure at the Ford Foundation, JL was continually at odds with both liberal and conservative political forces (which had their own agendas), while he was dedicated (as always) to *art*.

the magazine [. . .] watered down: *Perspectives USA.* JL did, in fact, prepare several supplements for *The Atlantic Monthly* on other cultures such as India and Burma.

101. TLS—2

[May 9, 1953] [Houston]

DEAR JAY:

I just got your letter and I thank you for your patience and understanding about this problem of getting the script ready for publication. Here is the introduction to the book [*Camino Real*]. I had meant to devote this AM, Saturday, to getting the book together, but last night a "crisis" occurred between myself and Windham. He accused me of "completely re-writing" his play [*The Starless Air*] while he was keeping "TV" and interview appointments, and have accordingly ruined it. It threw me into such a despondency I couldn't sleep and this whole day I have been immobilized except for sitting and taking notes on an afternoon run-through. But tomorrow, Sunday, I really will buckle down to the script [*Camino Real*]. I'm sorry to say the "Bigelow script" was hopeless. It was just a typed up copy of the prompt book and simply couldn't be published, as I say in this introduction. If I weren't involved in this directing job I could turn in a much smoother script for publication. However this one that I will mail to you on Monday will only need a little brushing up which I could do from proofs when I get back to New York about the end of next week. Affectionately,

10

« • »

introduction to the book: The "Foreword" for *Camino Real*. This essay had appeared, in slightly different form, in the *New York Times*, March 15, 1953.

102. TLS—1

Jan. 6, 1954 [Key West]

DEAR JAY:

I do hope this reaches you before you take flight to Europe as I wanted to wish you New Year and Bon Voyage and good luck with you know who. Fate struck me a hard blow in a bad place. I came down with an exquisitely painful and, worse, depressingly sordid condition called "thrombosed hemorrhoids" and have been in the hospital with it more than a week. They were going to operate, then decided to see if it would clear up naturally, which it has done, though it may be that I'll have to have the hemorrhoid veins taken out next Spring to avoid another attack.

I would have mailed the stories (and a few poems of dubious merit) if this had not removed me from work. I'll get them off in the next day or two. I'm being discharged from the hospital today and Grandfather and I are going directly from here to the airport to catch a plane to Miami. Frank came down to look out for Grandfather but, after driving the car down to Miami, will fly back to New York to pick up Mr. Moon and bring him down to Key West with us, all very complicated and expensive.

I haven't heard from Maria for a long time, the longest time she's ever gone without writing me. I'm a little worried, though perhaps she just doesn't know where I am.

I'll see you in the Spring.

Ever,
Tenn.

« • »

Mr. Moon: TW's first bulldog.

103. TL—2

10 March 1954 [New York]

DEAR TENN,

I am ashamed to see how much time has passed since I have been meaning to write you—at least five days. The truth is I didn't want to write at the office or through the Dictaphone because my secretary is new and I don't know how discreet, and anything connected with Jay and Maria I put out of my mind there if only because of the intricate position of Gertrude in the office setup. I know you'll understand! And during this period for one reason or another I've been almost pilloried to that office.

I don't presume to know what's happening in London, despite all that Jay tells me, and like you I could not even dare surmise! What you say about whether or not they love each other truly is so very right, and of course love itself is a chameleon. I sometimes think that the tragedy of so many of us is that our sexual type is often not the type we can live with! I don't mean to be suggesting anything here; I just never know, and always feel that I cannot judge other people's problems, no matter how much sympathy and understanding and intuition I can bring to them.

[. . .]

Yours ever,

Robert M. MacGregor

≪ • ≫

anything connected with Jay and Maria: JL and Margaret Keyser Laughlin had separated in 1951 and subsequently divorced. Although he continued his longtime affair with Gertrude Huston, who was still designing books for New Directions, marriage to Gertrude was not an option because of his aunt Leila's and his mother's disapproval. JL was captivated by Maria Britneva but also found her constant effervescence wearing. He feared she would not be the steady manager and calm haven for him and the children that he wanted on the home front. (See also note to JL's letter to TW of 12/18/48.)

SECTION XI

JL: Well, Tennessee got quite annoyed with me when I broke it off with Maria because he wanted . . . he wanted it. He enjoyed the threesome trips around Italy with Gore Vidal. He enjoyed that very much. It took some of the heat off Tennessee of keeping her amused, you know. I could keep her amused or Gore could keep her amused, and he was angry with me for letting her down. But I think gradually he got over it, I think so. The person who really told me no was Jack Heinz's wife Drue. They met her and Drue said, "James, I forbid you to marry that woman."

≪ • ≫

Jack Heinz's wife Drue: H. J. "Jack" Heinz (1908–1987) and JL were boyhood friends in Pittsburgh (even attending the same Presbyterian church). They reconnected as adults when Jack was the head of Heinz Foods of "57 Varieties" fame. They became skiing companions, and Jack Heinz was the only outsider allowed to own stock in the Alta Ski Lift Company. (The stock was returned to JL upon Heinz's death.) Drue, born Doreen Mary English, Heinz's third wife, had a keen interest in literature and after JL's death [1997] endowed the James Laughlin Award in Poetry given annually by the American Academy of Arts and Letters for a second volume of poems by an American poet to be published in the upcoming year. She continues to be an active patron of the arts.

104. TLS—3

5/29/54 [Tangier]

DEAR BOB:

Frank says he mailed the proofs to you yesterday. I'm sorry about the delay. I didn't realize you were in a hurry for them. I only came across one <u>serious</u> error, the omission of a phrase in "Hard Candy" which made a sentence meaningless, and I wrote the omitted phrase in the margin. Two or three stories are still here as I haven't yet read them. "Mattress," "3 Players," "Violin Case," <"The Vine," and "Widow Holly."> As you have correct Mss. on these 5 it will be easy to check the proof at your end. That is, if there is a need for haste. I felt so fatigued, so run down, when I got on the boat that I knew I would loathe the stories if I read them. So I put it off till the last day of the voyage, when I was beginning to feel recovered. I liked most of them, especially "Two on a Party," which I almost wish were the title story of the book. Frank is disturbed over having both "Hard Candy" and "Mysteries of the Joy Rio" in the book. I think there should be a note stating that the latter is actually a first draft of the title story but that we felt there was enough difference to justify printing both. I think it might obviate some criticism, and criticism should certainly be obviated wherever possible, don't you think? I wonder if obviated is the right word . . .

Now please do me this favor. Don't distribute the book anywhere that my mother would be likely to get her hands on it. That is, around Saint Louis. It must <u>not</u> be displayed in windows or on counters anywhere. Don't you agree? Or do you? My mother's reaction is the only one that concerns me. I think she would be shocked to death by "Two on a Party"—although it seems that she did get hold of "One Arm" somehow or other. It still makes me shudder to think of her reaction! She has aged greatly since . . .

Isn't it awful to have conventional blood ties? You just can't break them.

Soon as we landed in Tangier we found ourselves involved in the turbulent lives of the Bowleses. Jane is hopeless enamored of an Arab woman in the grain-market, a courtship which has continued without success for six years, and Paul's Arab, Ahmed, has moved out of his house, at least for Ramadan, a religious period of abstinence like our Lent, which is now going on here. A cannon which shakes the whole city is fired at 3 AM announcing that eating, drinking, fucking must stop. It is fired again at 7 PM to signal the resumption of these practices, but Ahmed says that total abstinence is necessary in the third practice. Paul is languishing, liver trouble and paratyphoid came on him with Ramadan.

It appears that we have inherited Maria for the summer. A letter was waiting for me at Gibraltar in which she declared that she was brutally jilted and cannot stay in London, as everybody is sending her wedding presents and congratulatory messages. She is on a Mediterranean cruise to escape this humiliation. But she proposes to get off the boat at Corsica and come to Rome as she can't face London again under the circumstances. Funny as it does sound, I do feel sorry for her. Why did Jay propose to her if he wasn't prepared to go through with it? I wanted to have a quiet summer. . . . Of course when she arrives I will be happy to have her with us as she really does brighten a scene with her unquenchable spirits and love of fun. Jay says he was frightened of her vitality. Perhaps someone should have held his nose and made him swallow it for his own good. I can't see how, unless he is going to marry Gertrude after all, he will ever find anybody that will give him the lively companionship he seems to want and need.

Ever & truly, Tenn.

≪ • ≫

Ahmed: Ahmed ben Driss el Yacoubi (1928–1985), internationally acclaimed Moroccan painter.

she was brutally jilted: Unable to face a confrontation with Maria, JL simply left for India and Japan in mid-March of 1954 on business for the Ford Foundation, leaving everyone else including TW and MacGregor to pick up the pieces.

105. TLS—1

12/3/54 [Beverly Hills]

DEAR JAY:

I was surprised as you by Maria's arrival on these shores. She had abandoned the idea when I last saw her or had any communication from her on the subject. Exactly five minutes after I had opened and read your letter, in Kazan's room here, the phone rang and it was Maria! I can't imagine how she made the trip. She sent me back the traveler's checks and the apartment deposit which I had sent her in Italy, fearing she might go hungry or something, but she got a small film job and some TV so I guess her situation improved. As I say she's a person who always gives more than she gets, she wants to be on the giving end and seems to resent, well, not resent but decline if possible any material assistance that she can do without. The help she needs is artistic and emotional, not material, primarily. Of course I am sorry if her presence in America complicates things for you or makes you uncomfortable. If I were you, though, I would see her whenever you can and just keep things on a warm, friendly basis. She says she is trying to get herself TV work in New York and it may be that I can find something for her to do in connection with the new play [*Cat on a Hot Tin Roof*], I do hope so. I will be glad to see her, myself, as I miss her jokes and companionship when I get anxious or blue over something, which is only too often.

Saw an advance copy of *Hard Candy* out here and it looks great. You will get a copy of the new play soon as we get the final draft typed up next week in New York. Now must have my swim and start packing.

See you soon in Manhattan?

Ever fondly yours,
Tennessee

« • »

106. TL—2

Jan. 9, 1955 [New York]

DEAR TENN—

Thank you so much for your Christmas card and message. I'm so pleased that you liked my little poem that Johnny Myers printed. As you will no doubt have guessed, it was written for G[ertrude Huston], but grew out of M[aria Britneva]'s repeated accusations that G had me "under her thumb." Well, if that's where I am, as the poem says, I don't much mind, and if there is any pressure it is certainly of a kind that I never feel. The "baubles," of course, are out of Goldsmith, again thanks to M, and the business about running from life to life from the sayings of the Buddha . . . all of which just goes to show how odd are the ways in which a poem gets itself felt and made. And I'm so pleased that you liked it. I have quite a few accumulated since my last little book and must soon get busy and put them together for another. Not that I have much ambition for them . . . they come of themselves, little personal fantasies that are things unto themselves . . . but I like them, or some of them, and am pleased when friends do too.

[. . .]

I was much cheered up by our telephone conversation. As you have gathered, all this business with M is driving me half crazy. I don't think anyone has ever upset me so much. She has wonderful qualities and if she would just get over her illusions—me, for one, and the idea that she has to be an actress for another—I think she would have a happy and useful life.

I do want to help her, but everyone whose advice I have asked thinks there has got to be a complete break in her mind. As long as she thinks I am helping her she thinks that means in the end I will accept her and it just prolongs the illusion and her misery. The very fact she went to such lengths to worm it out of the doctor where the help was coming from just proves that point. And her whole thought in going to him—as far as I can gather from talking to him—has been that by doing so she would alter her personality so that I would like her. In other words, she went to him not really to help herself, but just as a further means of getting at me. And she was much worse since going than before.

[. . .]

I want to talk to Bob Hutchins about it, of course, as you suggested. He is a really wise person, and a benevolent one. He flew in and out of town this week for a meeting, but I couldn't get him alone. However, he'll be back later in the month and I'll surely get to talk to him then. As you say, it's a real necessity for me, for my peace of mind and my sense of justice, to do the right thing. But I honestly think the right thing, for now at least, is the complete break. Perhaps later there will be other opportunities, when she gets rational and really starts on a new life. I hope so.

Thanks for being so nice to G when she was down there. She had a lot of fun going around with you. You can imagine how hard all of this business is on her. But she takes it with a smile and is very understanding.

I'm not just sure where you are now, so will send letter to Key West as well. Have fun, and let me know what develops.

As ever,

[James Laughlin]

« • »

my little poem: "It's Warm Under Your Thumb," dedicated "to Maria" in *Collected Poems* (1994) but without dedication in earlier and later printings.

Bob Hutchins: Robert Maynard Hutchins (1899–1977), American educational philosopher who became dean of the Yale Law School in his twenties and at thirty years of age became the wunderkind president (1929–1945) and then chancellor (1945–1951) of the University of Chicago where he introduced numerous reforms such as the Great Books Program. He and JL worked together producing the Goethe Festival in Aspen in 1949, which was partially sponsored by the university. In 1951, Hutchins, now assistant director of the Ford Foundation, invited JL to Pasadena for a series of meetings concerning the new Ford Foundation outreach into the foreign arena, intended to counter Soviet influence in Europe. This led to JL's employment by the Ford Foundation as head of Intercultural Publications Inc., which produced the magazine *Perspectives USA*. JL considered Hutchins a wise friend and mentor and often turned to him for advice.

107. TL—2

January 16th [1955] [New York]

Dear Tenn—

I hope that you had a good time in St. Louis and New Orleans, and that you found your Grandfather in better shape than you anticipated. As I told you, I am rooting hard for him to make it to 100, and feel sure that he will.

Audrey finally found a copy of the new play [*Cat on a Hot Tin Roof*] for me to read, and, frankly, I am still shaking all over. It is really shattering, a small atom bomb, and in parts as strange and true as Dostoevski—perhaps not the comparison you would choose yourself, but it hit me in the same sort of way.

You have certainly come to grips here with some of the most crucial problems of mortal existence and there are no holds barred. No doubt a lot of thin-skinned people are going to scream at you for this one—they just won't be able to stand up to this direct facing of truth—but I think that those who can take it will be carried away with the almost barbaric mixture of terror and love.

Brick is a terrific character, and his "position," if one can call it that, seems to me to fit in with what I learned out in India. If people will take the trouble, this play will give them a lot to think about— about the state of the world today, as it derives from the basic things in human nature—the role of strength, and the role of weakness, the drive for power, the hunger for love—it's all there, and boiled down into a tight pattern that is as taut as a watch spring.

You have written some parts there that it is going to be hard to find actors big enough to handle. It's almost like a composer putting down notes that the instrumentalist, or the singer, can hardly play or sing. I grope for the word to describe what I feel about some of these people; they are almost larger than life, as if more life—life as it really is—has been crammed into them than they can hold. I saw a German movie not long ago, about the Nibelungen, where the figures had this same sort of larger than life size—the passion and the drive were just swelling them up and bursting out of them. You get here, I think, into the realm of myth, almost.

I hope that Gadg will sense what is here and let it be played for what it really is. Forget the little laughs and little businesses and play it for the big values that are in it.

May we get Lustig started on a jacket for it? I'd like to have the book out as close to the opening as possible, because I think this one is going to raise the roof and the book should be available for people outside New York.

I'm going out skiing at Alta now for a week or two but will be back soon and will call you. Meanwhile, Bob can move ahead if you give him the word.

Best to Frank,
[James Laughlin]

≪ • ≫

to make it to 100: Reverend Dakin died on February 14 of that year at the age of ninety-seven. TW paid tribute to his grandfather with the character of the ninety-seven-year-old Nonno, "the world's oldest living and practicing poet," in *The Night of the Iguana* (1961).

108. TL—2

March 8, 1955 [New York]

DEAR TENNESSEE,

I had to rush back to the office early today so didn't have a chance to talk with you. But I just want to thank you for such a wonderful evening and say that I was deeply impressed with the "Cat!" As you know, I am never very happy about Gadg's "busy-busy" direction—he seems to be concentrating more on keeping all the actors wiggling all the time than on getting them to speak the lines beautifully—and I look forward to the day when you will direct your own plays and be able to bring out the full charge of poetry that is in them. It seems to me that in the theatres of London and Paris the directors don't feel obliged to have everybody running every which way all the time. When a writer can write beautiful lines, as you can, they're willing to let the actors stand still and recite them with depth and feeling. And it seems to me that all this hyper-activity is pseudo-theatre. Maybe it is necessary where you don't have really great actors, but I wonder.

Of the present cast, I think I like the boy best, and then old Burl Ives, though he is not so good when he can't be shouting. I thought he fell off badly in the last act where he had to convey a great deal in a subdued mood. He doesn't seem to me to be an actor who can do much with his hands or face. Perhaps you could write in a few lines in [a] poetic vein at that crucial point which would indicate that he has reached some kind of inner resignation.

And I wonder about the elephant story. It struck me as something of an intrusion, breaking the structural continuity of the play. Do you feel that a laugh is needed at that point? I didn't. But I may be wrong.

I think that BBG is not very good in her long opening monologue where she seems to be shouting and forcing, but gets much better when she quiets down and lets her suffering come through. Maybe you should cut the monologue somewhat if she can't get to playing it better. I found her quite moving in the last scene and I think she carries that off. I wonder why you sacrificed one very beautiful line that was in the end of the script I read. I can't quote it exactly from memory but the sense of it was to define Brick's nature in poetic terms. Somehow I felt that Brick's closing line of "I admire you" was not quite big enough to finish things off on the scale of values that the play has established. Why shouldn't the author have the last word here in a line which finally establishes what he believes about Brick, who is, after all, the central figure.

I was a little bit troubled by the negro spiritual background music toward the end. This struck me as somewhat Hollywood. Do you think it is really needed? It seems to me that you have built up a sufficient charge of emotion by that time so that no false stimulants are needed.

Finally, I am not too happy about the abstract set. It doesn't seem to me to be right for the texture of this particular play. Every time that Brick went out onto the veranda I had the feeling that he was doing some kind of mysterious ritualistic movement. Perhaps Gadg wanted this effect, but I can't, in my own mind, tie it in to the central purpose of the play.

From all the above you might get the impression that I was dissatisfied. That is not the case. Actually I was deeply moved and convinced by the play as produced.

I think it will be equally effective in book form and am eager to get forward with that as soon as possible. When do you think you will have a final script? Is Paul [Bigelow] helping you with this this time? Meanwhile, could we have a temporary one to show to Lustig to get him started on the jacket? I like your idea of printing both versions of the ending.

Please be sure to give me a call when you get back to town, as there is much to talk about, and meanwhile thanks again for a really exciting evening.

As ever,
J. Laughlin

≪ • ≫

a wonderful evening: *Cat on a Hot Tin Roof* opened on Broadway at the Morosco Theatre, March 24, 1955. JL must have seen the production three weeks earlier, during
its out-of-town tryout in Philadelphia when the kind of feedback he provides here
could actually have been incorporated into the production.

the boy: Actor Ben Gazzara (1930–2012) originated the role of Brick.

Burl Ives: Burl Icle Ivanhoe Ives (1909–1995), American folk singer and stage and
screen actor, originated the role of Big Daddy on Broadway and also played the part
in the first Hollywood film version.

BBG: Actress Barbara Bel Geddes (1922–2005) originated the role of Maggie.

109. TLS—2

April 4, 1955 [Norfolk]

DEAR TENNESSEE,

I have recently been reading through the work of a lot of the most
applauded younger American poets in order to make selection for
a group in the forthcoming number of *Perspectives*. These are the
people who are being published in the literary quarterlies and getting
their books published.

My impression, after reading them en masse, is that they are simply decorators. They have a lot of technique and produce a beautiful
surface, but they say absolutely nothing, and one gets the impression that they are afraid to touch real life or real human emotions
and problems. Your poems, on the contrary, have a way of getting
right into the marrow of life. They are charged with authentic emotion and they tell a story which people can understand and identify
themselves with. They are not slick in the way these other poets are
smoothed and polished, but after reading them, I begin to think this
is a considerable virtue in itself.

Therefore I would like to urge you once again, and more firmly
than ever, to put aside your modesty and get together for us a little
selection of poems. Now please believe me, I know what I'm talk-

ing about. I think that the public is getting sick and tired of elegant poetry that has no content. I think you will be amazed and delighted with the response that you would get to a volume of your own poems. There would undoubtedly be a few snippy reviews from some of the high-brow critics but I believe that the real reaction would be measured by the number of letters you would get from readers who were touched and deeply moved by your understanding of what really goes on inside people's hearts and minds.

And can you find for me, right away, a copy of the very beautiful poem you wrote for Maria at the time of Sandra's death? I think that would be a good one to put in *Perspectives* in one of our next numbers.

As ever,

J. Laughlin

[signed in his absence by a

secretary at ND]

≪ • ≫

Perspectives: A quarterly magazine for European distribution (with a small print run for the United States) published in English, French, German, and Italian. After initial discussions with Robert Maynard Hutchins of the Ford Foundation in 1951, JL proposed a beautifully produced magazine that would present American culture not only in literature but also in art and music, history and philosophy (and even architecture). The Ford Foundation funded Intercultural Publications Inc. (IPI) for five years. There were sixteen issues of *Perspectives USA*, the last appearing in 1957. In addition to the magazine promoting American achievement, JL believed in "reverse flow" and began producing sections on foreign cultures for an American audience that were published in *The Atlantic Monthly*, the first being *Perspective of India* in 1952. (See also note following Section X and note following JL's letter to TW of April 11, 1953.)

very beautiful poem [. . .] Sandra's death: "A Wreath for Alexandra Molostvova" was first published in *In the Winter of Cities* (ND 1956). Alexandra, called Sandra, was Maria Britneva's cousin, raised by Maria's mother.

110. TLS—1

8/20/55 [Rome]

DEAR BOB:

I have devoted most of the last three or four weeks to work on the long poem ["Those Who Ignore the Appropriate Time of Their Going"] and it is nearly ready to send you, so please don't move on the book till you get it. Also by that time I hope to come up with a better title, maybe the new title of this poem. I'm grateful for your patience about this: I think the end result will justify it. I believe that our public is fairly used to postponements of publication, so that's no great matter, perhaps it is even an advantage, it may work up a fever of expectation, people crowding Times Square for latest bulletins on its progress as on the eve of elections.

Today I am meeting Audrey Hepburn (with Hal Wallis who is in Rome) to discuss the possibility of her playing Miss Alma in *Summer and Smoke*. Then maybe tomorrow I am flying to Paris, Stockholm, and London, for a long junket before we sail (September 22nd) on the *United States* liner. This is a footloose summer. Since I think of settling down in Japan, I want to see everything in Europe that I still haven't seen or want to revisit.

Give Jay my love. I presume he's back, by this time, and can co-operate with us in the preparation of the poetry book. His sense of cadence, what I lack most, would be a great advantage, and why not use it.

Did you see Kenneth Tynan's review of the book [*Cat*] in the *London Observer*? He gave Kazan hell, rather unjustly, but said that *Cat* was the most important play since *Death of a Salesman* and that the original version was much better. I hope Kazan doesn't get hold of it. He will rage! We came to a total impasse on the film script when he suddenly sent me an outline for a new ending that shocked me almost shitless, it was such old mellerdrammer. I wrote him so. His reaction has not yet crossed the Atlantic. Having sold *Cat* to Metro for half a million, I think I ought to be much more scrupulous now about doing things in accord with my own conscience only.

I don't think the copy of "Soft City" you sent me is the final version since it repeats a passage, giving a loose, flabby texture to the poem. I'm enclosing a corrected copy of the light verse you took off the Caedmon record. We may be able to get everything in order before I sail, but since I am traveling around so much, it doesn't seem likely.

Fondly,

Tenn.

« • »

don't move on the book: TW's first book of poetry, *In the Winter of Cities* (ND 1956).

Audrey Hepburn: (1929–1993), British-born Hollywood actress.

Hal Wallis: (1898–1986), American film producer who produced the successful screen adaptation of *The Rose Tattoo* (1955).

Kenneth Tynan: (1927–1980), English theater critic.

Caedmon: TW recorded two albums with Caedmon Records, *Tennessee Williams Reading from The Glass Menagerie, The Yellow Bird, and Five Poems* (1952) and *Tennessee Williams Reads Hart Crane* (1965). TW comments on the latter in his letter of September 26, 1965.

111. TL—1

September 2, 1955 [New York]

DEAR TENNESSEE,

[...]

It seems strange to be back in New York after India.—a totally different world and way of life. Bob tells me that you are thinking now of going out to Japan. I know you will like it there—I did—but be sure not to forget about India, as it is even more marvelous, I think, in its very different way.

I am very pleased with the way things are going on your poetry volume. [. . .]

Cat seems to be going great guns, with a third printing on press now. People I have talked to about it have been particularly appreciative of the fact that you gave them both versions of the play, and, with hardly any exceptions, have liked yours better than Kazan's. I hope that if you work with him in future you will be tougher about not letting him change things around to suit himself.

Did you finish any new short stories over the summer? We would like very much to have another one from you for *Perspectives*, if you have one that would be suitable. By the way, we are running in Number 14 an article on "off-Broadway" theatres by Alice Griffin, which deals at some length with the production of *Camino* up in Connecticut, and has an illustration from it. I wish I could have seen that, as it sounds to have been very good.

I've talked with Maria several times on the telephone and hope to be seeing her soon. She sounds cheerful and benevolent, a mood which I hope will continue. She keeps giving me various messages from you about the poetry, but they aren't too clear, and anyway I guess we can wait until you get back to sort out the details.

With best wishes to Frank,

James Laughlin

≪ • ≫

112. TL—1

October 20, 1955 [New York]

DEAR TENN—

I've been trying to reach you on the telephone the last two days, but no luck. I have to go out of town tonight until Monday and heard from Bob that you were also heading toward Key West soon. I wanted to go over a few things with you on the poetry manuscript before you leave.

I have read them again carefully and am once again impressed by how moving and exciting they are. Nobody else is writing like that, or putting so much of his inner self into his poetry. There is a terrific emotional charge and many lines of a haunting beauty and insight. You have a freedom of imagery that is akin to that of the Surrealists, but your poems are better than theirs because you always hold them in focus on a theme.

I don't think I would suggest many changes: a few places where I think a line could be made a bit more musical. [...]

Thinking about a title, what would you say to something rather simple and severe like *Legends: A Book of Poems*? This suddenly came to me and I rather like it. It suggests the mythic quality that so many of the poems have. But if you would prefer something romantic there are plenty of fine images in the poems to choose from.

As to format—type and paper, etc.—I've suggested to Bob that he bring up to show you a complete set of our Poets of the Year series. Each one of these has a different design, many of them lovely, and I'm sure that one among them will appeal, and then we can follow that.

As ever,

[James Laughlin]

≪ • ≫

Poets of the Year series: From 1941 to 1945, ND published a series of short paper-bound volumes called the Poet of the Month series until the Book of the Month Club threatened ND with a lawsuit and the name was changed. JL intended each of the forty-one volumes of the series to be an example of fine printing as well as to showcase the work of an individual poet.

113. TL—2

Tuesday, July 17, 1956 [Westchester, New York]

DEAR TENN,

I've been meaning to write for a long time, in fact I feel very guilty that I haven't. No secretary, and impossible temporary help, too many books suddenly ready for publishing, too much life I guess. Although everything has been going forward, the amenities have suffered. Hope the voyage was a great rest, that Spain or wherever was exciting and pleasant. Hope you are having all you desire in Rome.

[. . .]

Jay, by the way, is in Germany organizing a supplement for *The Atlantic Monthly*, like his ones on Japan, India, etc., and I'm sending him your address in Rome, in case he gets there.

Have you seen any of the reviews of *In the Winter of Cities*? I think they are mostly rather good, although you were right of course and no one is willing to concede your importance as a poet separately from your importance as a playwright. I'll try to send you at least the *Time* magazine one tomorrow.

Incidentally, Thomas Merton has written Jay saying that he found much in the volume very stimulating and moving. He also admired the organization of the book itself, and hopes to do likewise with his own poems. Babette Deutsch wrote me that you "have Rilke depths," and that she was liking much of the book.

What are you up to? Did you find Paul Bowles in Tangier? How was the bullfighting? [Federico García] Lorca's brother reports that he really thinks things in Spain are simmering to boil over, that the Franco regime is wobbling, despite the support it is getting within the country from U.S. aid. He was there this last winter on a Bollingen grant (which we helped him get) in order to collect his brother's manuscripts while people who knew him are still alive. Perhaps you read that the nephew was arrested for leading the student demonstrations. This was the boy who has been typing up Federico's manuscripts, in some cases for us—*The Butterfly's Evil Spell*, for instance, which [we] hope to have published in translation of course late this year. How's the new bulldog? She was certainly killing with that mirror at your apartment.

My very best to Frank.

Fondly,

[Robert M. MacGregor]

≪ • ≫

Merton: Thomas Merton (1915–1968), American Trappist monk, author, poet, and contemplative. Merton and JL became close friends—ND published twenty-nine titles by Merton. (See also note following letter from JL to TW on June 9, 1949.)

Babette Deutsch: (1895–1982), American poet and translator.

Lorca's brother: Francisco García Lorca (1902–1976), brother of the martyred Spanish poet and playwright Federico García Lorca, whose work was published by New Directions. A diplomat and scholar, Paco (as he was known) became friends with Robert MacGregor in New York where he lived in exile from 1939 to 1957, teaching at Columbia University. ND published his *In the Green Morning: Memories of Federico* in 1986.

the nephew: Manuel Fernández-Montesinos (1932–2013), nephew of Federico and Francisco García Lorca, became family spokesman after the death of Francisco. He presided over the Fundación García Lorca in Madrid from its founding in 1984 until his death.

114. TL—2

August 16, 1956 [New York]

DEAR TENN,

[. . .]

I could not have been more pleased by the news of Maria's wedding. She deserves a good break and I hope she gets it. I sent a clipping of the *New York Times* story to J. L. in Germany, but I'm not sure that he received it since he was traveling around. He should be home at the end of the week and I gather that he did not have the time to go to Italy after all. I expect he was pleased by the news of Maria's marriage and I am sure that you were, too. Do you know anything about the gent?

[. . .]

Fondly yours,
Robert M. MacGregor

≪ • ≫

Maria's wedding: In 1956 Maria Britneva married Lord Peter St. Just, a childhood friend whose mental instability resulted in repeated stays in various hospitals and treatment centers. Eventually she inherited the family "stately home" of Wilbury Park in Wiltshire, England.

115. TL—2

November 10, 1956 [Norfolk]

DEAR TENN—

I was distressed to discover, when I was downtown this past week, that you had already gone back to Key West. I'd hoped to catch a glimpse of you, and particularly wanted to arrange a get-together with Ann, who is eager to meet you. Please be sure to let me know if you come back up North, won't you?

If you are likely to be up around Thanksgiving time we would like very much to have you and Frank come to an evening when we will have the Indian sitar virtuoso, Ravi Shankar (brother of the dancer), and his wonderful drummer, Chatur Lal, playing for a few people at the apartment. This is really the way to hear them best, when they sit right on the floor in the middle of a small group, and you get right into the "jam"—which is about what it is like, or, rather, a sort of mixture of quite intellectual chamber music and a jazz jam session. They start off rather formally on a raga and then it gets hotter and hotter and the rhythms are terrific. I think you would like it, and they would be interesting people for you to know when you make your trip to India. I don't know the exact date when the party will be, but will let you know, and hope you can make it.

[. . .]

Have you read James Baldwin's novel *Giovanni's Room*? If you haven't, be sure not to miss it—one of the few things I have read recently that was really good. Don't be put off by Anthony West's smart-aleck review in the *New Yorker*, it is really a beautiful book.

Here is one thing I have on my mind that is quite important: would you feel like joining in a petition to Eisenhower for the release of Ezra Pound? It would be a very carefully staged and managed effort, with perhaps only about a dozen big literary names signing a letter asking clemency which would go to Ike through a private channel, entirely reliable, that has opened up. As you probably heard, Ike asked Faulkner to get ideas from leading writers about ways of improving relations with writers abroad, and Bill Williams gave one of the best answers, I think, when he told them that one of the easiest things they could do to make us be "liked" by writers abroad would be to let our leading poet out of the coop where he has been languishing these past ten years. This attempt would follow along that approach. It wouldn't try to argue the degree of his "guilt"—I have always felt that his political behavior was just a part of his whole illness—but just point out that, whatever it was, he has been locked up for ten years, and that is enough; that his illness is not getting any better where he is, and that he is not violent or dangerous; and, finally, that it is getting to be a national disgrace— at least so it is widely viewed abroad—to keep one of our greatest poets behind bars.

I'll keep you posted on how this develops—the ground has to be prepared very carefully—but would be glad if you could let me know right back if you are willing to help—subject to liking the actual letter, that is.

What do you hear from Maria? I would certainly be glad to hear that things were better for her. I think about her often and send up a little silent prayer that things will straighten out. She just wasn't for me, but she is a wonderful person, with very rare gifts, and she deserves much better luck in life than she has had so far.

Bob and I have been trying to pry a script of *Orpheus* [*Descending*] out of Audrey, and it is promised for this week. I'm eager to see how you have changed it from *Battle* [*of Angels*]. I hear that Magnani is out of the picture now, which is too bad, but she did sound hopelessly difficult.

Baby Doll must be cold tonight over there in Times Square, all 168 feet of her (Get me some of that, man, the taxi driver said as we drove past her the other evening) as winter seems to have come and it's down below freezing. Hope it is nice down there.

As ever, and best to Frank,

[James Laughlin]

≪ • ≫

Ann, who is eager to meet you: Ann Resor Laughlin had married JL in the spring of 1956. An intelligent and cultured Radcliffe graduate, Ann was eager to help JL in his literary and cultural endeavors. She provided funding from her own considerable assets for various ND titles and even underwrote the education expenses for the children of several long-term ND employees.

Ravi Shankar: (1920–2012), Bengali musician and composer who popularized the sitar. JL sponsored the first party held for Shankar in America on November 29, 1956.

Chatur Lal: (1925–1965), Indian tabla player.

a petition to Eisenhower for the release of Ezra Pound: In 1956, the long campaign among primarily American writers to have Ezra Pound released from St. Elizabeths Hospital in Washington, D.C., was building. He had been incarcerated at the institution for eleven years after being declared unfit by reason of insanity to stand trial for treason over his wartime broadcasts on Italian radio. Archibald MacLeish, poetry consultant to the Library of Congress, organized (with JL's help) a letter to President Eisenhower that was signed by T. S. Eliot, Robert Frost, Ernest Hemingway, and many other authors of world standing. This is the "petition" that JL is asking TW to sign. Although there is no evidence that TW signed the letter, he did visit Pound at St. Elizabeths early in 1957, accompanying Maria Britneva St. Just, who reported to her friend Mary de Rachewiltz, Pound's daughter, that "he gave Tenn a nice hug when we left and kissed my brow" (letter postmarked New York, 2/25/57). JL used the back-channel of his brother-in-law, Gabriel Hauge, special assistant to the president on economic affairs, to make sure that the letter got to Sherman Adams, Eisenhower's chief of staff, in February 1958. The same month, Frost had dinner at the White House and brought the matter up directly with Eisenhower. All charges against Pound were dismissed on April 18, 1958, and he was released from St. Elizabeths and returned to Italy.

all 168 feet of her: As part of his sensational and successful promotion of the film *Baby Doll* (based on TW's one-act plays *27 Wagons Full of Cotton* and *The Unsatisfactory Supper*), director and producer Elia Kazan had a gigantic billboard posted in Times Square that featured actress Carroll Baker, who played the title character, in a baby crib wearing a short, flimsy nightgown, and sucking her thumb.

116. TL—2

January 22, 1957 [New York]

DEAR TENN,

Just a hasty line to tell you that, quite unexpectedly, Ann and I are off for a couple of months in Burma, to assemble material for a "Perspective of Burma" collection for *The Atlantic Monthly*.

This is very unexpected, because I had thought that the [Ford] Foundation was all finished with us, and that I was again a free man. But they assure me that this is the last one, and I must confess that I'm not too unhappy about going to Burma because it is such a wonderful country and such really delicious people. If you get bored with Key West, fly out and join us! I know you would like it.

Audrey kindly let me read a script of *Orpheus Descending* and I was much taken with it. It really packs quite a wallop. And it was especially interesting for me to see the way you had developed the original theme of *Battle of Angels*. The dramatic structure is now much tighter, and I think that the characterizations have been deepened. You've added a lot, of course, and I like the symbolism and the way the thing drives ahead relentlessly to its tragic conclusion. There are some very lovely poetic passages, and also your usual fine ear for the way people talk. Needless to say, we want to publish the book and hope that we can get it out as soon as you have the final playing script in shape. Bob will be following along with you and Audrey while I am away, and I'm sure that everything will go smoothly.

Ann and I enjoyed *Baby Doll* very much, though we felt it was uneven. A question of the direction, I would say. There would be moments of the greatest poignancy and authenticity, then suddenly it would seem as though the director had become afraid to go the whole way and the tone would switch over into a kind of artificiality. Then a moment later it would switch back to the real thing. It's a pity that this film couldn't have been made in Italy, because I'm sure that what caused the trouble was the famous Hollywood production code. The acting, of course is terrific, and so is the background setting, those wonderful colored people slouching about, and the whole eerie atmosphere of the ruined mansion. That one flash where the colored man laughs at the husband out of the window of the cotton gin is pure inspiration and quite unforgettable.

I was so sorry that I didn't get a chance to see you when you were last in New York. Life runs along, so rapidly, and one never seems to manage to make it stand still and fully yield itself up. I do hope that you'll be around when we get back in April so that you can meet Ann and perhaps come up to see us some day in the country, where you have never been, and I wish you would come.

You'll be glad to hear, I'm sure, that New Directions is going to publish James Purdy. It was a bit of a battle to arrange it, because a number of other publishers were after him, but he felt himself that we were the right firm for him, and I am very excited about his possibilities. The first book will be a short novel, plus the short stories that were in the two volumes he privately printed.

You never did tell me whether you would be willing to sign a petition for poor old Ezra. Do drop a card about this, because the matter is moving forward, and your support would be very valuable. Just write me care of New Directions and they will send it out to me in Burma by airmail.

Hope you are having fun down there and that the swimming is good. I believe there are crocodiles in Burma, but maybe I can find a pool, as it will be hot out there.

With best wishes,

As ever,

J. Laughlin

≪ • ≫

James Purdy: (1914–2009), American novelist and short-story writer. ND published Purdy's collection of short stories *Color of Darkness* (1958) and the novel *Children Is All* (1962).

117. TL—1

March 13, 1957 [New York]

DEAR TENN,

Thought you might be pleased to know that *In the Winter of Cities* has been chosen as one of the "fifty books of the year" by the American Institute of Graphic Arts.

The year, of course, is 1956 and the "best" is best designed. This means that the book will be on exhibit at the New York Public Library probably in April and in five other cities, either in art museums or libraries. They also publish a catalog, a copy of which I shall try to get you.

I am delighted to hear that *Orpheus Descending* is getting such enthusiastic receptions out of New York.

Yours in haste,

Robert M. MacGregor

≪ • ≫

"fifty books of the year": Graphic designer and visual artist Elaine Lustig Cohen (1927–2016), who assisted her first husband Alvin Lustig (1915–1955) on a number of book covers for ND, was the designer of this book.

118. TLS—1

6/13/57 [Havana, Cuba]

DEAR BOB:

It was harder than I expected to pick up the manuscripts of *Orpheus* again. I took them to the hospital but couldn't touch them. I am sure when I get back to New York I can prepare the book ms. in a single morning. Perhaps we could get together for the ceremony and you could take the prepared script away with you. It only involves one or two little inserts and pages removed from one typed copy and put in another with a few notations . . .

I am entering the Austen Riggs Institute, Stockbridge, Mass. on the 18th of this month, to start analysis or psychotherapy there. Will be in Miami till then, or two days before then. Expect to fly up to New York this coming Sunday, the 16th. We could get together Monday. I am most apologetic about this delay but you know what a terrible state of nerves and even worse state of mind I have been in these last two months.

Give Jay my love, if he's back or you write him.

Love,

Tenn

≪ • ≫

the Austen Riggs Institute: It is at the Austen-Riggs Center that TW began psycho-analysis with Dr. Lawrence S. Kubie, which lasted approximately one year.

119. TL—1

January 20, 1958 [New York]

DEAR TENN—

Just a line to tell you that both Ann and I were enthralled by the new play [*Suddenly Last Summer*]. It really is a smasher, and beautifully acted and directed. I don't know how you do it, it's some kind of magic, to make something so poetic and beautiful out of such a frightening theme. It cleaned us both out emotionally, a true katharsis.

I think it will be just about as strong to read, too, and I was glad to hear from Audrey and Bob that we can start right in on the book. I'd like to see a rather unusual format. By that I don't mean something wildly modern, but a type face that has a lot of character and a design that will set off the poetry of it. I see it as a rather tall and narrow page, with the character names set above the lines of the speeches as is often done for poetic drama. I'll get a sample page set up to show you what I mean, and hope you will like it.

Audrey has brought up the question of a possible volume which would collect together some of the earlier plays. How do you feel about this now? I recall that the last time we discussed it, some years ago, you felt you preferred the separate volumes, for the time being at least, and wanted to wait. But, you may feel differently now, and we would be keen to tackle it, of course, if you'd like it now.

Did you ever find the statement that you wrote about Purdy's book? Hope you can turn it up because we want to start a new series of ads and would like to use it. The book is beginning to pull now, and we're going into a second printing. Purdy tells me that he has been working on a play—experimental in form—but I haven't seen it yet. He works very slowly and is shy about showing things till he is satisfied with them.

[. . .]

That Meacham girl is terrific. I liked her in Jim Merrill's play, too, but here she has more to work with and throws everything into it.

As ever,

[James Laughlin]

[Typed note from JL to RM clipped to RM's copy of the above letter:]

Bob—

Trust you approve. Let's not let Ste[f]an [Salter] do the design. I'd like something really elegant, about the shape of the Watkins Heine, perhaps using a face like Perpetua or Weiss, something rather tall and graceful, and on an interesting stock. Since it's fairly short, and shd sell well if we can get it right out, I think we can well afford to do something distinguished. Yes?

J.

≪ • ≫

collect together some of the earlier plays: First mention of the idea that was realized as *The Theatre of Tennessee Williams* series in the early seventies.

Meacham girl: Anne Meacham (1925–2006), American actress who originated the role of Catherine Holly in *Suddenly Last Summer*.

Jim Merrill: James Ingram Merrill (1926–1995), American poet.

Watkins Heine: Heinrich Heine's *The North Sea*, translated by Vernon Watkins (ND 1951).

120. TL—1

March 11, 1959 [New York]

Dear Tenn,

I am still limp—pulverized is the word, I guess—from *Sweet Bird [of Youth]* last night.

They really brought it off. That girl is terrific, and the boy almost as wonderful. They manage somehow to get enough change of pace—between the tragic and the human—so that the intensity is bearable.

And I like the new ending—the direct statement to the audience—this is <u>you</u>, too. And it is. I know. The corruption is in all of us, and our only chance is to recognize it, and live with it.

We want to start on the book as soon as possible and I've asked Audrey about getting a script with the new lines in it.

Hope to see you soon. Would you—and Frank—by any chance be free this coming Monday evening—the 16th? Patchen is in town and doing a Poetry-cum-Jazz program with Charlie Mingus at the Living Theatre. It might be fun, and we'd love to take you and Frank to dinner and that if you'd like to.

Bob is in Japan and writes that it's marvelous.

Best ever,

James Laughlin

≪ • ≫

That girl: Geraldine Page (1924–1987), American stage and film actress whose career took off when she played Alma in the 1952 revival of *Summer and Smoke*, off-Broadway at the Circle in the Square Theater, directed by José Quintero. (See note on Quintero to letter from TW to JL of June 27, 1960.) Page went on to originate the TW roles of Alexandra del Lago in *Sweet Bird of Youth* (1959) and Zelda Fitzgerald in *Clothes for a Summer Hotel* (1980).

the boy: Paul Newman (1925–2008), American stage and film actor.

Charlie Mingus: (1922–1979), American jazz composer, bassist, and bandleader.

the Living Theatre: Founded by Judith Malina and Julian Beck in 1947, The Living Theatre is the oldest experimental theater company in the United States.

SECTION XII

PF: What do you remember about the infamous Dr. Max Jacobson?

JL: Well, now let's see. Who was using Dr. Max? Somebody that we knew. Dr. Max, of course, was the doctor of JFK.

PF: Right.

JL: And somebody Bob knew well had had great benefit from these little potions Dr. Max would give his patients. So Bob went to him, and then Bob liked him and Bob thought he was helped by these things and stuck with him over quite a long time.

PF: And he didn't realize—what were they, amphetamines?

JL: They were little brews. The picture I got of it was that Dr. Max would pour different things out of different little bottles and into the little plastic containers he was giving Bob to take home and take. God knows what was in them. I don't think that . . . I mean he has the reputation of giving certain people dope, but Bob certainly didn't think he was getting dope.

PF: He really thought he did feel better?

JL: He did, yes. He felt better. Bob's big trouble was that he was a reformed alcoholic, and he was sticking to it. He was not drinking at all, ever, but I think maybe, I don't know, maybe that situation leads to a sort of depression, a physical feeling of lack.

PF: So he felt he needed something to give him a boost?

≪ • ≫

Dr. Max Jacobson: (1900–1979), German-born physician who became known as Dr. Feelgood for his "miracle tissue regenerator" cocktail that included animal hormones, enzymes, human placenta, painkillers, steroids, and amphetamines, with which he treated celebrity patients via intramuscular injection. Some side effects of the shots (among others) were mood swings, impaired judgment, and hyperactivity. Though strictly cautioned not to combine the injections with alcohol, TW did and the results left him with weird tics, an irregular heartbeat, and severe paranoia. It was most likely the sustained combination of Dr. Jacobson's shots, antidepressants, and alcohol that led to TW's complete physical and mental collapse in 1969.

121. TL—2

June 27, 1960 [New York]

DEAR TENN,

I thought you'd be amused at this clipping from today's *Publishers Weekly* showing that your books will be prominently displayed at the Olympics in Rome.

Are you going to Rome for the shooting of *The Roman Spring of Mrs. Stone*? I gather from one of the papers that Quintero is already on his way there. If you are in Rome during the Olympics I want to see that you meet Sawabo Arioyshi, a young Japanese lady playwright, who has been most of this year on a Rockefeller grant. She is evidently going to cover the Olympics for Asahi in Tokyo. I think you will find her very amusing; she is a pretty good friend of Yukio's too I think.

Everyone tells me that you and Yukio were very good on television recently, another reason why I think I'm going to have to get a television set. I'm also told that Chris Isherwood pinch-hit for you a week ago, and spoke at length about *In the Winter of Cities*. That would endear him to me if there were no other reasons. There certainly are many reasons—he is just a thoroughly good person, isn't he—and I dropped him a note of gratitude.

I imagine you have seen the letters in yesterday's *Times* magazine section following the publication of your reply to Marya Mannes. It seems to me that the *Times* very unfairly published the letters supporting Miss Mannes first, so that those supporting you were all on pages toward the end of the [magazine]. Be that as it may, I was greatly cheered by your reply to her article, and I wondered why we don't try to publish a volume of your prose pieces. What would you think of the idea? Quite a few are published as introductions to plays, but I can think of quite a few that aren't, and these pieces would make a very nice little book.

[. . .]

Fondly,

Robert M. MacGregor

≪ • ≫

Quintero: José Quintero (1924–1999), Panamanian-born American stage director. Quintero directed the 1952 landmark revival of *Summer and Smoke* at Circle in the Square Theatre in New York and later directed the Broadway productions of *The Seven Descents of Myrtle* (*Kingdom of Earth*) (1968), *Clothes for a Summer Hotel* (1980), and the celebrated film adaptation of TW's novella, *The Roman Spring of Mrs. Stone* (1961).

Yukio: Yukio Mishima was the pen name of Kimitake Hiraoka (1925–1970), Japanese novelist, poet, playwright, and actor. ND published three titles by Mishima.

on television recently: Edward R. Murrow conducted an interview with Tennessee Williams, Yukio Mishima, and Dilys Powell for his CBS program *Small World*, which aired May 8, 1960.

your reply to Marya Mannes: After several years of undisguised contempt for the plays of TW, theater critic Mannes wrote a piece for the *New York Times* entitled, "A Plea for Fairer Ladies," in which, among many other complaints, she decried "the public appetite for theater of violence, aberration and decay," and identified TW as one of the primary purveyors of the kind of theater she felt was ruining Broadway. TW challenged Mannes's premise with good humor in his own essay in the *Times*, "Tennessee Williams Presents His POV." Perhaps his best retort to her insistence on the need for morally uplifting entertainment was, "It is not the essential dignity but the essential ambiguity of man that I think needs to be stated."

very nice little book: TW's major essays were later collected by ND in *Where I Live: Selected Essays* (1978), which was revised and expanded as *New Selected Essays: Where I Live* (2009).

122. TLS—1

July 26, 1960 [Key West]

DEAR BOB:

Sorry I couldn't answer your letter quicker but the heat of a Key West summer had all but knocked me out, I could just barely get through my little day's stint of work. I don't know what possessed us to pass a summer there. Well, we did spend about six weeks constructing or supervising the construction of a big patio about the house, taking out walls for sliding glass window-doors and putting up "planters" with tropical plants, Etc., and it has become all but impossible to travel with the menagerie of two dogs (one huge black Belgian shepherd who looks like the wolf at the door), a parrot—Frank won't travel without them and I can't travel much without Frank and, well, maybe [the] trip around the world last year has killed or at least anesthetized the travel-bug.

About *Period of Adjustment*. I don't see much reason not to start on publication whenever you want to. I turned all my revisions over to the director, George Roy Hill, and I know that he has completed the collation of Act One and he said that Act Two will not be substantially altered. However I have not yet been given a copy of this final or semi-final draft. I think you might check with Audrey or Cheryl Crawford about getting a copy for ND. And mention me, too, as a would-be recipient of one.

I have just completed a fairly final draft and assembly-job on *Night of the Iguana* which goes into rehearsal today in New York for its try-out at the Coconut Grove Playhouse (Miami). It will open there about August 20th with the same cast that played it so beautifully in its shorter version at the Spoleto festival last summer. I think it's a more interesting and poetic play than *Period* and when copies are out I will get one to you.

I am tired of writing and writing is tired of me: yet I can't think of anything else to do. I am like old Aw Boon-Haw, the tiger balm king of the Orient who kept building and building his palaces and gardens till they became grotesque because a fortune-teller told him that he would die when he stopped.

I hope we can have a quiet pleasant evening sometime during the madness of the rehearsal period that starts the middle of September. Frank and I both miss seeing you, and that is not a statement I could make sincerely about many people in New York.

Give Jay my fondest greetings.

Love,

Tenn.

≪ • ≫

Aw Boon-Haw: Hô ˙Bûn-hó˙ (1882–1954) was a Burmese-Chinese herbalist who introduced "Tiger Balm" ointment to the West.

123. TL—3

December 9, 1960 [New York]

DEAR TENN,

We are promised copies of the revised edition of *Period of Adjustment* today, and if one comes along, I will shoot it right to you.

[. . .]

Incidentally, all sorts of people have commented to me on the four figures in the wedding band, and I tell them that they are your work of art. Guess you could become a real child artist without even graduating from kindergarten!

[. . .]

I'd hoped to have a chance to talk with you further about the idea for *The Glass Menagerie* that I broached in the middle of 6th Avenue with both you and Audrey looking for cabs. As I said, probably incoherently, the New Classics series in which *The Glass Menagerie* has been these many years, although it is hardbound with a jacket and only slightly more expensive than paperbound books, has been losing out to the evidently more glamorous paperbooks in all the bookshops. In fact, we find it very difficult to get bookshops to stock the New Classics series at all anymore. Possibly, this is a passing phase, but there it is, and as each title in the New Classics series goes up for reprint, we solve the problem by putting them in paperbound form in our so-called quality paperback series. I think you've seen several of them and know what they're like. The paper is good, and the binding is sewn or perfect-bound, depending on what bindery is doing the job. The covers in the whole series are photographic, and this was the idea of Lustig, although he only lived to design a couple of the covers in the series. Evidently because there are so many covers in paperbound bookshops, our black and white ones stand out, particularly when they're grouped together, as we always try to have them. We end up spending an enormous amount of time finding just the right photographs or other material, but it's also a lot of fun and we think it is worth it.

Anyway, we would like to put *The Glass Menagerie* in this series, and this would mean a sort of new publication with review copies sent out, etc. Incidentally, neither Audrey nor I, who discussed this a fair amount, believe that that *The Glass Menagerie* will ever be of interest to New American Library, or that kind of paperbound reprint distributed on a mass [market] basis, because the publishers in that field evidently do this when a movie is imminent and they can have tie-ins. Since *The Glass Menagerie* has already been made into a movie, that's evidently that.

[. . .]

Anyway, let me know how you feel. I gather Audrey thinks it a good idea.

[. . .]

My best to Frank.

                                        Yours,

                                        Robert M. MacGregor

≪ • ≫

the four figures: The rough sketch of stick figures on the jacket design for *Period of Adjustment* was drawn by TW.

more glamorous paperbooks: Early on, JL insisted on calling his paperbacks "paperbooks," which in his mind indicated quality paperback books (known as trade paper editions) as opposed to the cheaply made, mass-market paperbacks.

will ever [. . .] New American Library: ND eventually did lease the paperback rights to *The Glass Menagerie* to New American Library in 1987, reclaiming them in 1999.

124. TL—1

                                    February 20, 1961 [New York]

DEAR TENN,

Just a line to tell you that I thought the D. H. Lawrence play was really tremendous on TV the other night. I've always liked it very much from reading it, but it came out even stronger as they played it. What a wealth of understanding you have packed into that short play. I doubt if any artist has ever understood another so well.

I liked the others too, though I thought *The Purification* was a bit overdone as they staged it, but the *Phoenix* [*I Rise in Flame, Cried the Phoenix*] was really sensational. I hope someone will stage that around New York soon, perhaps with the same cast. I wonder if the woman who played Frieda had ever known her? I thought she had her to the life. I never met Lawrence himself, but that actor seemed just right for him, as I've always imagined him.

I hope you are having good weather down there in the islands. We haven't been able to get away at all as my dear old aunt is still very ill, and we have to stay near her. It's been quite a winter—I've never seen so much snow in Connecticut.

Your brother Dakin writes me that he is giving up the army. A step with which I can certainly sympathize, but I hope he didn't take it on the strength of my encouragement for his literary effort.

I doubt if you will be up here, but if you should be around on Sunday, February 26th, there is to be a reading of Bill Williams's play *A Dream of Love* (with good actors, I'm told) at the National Arts Club. This is the play of Bill's that I think is so extremely beautiful, and it really ought to be produced. I'll send you the complete book of his plays, when we get it out, in a few months' time.

As ever,

James Laughlin

≪ • ≫

on TV the other night: A syndicated television program, *Play of the Week*, presented *Four by Tennessee* on February 6, 1961, which included the one-act plays *Hello from Bertha*, *The Lady of Larkspur Lotion*, *The Purification*, and *I Rise in Flame, Cried the Phoenix*.

the woman who played Frieda: Jo Van Fleet (1915–1996) played the role of Frieda Lawrence in this television production of *I Rise in Flame, Cried the Phoenix*.

that actor: Alfred Ryder (1916–1995), English actor.

the complete book of his plays: *Many Loves and Other Plays: The Collected Plays* (ND 1961). The publication marked the return of W. C. Williams to the ND list after his ill-fated move to Random House with David McDowell.

125. TL—2

April 5, 1961 [New York]

DEAR TENN,

Just after receiving your letter of early last month I sat down and typed something out, but then it seemed more illegible even than my handwriting, and I planned to get back to it. I never did. Please, please forgive.

Anyway, I hope everything has somehow worked itself out. I will be fifty myself August 5th, but at least for the moment, it doesn't worry me as reaching the age of forty did. Somehow I have reached an agreement with myself, and I don't know how it was brought about, except that I really do like my work, and there is always more of it than I can possibly accomplish so that I just have to plunge on without thinking of the passage of time. I also think that Dr. Max Jacobson has a great deal to do with it. He has done marvels for me or with me, but then I have stuck with him even when his experiments weren't working and given him time to adjust them until they did again. (I am a lethargic, stubborn kind of fellow and don't give up easily.) I also don't mind his crazy, temperamental bantering. One soon learns that it is fundamentally very good-natured and largely a sort of technique for dealing with the difficult people who come to him. You know that he did a wonderful job for Alvin Lustig in his last year and a half, after of course there was no hope (there probably was no hope anyway). What he did do for Alvin with his concoctions of hormones and vitamins and enzymes was to give Alvin courage to make it possible for him to function in a miraculous way. I don't believe in urging people to go to doctors or as a matter of fact to do anything with their personal lives. These are things they must solve themselves, but you will remember that when I asked him, Dr. Max said, "Maybe both of us have learned something in the interim and now I can be of real help to Tennessee."

[...]

Fondly yours,
Robert M. MacGregor

≪ • ≫

126. TL—2

May 3, 1962 [New York]

DEAR TENN:

On the way by subway and bus out to Idlewild [now JFK Airport] yesterday with George Zournas to meet the four young Tibetan monks selected by the Dalai Lama to study English and American ways with George's Tibetan teacher in New Jersey, I saw in the *New York Post*, which I almost never see these days, that you along with Julie Harris and Thornton Wilder have accepted dinner invitations to the White House a week from Friday. At least you can talk to Jackie about Dr. Max, who has been treating her for about a year (I gather he is also treating the President).

[...]

Yours,
Robert M. MacGregor

≪ • ≫

George Zournas: See endnote of letter from Robert MacGregor of April 20, 1951.

Julie Harris: (1925–2013), American stage and film actress.

127. TLS—1

9/24/62 [Key West]

DEAR JAY:

It's always wonderful to get a letter from you and it is still more wonderful, I guess when I have the leftover energy after a hard day's work to answer a letter from you or anybody that writes me, but I know you understand that.

I am back in the benign tedium of Key West, putting the finishing touches on the milk train [*The Milk Train Doesn't Stop Here Anymore*]. I have told Audrey that this play is not, under any circumstances, to appear first in any magazine including the one for gentlemen, desperately interested in being hip, not square, and consequently being squarer than square [*Esquire*].

You'll get the acting version as soon as the actors get it so you can aim at a publication date sometime prior to its execution on Bd'way. I am also finishing up two long-short or short-long plays [*The Gnädiges Fräulein* and *The Mutilated*] under the common title of *Two Slapstick Tragedies*. I think they have a new quality for me, perhaps they're my answer to the school of Ionesco, but they're not just funny, they're also supposed to be sad: I mean "touching." Who is touched and by what is the big question these days which are the days of the untouchables, the emotional astronaughts [sic]. In which I'm beginning to feel like Louisa May Alcott or the early Fannie Hurst.

Although I hopped all over Europe last summer, including London, I didn't get a glimpse of Maria. She was summering with his Lordship who was out of the "bin" for a bit. She kept wiring me to join them in Geneva or Trouville but I didn't feel up to an encounter with his Lordship, he is not my cup of tea, but I am glad for Maria that he is taking an interest in her and the children again.

I am reading a trio of novels by Muriel Spark, a marvelously witty English writer, one of the few lady writers that I like to read. Her best, I think, is *Memento Mori* which is chillingly brilliant. She's sort of like Mary McCarthy would be if Mary had a narrative gift and a sense of character, however mordant, and she is just about the only contemporary novelist that Mary couldn't put down on her own critical terms.

I saw Paul and Jane Bowles in Tangiers and both were doing well, after their fashion. By this time they must be in the States as they were planning a trip over in September. Can't you do something about Jane's stories or a revival of her novel *Two Serious Ladies*? You can reach her through Libby Holman at Tree-tops, Greenwich, Conn., if you want to discuss her work with her. My best to Bob. I hope to see you both soon.

Ever,

Tenn

≪ • ≫

Ionesco: Eugène Ionesco (1909–1963), Romanian-born French playwright whose work is most associated with the playwriting style known as Theatre of the Absurd. In a January 1962 interview, when asked to name some modern playwrights that he liked, TW first responded, "I'm not crazy about Ionesco."

Muriel Spark: (1919–2006), Scottish novelist. ND has reissued fourteen of her novels and brought out her memoirs and collections of her stories, poems, and essays.

Mary McCarthy: (1912–1989), American novelist, critic, and political activist.

Libby Holman: (1904–1971), American torch singer and stage actress.

128. TL—2

October 1, 1962 [New York]

DEAR TENN—

Many thanks for your much-enjoyed letter. You write good ones, and I wish there were more, but it's probably my fault—I just don't seem to have the steam I once had for correspondence, and have never managed to master the machine, that is the Dictaphone, which makes, with me at least, everything come out sounding like mashed potatoes . . . if you can imagine the noise they make.

That's good news that the *Milk Train* is coming along well. Since I wrote you last Bob showed me a very interesting report on it by some dame who had seen it at Spoleto and it really sounds fascinating. We'll be very eager to see the script and hope to push into proofs with it rapidly so that [the] book can be ready by the time of the New York opening. And naturally I'm much pleased to hear about the ban on *Esquire* this time. I don't think there is any doubt that magazine publication takes the edge off the book sales. Audrey always claimed that the ads *Esquire* took helped the theater attendance, but I wonder if they really pulled that way.

Your phrase the "emotional astronaughts" [sic] really hits it on the button, the kind of daze into which the whole population seems to have fallen, drugged by all the bilge that comes over the air and off the page, so that there is this unbelievable apathy about the nuclear arms race while people sublimate what's left of their "souls" playing Walter Mitty-John Glenn on trips to the moon . . . I must say I am disgusted with Kennedy. I had great hopes that he would turn into somebody with a touch of greatness, but as far as I can see he's just a politician, and next thing will be trying some crazy stunt in Cuba, or elsewhere, if he calculates it will get him re-elected. And let's not arrest the Governor of Mississippi until after the big weekend football game . . . *that* is sacred.

I would love to see you really tear into this un-life (as dear old [E. E.] Cummings would have called it) situation with a tremendous, give-em-hell satire. Maybe that's what you're getting toward in the *Slapstick Tragedies* . . . There are passages in many of the earlier plays which indicate to me that you could move right into Swift, and be terrific at it—just turn loose, no holds barred, on everything that is wrong with our so-called "culture." I don't know what the form would have to be—perhaps the sort of thing Brecht did, or some of these new dramatists. I haven't followed them as closely as I should have, probably. It seems to me that life is absurd (as the Existentialists claim) but that these birds who are writing "theater of the absurd" haven't quite found the equation for making high drama of that fact. They let themselves fall into a kind of self-deluding verbal comedy. I dunno . . . I'm no critic, and can't manipulate ideas like the PR boys.

What I suppose I'm trying to say is that I hope you will let yourself go in one play, be wilder, perhaps savager, pour out all your resentments at the state of things, a bellow of thunderous rejection . . . regardless of whether it fits into the conventions of formal drama, the well-made play etc. *Camino Real* was, I've always felt, a protest play, and very good, too, one of your best, but I think there are other ways of doing it, too, that you ought to explore. Impertinent, I guess, of me to try to suggest what you might want to do, but nobody writing today can beat you in insight into people or command of language to figure what you have seen, and I would love to see you really let fly. You are a very disciplined writer, have made yourself that by long industry, working about every morning of your adult life, I guess, changing, testing, building up mastery of stage techniques. Now I wish that one time you would try being undisciplined, perhaps almost "automatic," uncensored . . . Maybe it wouldn't end up as a play . . . it might be more like a long prose poem, not a narrative, just a sequence of reflections, moods, attacks, jabs, punches, cries of rage . . . a contemporary Maldoror, if you will, a non-dead who has seen it, had it, to the gills, and now is spitting it back out at them, hate and love intermingled . . .

Or am I trying to impose on you what I would like to try myself if only I had the talent to even begin to attempt it? I suppose I'm still a thwarted would-be writer . . . who never got going, having been diverted into the substitute activity of publishing—though I've no regrets about that, it's been fascinating, occasionally frustrating because there weren't the means to operate more ambitiously, but always interesting.

I'm glad you reminded me about Jane Bowles's book. I like it a lot. Bob seems a little less keen about it than I am, but I think he could be brought around to a paperback reprint, particularly if we could sell you on the idea of doing an introduction for it. She isn't very well known, unfortunately, despite the good play that was on Broadway some years back, and something is needed to stir up fresh interest. Just putting the book out again probably wouldn't do it, without some strong shots in the arm to get people talking. I'll get my copy back from Sandy Richardson at Lippincott (I was trying to persuade them to do it) and see what can be done. He (Sandy) by the way, was the one who brought Muriel Spark to their list. I agree with you about her, a wonderful writer.

Please forgive me for gushing along so much, and do be sure to let us know when you get back to New York so we can have lunch or something.

As ever,

[James Laughlin]

« • »

E. E. Cummings: (1894–1962). A selection of his poems was published in the first *NDPP* anthology in 1936. Laughlin made overtures to Cummings in 1937 to publish his work, but, wanting to offer the poet something substantial, he waited too long and Cummings's *Collected Poems* came out from Harcourt, Brace. The two men remained friendly, however, and JL credited Cummings's style, including lack of punctuation and capital letters, and using typewriter spacing, with inspiring his own "typewriter metric."

Maldoror: *Les Chants de Maldoror* is a long prose poem, structured in six cantos, by Isidore-Lucien Ducasse during 1868 and 1869. Ducasse was a Uruguayan-born French author whose pseudonym was Comte de Lautréamont. ND published a translation of *Maldoror* in 1943.

Lippincott: J. B. Lippincott & Co., a once-large American publisher founded in 1836 and based in Philadelphia. At this time Lippincott was ND's distributor and there was close cooperation between the two firms. After Lippincott was acquired by Harper & Row in 1978, ND began an association with W. W. Norton and Co. for distribution and warehousing that continues to this day.

129. ANS—2

[no date]

J

Your letter to Tenn is wonderful. I don't know if he could—or even should—write the way you'd like him to. Tenn, as I see it, is subjective rather than Swiftian; but of course he has the passion and the disgust as well as skill, and I think he'll even be flattered at your suggestions.

Earlier he wouldn't write an intro for Jane Bowles, but maybe he would now.

Bob

≪ • ≫

130. TLS—1

11/17/62 [New York]

DEAR J.—

Finally got hold of Tennessee on the phone and in fact talked with him for a long time. I may see him tomorrow night, at a small birthday party he is giving for his sister. If I can go, I'll try to give you a full account.

It seems Tenn doesn't at all remember having suggested to you that he wanted to have the play [*Milk Train*] published quickly and in time for the opening—which certainly seems strange considering I had written him a reminder and sent it both to 64th Street and Key West, but of course this is our Tenn! Says he thinks it would be a great mistake to rush ahead at this point, as he expects to make many changes after the play goes out of town—to New Haven on December 4th. At the moment he is evidently feeling very pessimistic about it—"bearish" as he put it—and he evidently can't stand being at the rehearsals so he may be going to Key West on Wednesday or so until the move to New Haven. He's having many second thoughts about Machiz, who evidently is being very temperamental with T.W. and doesn't want him at rehearsals, etc. etc.—He's terribly uncertain about whether or not he hasn't given the young man too much mysticism in his role as "Angel of Death," and will want to tone it down when he can see how audiences react.

Although this may mean one of those agonizing periods of trying to get the script—makes me shudder to think of—I expect we'll probably get a better play to publish, but of course if we don't get it out fairly early in the run we lose a lot of sales I suppose. It rather looks as if we have no choice, although if you want me to try to get him to change his mind, call me by Wednesday morning and I'll try.

[. . .]

Seems his new secretary is a poet named Frederick Nicklaus (Strike any bell with you? It does a faint one with me.), and Tenn thinks very highly of his poetry, wants me to see it and you to see it (hrumph!) of course I have the excuse (and valid enough) of not knowing much about poetry, but you . . .

Hope there's some snow, and that you find all the lift business in order.

Best, Bob

《 • 》

his sister: Rose Williams. See notes to the letters dated June 3, 1949, and April 7, 1976.

Machiz: Herbert Machiz directed the original productions of TW's *The Milk Train Doesn't Stop Here Anymore*, *Suddenly Last Summer*, *Something Unspoken*, and *In the Bar of a Tokyo Hotel*.

Frederick Nicklaus: (1938–1993), American poet whom TW began seeing on and off for several years, beginning prior to Frank Merlo's death. Nicklaus's poetry collection, *The Man Who Bit the Sun*, was published by ND in 1964.

SECTION XIII

⸙

PF: Well now, what is your recollection of the sixties? *The Night of the Iguana* was the last real success.

JL: Right.

PF: Do you remember what the interaction was between you and Tennessee or you and MacGregor and Tennessee once he stopped being the darling of the critics?

JL: I don't think it affected either Bob or myself in any way because we liked him so much. We just hoped that he would go on writing. We wished him well and wanted him to find his way.

≪ • ≫

The Night of the Iguana: On December 29, 1961, *The Night of the Iguana* opened on Broadway starring Bette Davis, Margaret Leighton, and Patrick O'Neal, ran for nine months, and won the New York Drama Critics Circle Award for best play of 1961.

131. TL—1

January 22, 1963 [New York]

DEAR TENN—

Bob tells me that you are back in Key West and working again on the novella [*The Knightly Quest*], which sounds fine. I have always liked your fiction a great deal—you get a terrific style-atmosphere if that is the term I mean. What I'm trying to say is that the story is always interesting and then, on top of that, there is something extra in the way the language creates a mood which enchants the reader to believe the story.

Bob showed me the Rastrofrarian [sic] poem ["A Mendicant Order"], which is nice. Did I tell you that my daughter, who is out in India, has become a disciple of the wonderful old saint Vinoba Bhave, the one who was Gandhi's guru, and goes hiking through the countryside with him for weeks at a time? They sleep on the floor in peasant villages, the floor being mud, going from place to place, walking, she says, about ten miles a night, when it's cooler, and then he lectures the rich to give some of their land to the poor, and many do. Quite an experience for an American kid and she really seems to be eating it up.

Did you ever get my letter I sent to Jamaica, enclosing re-typing of the long poem ["Lost Island"], and saying how pleased I was with the way you worked it out. It's a very fine poem, I believe, and I wouldn't change it any more, if I were you.

I hope it's nice in Key West and life serene. I always remember my visit down there with you, the time Gertrude was along. Poor Gertrude, she has been having a rough time. She had to go into the hospital and have her insides removed. She seems to be recovering all right but I guess this is always a big psychological shock to the intrinsic female. On top of this her husband, who must be something of an odd duck, sent their dog to the SPCA to be put away because the dog, a very nice Airedale, apparently got upset when G left home for the hospital and expressed its feelings by peeing and crapping all over the place. A sad tale.

Best to all, as ever,

[James Laughlin]

≪ • ≫

my daughter: Leila Laughlin Javitch, JL's daughter by Margaret Keyser Laughlin, born in 1944.

Vinoba Bhave: Indian advocate of nonviolence and human rights (1895–1982), considered to be the spiritual successor of Gandhi.

her husband: After JL's marriage to Ann Resor, Gertrude Huston married James Awe, who had been involved in two productions of TW's plays.

132. TLS—1

1/23/63 [New York]

J -

Went yesterday from Burnshaw's friends to TW's for lunch before he and Frederick Nicklaus were to go to Idlewild. Found even more confusion than usual, with Tenn ransacking and turning into a greater mess papers and parts of manuscripts from shoeboxes and old suitcases from the top shelves of closets in a desperate effort to find the only scripts of two plays never produced or published, which were not in the warehouse where he went the day before with Andreas Brown, the young fellow who's doing a bibliography of T.W., is a collector, and is evidently the fellow who has arranged the gift to Texas. Brown had been there alone on an earlier day without Tenn, and I certainly sounded a note of caution about that. As I think over many things I learned yesterday I think I may write

Tenn about the experiences at Buffalo with Bill Williams's papers and at UCLA with Henry [Miller]'s.

[. . .]

In haste
Bob—

≪ • ≫

Burnshaw: Stanley Burnshaw (1906–2005), American poet.

Andreas Brown: Bookstore owner and rare book dealer, Brown owned and ran the famous Gotham Book Mart from 1967 to 2007.

133. TL—2

February 15, 1963 [New York]

DEAR TENN:

I hope you will take the trouble to read all this through carefully, even if it is such a bore.

I have been meaning to write you anyway about the Andreas Brown situation. Frederick had told me that day I was at your apartment and you were looking for lost manuscripts, that Brown had been going to your warehouse with you, and I gathered that he was the one who thought up and engineered the Texas deal. I'm sure you now know him much better than I do, but I must say that the time he came to see me, about his bibliography of your works, he made me extremely nervous. He is a collector himself and interested in raising the value of his personal holdings of your works, both by his bibliography and by everything he can learn.

I do not know if you have run into this world of collectors, but I find it full of intrigue, dangerous prying and even treachery. Henry James' *The Aspern Papers* was written when the whole thing was quite in its infancy, and the greed, avariciousness and blackmailing even of collectors today is almost unbelievable. This includes so-called "reputable dealers" and I rather think all dealers in manuscripts and rare editions, and individuals in university libraries, are probably turning out to be the worst of the lot.

Brown made me particularly nervous because he already knew so much about you, evidently from private letters he had bought or seen, and quite a few of his questions had nothing to do with bibliographical material but were personal and, I felt, highly dangerous.

I also wanted to tell you about two experiences we have had with others who have given their papers to libraries. William Carlos Williams allowed some woman from the Buffalo University Library to go through his attic quite a few years ago, before anyone would have thought that papers of WCW would have monetary value. Bill and his wife Floss did not even know what the woman had taken, but it was all supposed to be for posterity, and I guess Bill was flattered that Buffalo thought of him in terms of posterity.

We discovered about 1957 from a scholar who had been working at the Buffalo Library that a lot of letters of a highly personal nature from J. Laughlin to Bill, whom he at one time looked on as a kind of father confessor and advisor in personal matters, were there at Buffalo for anyone to see. Bill could not withdraw the letters, but because Buffalo hopes to get other things from him and from ourselves, we were able to get them to put a restriction on these letters so that no-one, presumably, is allowed to read them again, without J. Laughlin's written permission.

The same thing more or less happened at U.C.L.A. where Henry Miller had given all his trunks full of papers. Here a young fellow apparently came across the letters from Durrell to Miller, transcribed the full correspondence, went to work and persuaded Durrell and Miller to let them be published, as they are this month, and is building himself a career on the basis of being an authority on Miller and Durrell. This is all very fine and may be useful, but I have often thought that it would have been much better if Miller and Durrell had been able to pick their own editor. So it goes!

I go into all this because I do hope you will be cautious with Brown or anyone who appears. The world seems to be full of the hangers-on who hope somehow to benefit from you or from us! You remember that chap who got you to go up to Fordham to broadcast about Dylan Thomas. He has appeared from time to time on our horizon, always in new fantasy guise, although you would think he would not have the nerve to show his head again in New York.

Hope that the weather is fine down there.

Fondly,

Robert M. MacGregor

≪ • ≫

young fellow: George Wickes, professor and Henry Miller scholar.

Durrell: Lawrence George Durrell (1912–1990), British novelist, travel writer, and poet.

letters from Durrel to Miller: The edition referenced here, *Lawrence Durrell–Henry Miller: A Private Correspondence*, was edited by George Wickes (1963). ND would publish a full run of the correspondence, which continued until Miller's death in 1980, in 1988, edited by Ian S. MacNiven.

134. TLS—2

2/18/63 [Key West]

DEAR BOB:

I'm glad that you've confirmed my instinctive distrust of Mr. Andreas Brown. I thought I was being paranoiac but you show me I wasn't. As you say, his activities and his queries go far beyond the legitimate function of a bibliographer, and a bibliographer was as unexpected to me as it was to William Carlos Williams. This man has sent me photostatic copies of love-letters that I wrote in 1940. He has ransacked the trunks in Manhattan Storage and come out with things that he says are so personal he doesn't dare show them to Audrey or Alan Schwartz. And you know how foolishly I have exposed the truth of my life in letters and journals. If he is really a blackmailer, and I am susceptible to blackmail, he has really made a big haul.

What most frightens me about this situation is that he was obviously brought into my life by Audrey, and his invasion of my privacy is fully apparent to that brilliant, hard-boiled little lady, and she appears to approve it, as does Mr. Schwartz.

Gilbert Maxwell is now in Florida, having received a two thousand dollar advance on a book he's doing about me, and he gleefully reports that he spent several evenings with Mr. Brown and that they both "let their hair down" in their discussions about me. Gilbert assures me, and perhaps he means it, that the book will not be published without my approval. But Gilbert is understandably hungry for money, and how do I know that his publishers, Harcourt, Brace, and a newer firm joined to them, won't seduce Gilbert with further monies, to do a disgracefully sensational and distorted book about me. Poor Gilbert is a poet who only wrote five or six fine poems and is now scratching for a living as a prose-writer without much gift for prose. Audrey and Schwartz, as well as the bibliographer, are aware of this, too. And I suspect they could have prevented the use of that disgusting dust jacket on "Mother's book" [*Remember Me to Tom*, 1963].

For these reasons, and others, I have so far refused to sign the contract paper with Ashley-Steiner, the agency that Audrey is now attached to. Of course, if coercion by an implied threat of exposure of my privacy is attempted by these representatives of mine, I will not give an inch. I'd rather go into exile and give up all future work in the States than dishonor myself and intimate friends by submitting to such a thing; I would even rather meet them face-to-face in a courtroom. After all, I have no criminal record. My only record is a record of struggle to live the only way I know how and to create a deeply felt and honest body of work for the American theatre.

Last week I made out a codicil to my will in which I removed, as literary executors of my estate when I die, all present representatives. I took the liberty of naming New Directions (you and Jay), the executive secretaries of the Dramatists Guild, and the head of the English Dept. at the university where my manuscripts will be deposited as the new custodians and arbiters of my posthumous Mss., feeling that in this way I could be protected, posthumously, from a commercial exploitation of whatever unproduced and unpublished works I leave behind me and revivals of the ones done before.—I don't want my work to fall into the hands of Hollywood and Broadway hucksters, and I think that you all would keep me from turning in my grave so violently that I would plough up the graveyard. I know I am writing morbidly about this, but I have been so far from well these past few months that it would be foolish not to consider these kinds of eventualities.

I have leveled with Audrey about my reluctance to make a 3-year commitment with Ashley-Steiner at this time, and if she still holds any of her past understanding and sympathy, she will not press the matter, and meanwhile I am in touch with the Dramatists Guild (Louise Sillcox and Mills Ten Eyck, Jr.) about the future steps to be taken. Of course I would like your opinion of all this. Miss Sillcox says that she thinks that, whether sick or well, I would still be following this instinct.

Frank Merlo is now down here in Key West and Fred [Nicklaus] and I see him daily. He is heartbreakingly thin and ill-looking, but he still dances at the bars and walks down the street like the brave little man that he is, little only in physical size, but great in spirit, and he and Freddy not only accept each other but are warmly friendly together. I realize that I have always had only one close companion at a time and that each of them has been superior to me in human dignity of behavior, and my only excuse is that I have steadily been burning myself out in my work, such as it may be, which I can't guess.

It was Andreas Brown who persuaded me toward Texas. I had no idea that there were already mss. deposited at Harvard. But in the long run, I don't think it will make much difference. I am embarrassed, though, about the unintentional offense to Harvard. I had not imagined that any university would want to preserve my papers. I thought that they mattered that much only to me.

[...]

Yours ever,
Tennessee

≪ • ≫

my instinctive distrust of Mr. Andreas Brown: Not only did the University of Texas at Austin purchase a massive acquisition of Williams papers based on the work done by Andreas Brown, but also TW and Brown eventually became good friends. Brown also became an important bibliographic source for theater professionals and scholars prior to any published bibliographies and a champion for the work of biographer Lyle Leverich.

Alan Schwartz: TW's lawyer at the time.

Gilbert Maxwell: (1910–1979), actor and author of *Tennessee Williams and Friends (An Informal Biography)* (1965).

Frank Merlo is now down here: See note to letter of August 31, 1963.

135. TLS—1

Rec. 3/27/63 [Key West]

DEAR BOB:

Season in hell, everything going to pieces, all at once. Today I said to myself, Face it, baby, you're dying. Can you do it decently or will you make a mess of it like most things in your life?

Suspect following circumstances: lung cancer, since I hack away like Camille as played in a road company directed by Herbert [Machiz]. Face swollen up like a pumpkin from glandular or lymphatic infection that doctors here try to tell me is non-contagious mumps, as if I didn't have one marble left in the head-box. Nerves like dancing monkeys all the time. Dreadful realization that no one here is likely to pity me much except myself and Frankie, and so weak in my pins I don't see how I can get on a plane to Miami [then] to New York.

But Frankie is here and he is a true comfort to me. As for poor little Freddie, I think he is probably one of the best poets in America. I seriously do think so. But he nearly strangled me to death a few nights ago because I woke up at three AM and tried to revive him, sleeping on the sofa, by pouring ice-water on his head, and he says that I called him a whore.

I should have known better since he has often warned me that his quiet exterior is the facade of a terrific violence in him. Which is a necessity of true poets.

Bob, please write me care of Gen. Delivery, Key West, what you and Jay think of his talent and his poems. I will, of course, keep it strictly confidential because he is, after all, a vulnerable as well as a violent creature and until lately was very kind and gentle.

[. . .]

I don't at all object to your doing the three-in-one volume but I think you might take a look at the re-write of *Summer and Smoke* that I prepared for its London production after the original had already gone into rehearsal so the re-write couldn't be used. The re-write is titled *The Eccentricities of a Nightingale* and is much better, and basically different, from *Summer*.

Give Jay my love, and will you tell me what is best for me to do? I don't seem to know anymore.—But I am re-writing *Milk Train* for more serious values and I just might make it good enough to publish, at least in a limited paperback edition.

Yours,

10.

‹‹ • ››

136. TL—2

March 29, 1963 [Norfolk]

DEAR TENN—

Bob just showed me your letter, and I'm so distressed that you have these worries and problems. I just wanted to send you at once a word of encouragement and affection. We don't see each other too often—my nature seems to lead me more and more toward a self-contained life; I may end up as a hermit!—but I think you know how I feel about you as a friend, one of the truest, most understanding I have ever had—and how much I wish I could do something to cheer you up, or help out, in this tough period.

I wanted very much to take you up on your kind invitation to stop by in Key West on our way back from Grenada in February. Then suddenly Ann's mother had to have a bad operation, so we had to rush back here. Since then it has been one thing after another in the way of urgent work, though I do hope to get off this Saturday to Utah with my boy Paul for a week of skiing during his Harvard vacation. But I would more than gladly change that plan if my coming down to see you would brighten things for you at all.

[. . .]

Now about your own health. If you are worried about the possibility of a cancer—and who isn't these days?—the only thing to do is to get thorough testing right away and put your mind at rest. A few months ago I had a worry of this kind, but a specialist here in New York did thorough tests and was able to relieve me of worry immediately. But I would come to New York, or one of the wonderful Boston hospitals, if I were you, as I don't think the Florida doctors are much. We found that out when my Aunt was ill down in Sarasota.

[. . .]

I hope you are not upset because *Milk Train* did not have a long New York run. I'm sure the newspaper strike didn't help any, but in my opinion the acting left much to be desired. It didn't bring out at all what I found in the play when I read it before seeing it, the depths that are there, the poetry, the compassion, the understanding of what death means. I felt that Hermione just let herself go overboard hamming it up. She made Mrs. Goforth repulsive and almost unbelievable, while in the written script I found her clownish, but also a bit tragic and touching. As for the boy, he sure is handsome, but why did he have to be so wooden in his delivery? He seemed to be so busy projecting himself as a symbol that he never got to be a person. I suppose these things are the director's fault, but I guess Hermione is a tough one to "control."

[. . .]

You ask about Fred[erick Nicklaus]'s poetry. I think he is very gifted, but because he is writing in the traditional vein, it may be hard for him to win immediate success. I hope he will be patient, and will stick to his guns and write the way he feels, without trying to copy the latest fashionable trends. Surely he is ready for a first small book and we would be glad to undertake it. But he shouldn't expect instant choruses of acclaim. Unless you write something sensationally different, it usually takes about 15 years for a new poet to build a reputation. Even with Dylan Thomas, I recall, it was a good ten years before full acceptance.

Well, Tenn, as somebody said once: Keep Breathing. Inhale and exhale, don't neglect your food and have some good swims. These dark days will pass, even though at the moment things look black. You've had a rough life, not the glamorous ease that is supposed to go with success, but look at the wonders that have come out of it. And I don't just mean the great plays and the beautiful poems and the stories that cut through to the truth, but also the hundreds of kind things you have done for people, and can still do. You are a good human being, Tenn, and don't forget it. You mean a lot to a lot of us, as well as the public, and we want you around for a long time.

As ever,

[James Laughlin]

≪ • ≫

Milk Train: The first Broadway production of *The Milk Train Doesn't Stop Here Anymore* starring Hermione Baddeley, Mildred Dunnock, and Paul Roebling, directed by Herbert Machiz, ran from January 16 through March 16, 1963, during a blizzard and a newspaper strike, and received consistently negative reviews. A revised version of the play opened on Broadway January 1, 1964, also during a blizzard, directed by Tony Richardson and starring Tallulah Bankhead, Tab Hunter, Marian Seldes, and Ruth Ford, but fared no better critically than the first incarnation and closed within a week.

my boy Paul: JL's son by Margaret Keyser Laughlin, born in 1942.

137. TLS—1

4/16/63 [Key West]

DEAR JAY:

Aside from the unsightly swelling of the lymph nodes in my face making me look like a victim of mumps, the worst symptom I suffer from this still-unexplained malady is a terrible fatigue and depression which has kept me from doing many things I would like to, such as answering your beautiful letter to me.

Bob MacGregor called me and we had lunch together the week I was in New York for medical tests. I turned over to him a short story, a poem, and my "last will and testament" with the request that he have it examined by one of your firm's lawyers. My greatest concern is that revivals of my plays should not be left in the hands of an agency which I know would have special interests that would not be mine. Of course I want to pay for this service, it's very important to me, and while I may not be as sick as I feel, I will certainly rest better when a definitive will has been made out, and I'd rather have it in a publisher's hands than an agency's.

I have gone back to prose and am completing a novella I started ten years ago. There are some passages in it that I think equal the best of my prose writing, it's called *The Knightly Quest*.

Please be careful with Andreas Brown. He is extending his activities far beyond the legitimate range of what he calls himself, "My official bibliographer." He may be quite trustworthy. On the other hand, he may not be. At any rate, he presents a very smooth surface and one can be taken in by such surfaces I have found in my years on Broadway.

More later. I will be back in New York, before sailing for Europe, in a couple of weeks, and then I hope we can meet.

Yours ever,

<u>10.</u>

« • »

138. TL—3

April 30, 1963 [Norfolk]

DEAR TENN—

I'm so sorry that I missed you on your visit to New York, but was greatly cheered by your letter of the 16th with its report of improved health and rising spirits. I hope you will feel a lot better when you get to Europe. I have never found the Florida climate, pleasant as it is, very peppy. Usually when I am down in Sarasota I find myself just lolling about and not getting much work done. The mountains are where I feel the best, but I know you love the beach and the swimming.

Bob has been keeping me posted on his talks with you about your will, and has shown me a copy of Mr. Ortloff's letter of comment of it. It looks to me as though Ortloff has some good points and that it would be well to get them straightened out so everything is quite clear. I have been involved with a couple of family wills where the wording was not too clear, and it led to a lot of hassle and fret.

[. . .]

Well, enough of these matters. I don't like thinking about such cheerless topics, and I hope you will live to a ripe and beautiful old age the way your grandfather did, but I did want to assure you that I would always do my best, as unselfishly as I can, to carry out your wishes.

That is good news that you are working on a novella. I'll be eager to see it, and also the new poem and story that Bob is saving for me down at the office.

I think Bob wrote you of my thought that it would be great to do the new edition of the *Winter of Cities* as a paperback. I have always loved your poetry and would like to see more people, especially the young around the colleges, able to have access to it. These days we find that the college kids are not buying many expensive hardbound poetry books, but a great many of the paperbacks. Actually, it runs about ten to one. I would like to see your poetry reaching that public, and I hope you will consider the idea. We would make it a very nice-looking paperback, of course, with decent paper and a good cover. A dignified job, not one of those drugstore kind.

I note your advice about Brown and will limit myself to matters purely bibliographical with him. He certainly is a fast talker.

Please give my best to Frank. I hope he is picking up after his ordeal in the hospital. He is a very plucky guy and I wish him all the best.

Do try to let me know a bit ahead the next time you're coming up to New York so that I'll be sure to be in town and won't miss you again. The number here in Norfolk is Kimball 2–5388, though I'm usually down in New York the middle days of each week.

As ever,

[James Laughlin]

« • »

Mr. Ortloff: Frank Ortloff, ND's lawyer at the time. He was a Quaker and a friend of Robert MacGregor.

139. TLS—2

May 6, 1963 [Key West]

DEAR JAY AND BOB:

I want to thank you both for giving your time and consideration to this matter of my last will and testament. I also received a long letter from the Quaker lawyer. I haven't answered yet, because I am trying to figure out how the whole thing can best be simplified and expedited and still be legally feasible. What occurs to me is this: couldn't my whole estate, aside from writings unpublished and unproduced as yet, be left to "The Rose Isabel Williams Foundation," the first consideration being the maintenance of Rose at Stony Lodge where she seems to be happy and well-cared-for. Then what's not required for the first purpose, The Foundation could distribute as needed to a list of beneficiaries not as out-right <u>settlements</u>, cash-settlements, but as "grants" to those persons on the list which I would compose of persons close to me in my life and to whom I feel grateful or loving, in varying degrees, very varying degrees. Of course this list of persons would have to be very carefully considered by me. No worry about Mother. She's already very well-fixed. Some worry about Dakin. (Incidentally, his name is not "Mr. Dakin," as the lawyer called him in his letter, but Mr. Walter Dakin Williams, called Dakin by his brother.)—No worry about Frank Merlo, unless some divine intercession prolongs his life-expectancy beyond the time his doctors give him, which is the stingy limit of June of this year.—Some worry about Frederick Nicklaus, although I don't think you choke a person to where he can't catch breath if you love him—the worry about him is for his talent which I think is precocious although traditional, and I love his poems. No worry about the banana queen, Marion Vaccaro who gambles twenty-thousand a day on the stock exchange, I see no reason to have financial worry about someone who does that and who is over sixty, and drinks two quarts per day.—For Maria, not much worry, since she married a wealthy man who fathered two children by her, but still great friendship for her and I want to express it, posthumously, by giving her artistic control of *The Eccentricities of a Nightingale*, which was my re-write of *Summer and Smoke* for the London production but wasn't finished till after the original *S. & S.* was already in rehearsal and so couldn't be used although it is ever so much better. She should have a sort of artistic proprietorship over that and a cut of, say, about fifty percent of its earnings.

Others on the list, to share what's left over from The Foundation's maintenance of Rose on the present level:—Donald Windham, if he's in financial trouble despite the strong and beautiful quality of his work, Oliver Evans, same reason, Carson's sister, Rita Smith, because of her lovely nature as a person, my colored maid in Key West, Leoncia McGee, because of her affectionate loyalty and decline into age and her courage, never declining.—There are a few others. I don't need to leave anything to McCullers because she is now well-fixed financially and I suspect her life-expectancy is as short as mine.— And of course, Dakin, my brother: his income, which isn't small and whose prospects are not small, either, since he will receive Mother's estate when she dies and I think she's going to outlive me. Bigelow?— if The Foundation can afford it, a hundred dollars if it appears that he is in some genuine crisis despite his fabulous gift for latching onto wealthy, elderly ladies, say, once a year unless he is taken ill, and there's no wealthy old lady to take care of him.—I think he sincerely liked me at one time but he never writes me now. Andrew Lyndon if poor old Mrs. Crane doesn't provide for him decently when she goes forth. Enough about money distributions from The Foundation for now, we can discuss them more thoroughly when I get to New York, which will be in one or two weeks.

Now about my so-called "literary estate." It <u>must not</u> be left to the discretion of an agency or an agent. That is obvious to us all. Bob and I arrived at a good list of literary executors the last time I was in New York: New Directions (Jay and Bob), the Dramatists' Guild (its executive secretary), and whoever is my legal representative at the time of my death.

Now I should warn you that nearly all my capital is in my corporations and that when I die, the officers of the corporations would be brother Dakin, and the tandem of Audrey and Alan Schwartz. This is frightening since Audrey and Alan seem to work hand in glove, now, and their interests may not be mine, and Dakin would be out-voted and out-witted, I'm afraid, since he's not a worldly person, but touchingly naive, despite being a lawyer, and is so hung up on Catholicism that he might want to put Rose into a little Catholic asylum to save her soul and deprive her of things she enjoys in her life—possible solution—2 more officers or a replacement for Schwartz or Audrey.

I know this involves drawing up a complete new will, but I think it could be done simply and quickly, if it makes sense to the lawyer, either lawyer of yours, any good lawyer but my present one.

I am stressing expedition (and simplicity) because I have to grow a beard to cover up, partially, the swollen lymph nodes on either side of my face, and I know that when the lymph nodes swell up it means that there is a reservoir of aberrant cells in the blood stream, bacterial or malignant, and I also know that when doctors give contradictory diagnoses, or none at all, you're in bad trouble. The local doctor told me I had non-contagious mumps and just go home and lie down with a bottle of booze by the bed. Others said I had non-contagious but infectious mononucleosis which makes me think of what Jabe said to Myra in *Battle of Angels*. "Do you think I had a tumor of the brain and they cut out the brain and left the tumor?"

I think my liver is going, that's my personal diagnosis.

I should have mentioned that I have three real-estate properties which should also go to the Rose I. Williams Foundation, a rental property in Coconut Grove, Florida, my house in Key West, and a $90,000 apartment building in New Orleans, (now being handled by the realty firm of Miss Blackshear) bought on mortgage, and the increment from the rental units paying off the mortgage, with the little left over being banked in New Orleans by Frosty Blackshear. Also a custodial (investment) account with Chase-Manhattan.

Please let me know soon as possible if these suggestions of mine can be quickly and simply made into a will. I know this is far outside the concerns of publishers, but I think you know I regard you both as my friends, not just publishers (sometimes of rather corny things, I'm afraid). And there's just no one else I can safely turn to in this matter.

I will bring to New York with me a nearly complete novella called *The Knightly Quest*, and I think with two or three short stories not yet published, it might make a good book of prose.

I thought I told Bob that the paperback edition of poetry was OK. Just hold off a bit on it till we decide if there are any poems that should be added to it.

I am working daily on my re-write of *Milk Train*. I think it will be considerably shorter and stronger, despite my debilitation. David Merrick wrote me yesterday he would like to do it in London. There's also the Royal Court Theatre, which I'm very fond of in London. And the "Arts Theatre" which did *Suddenly Last Summer*, but I don't want *Milk Train* directed by Machiz again. He camped it up too much. It needs more serious treatment by a more consistently serious director. Well, forgive this long, Gothic letter.

Yours ever,
Tennessee

≪ • ≫

Marion Vaccaro: Marion Black Vaccaro (1906–1975), TW's longtime friend and reliable drinking partner, she is the inspiration for the character of Cora in his short story "Two on a Party."

Leoncia McGee: TW's housekeeper in Key West and one of the few people singled out in his will—he left her a monthly stipend.

Andrew Lyndon [. . .] *Mrs. Crane*: Mrs. W. Murray Crane was a rich philanthropist widow to whom Andrew Lyndon, a close friend of TW's and Truman Capote's, devoted himself, reading to her every afternoon for nine years and holding dinner parties at her home.

David Merrick: (1911–2000). See note on page 11.

140. TN—2

J—

Tenn called this morning and said he wanted all his manuscripts back. I had probably made a mistake in telling him yesterday that I thought there were several things there he may not have intended to give me.

I was to give them to Nicklaus this afternoon but while I was out to lunch [with one of the manuscripts]—actually with two, the short story about his father [the essay, "The Man in the Overstuffed Chair"] and 1-act play [unidentified], which I'd not yet read—he appeared at the office and Rhoda gave him the envelope that was on my desk.

Evidently there is a lot of sort of upset with Frank coming out of the hospital possibly tomorrow. 10 may go to Abington Va. tomorrow, where the Barter Theatre production would or will be, Frank perhaps going to Key West and Tenn with him or soon after.

Anyway everything seems chaotic and emotional. This morning I thought Tenn sounded offended or at least irritated about something, but this afternoon when he called about the two Mss. he discovered he didn't have there was no trace of this. Said there was only one poem he wanted now to be published, and he said he'd send it back so we could get going—but I'm not at all sure he will.

At least when he's been in this kind of state before—I've never seen it all quite as frenetic, the Mss. just don't ever reappear.

I'm glad I took the one about his father, which I read at lunch at home. It has enormously powerful parts and is very moving. Actually it's a kind of fragment of autobiography. [. . .]

[Robert M. MacGregor]

≪ • ≫

141. TLS—1

[probably August 31, 1963] [New York]

DEAR BOB:

I'm sure that a man as kind and perceptive as you are must understand and excuse my fantastic behavior yesterday. Still, it was offensive, and I apologize for it. You know what I'm going through: the worst period of my whole life. I'm not sure it doesn't unbalance me at times.

Please do get me the prescription for those enzyme drops. They picked me up so marvelously that day and gave me a feeling of mental clarity which I don't always have, as you know.

I got up at two-thirty this morning and revised the bad section of "The Man in the Overstuffed Chair," eliminating most of the material about mother's bad taste in house-furnishing, which was both exaggerated and bitchy.

I still think more than two poems should be added to the prospective reprint of the poetry book and perhaps you and Jay can help me to revise the longer poems. Certainly "Lost Island" should not be dedicated to Frank unless certain things are taken out, things that were endearing to me but wouldn't be to others, such as his habit, our last two years together, of passing out stoned on the floor and me pouring a pitcher of ice-water over him in a useless attempt to revive him.

These additional poems could go under the heading "uncollected poems" as some of Hart Crane's last poems were headed in his collected works.

Well, it's five AM now and I am going back to bed. I have been giving dear Frederick, who certainly doesn't deserve it, a pretty hard time of it, too, but he is patient and understanding with me. We talk. Nothing is left unsaid. We both feel it's better that way, since both of us have suffered so much from a difficulty in communications with people outside of our work.

Yours,

10.

<Frank is being released from the hospital tomorrow—I mean today. Reports encouraging.>

« • »

"Lost Island": Most likely an early title for "A Separate Poem."

Frank is being released from the hospital: Frank Merlo died of lung cancer on September 20, 1963. TW and Merlo had been estranged during much of Merlo's illness. Their final encounter is dramatized in TW's 1981 play, *Something Cloudy, Something Clear*. TW gave the eulogy at Frank's funeral.

The letter dated 8/31/63 (above) was forwarded to Robert MacGregor by Audrey Wood on December 11, 1963, with a note saying it was meant for him but "written earlier this year."

142. TL—1

January 8, 1964

DEAR TENNESSEE,

I hope it is nice down there, and that you are getting some good swimming and a bit of respite after all the nervous strain of the recent weeks up here. I was so terribly sorry to hear about the untimely closing of *Milk Train*. That certainly was bad luck, but I hope you are not letting yourself be depressed about it. All of us who have read the revised version of the play think it is very fine indeed, and if the director and the actors couldn't put it across, then the fault, I think, is theirs. Unfortunately, I didn't get down to see it myself, thinking that it would be running for some time. By the time I got the news it was too late.

Well, we are pressing forward with the book, which should be ready soon, and then all can see for themselves how good it is.

Bob showed me the new poem, the one for Frank ["A Separate Poem"], and I think it is extremely beautiful. Knowing the circumstances, I am particularly moved by it. But even if I didn't know the inside story, I would rate it high among your poems. David [Ford] tells me that there will be no problem about fitting it into the end of the new edition of *Winter of Cities*, as it just fits. I have typed out a fresh copy of it, which is enclosed for you, and I will keep other copies for you here, in case you need them. I hope I have gotten your markings for the spacing correct. If anything looks wrong, please mark it up again and shoot it back to me by airmail, so we can catch it in the proofs for the book.

I gather from Bob that, for the present at least, you would prefer not to go ahead with that idea I discussed of letting the Graphic Arts Center of the Pratt Institute do a handprinted portfolio with illustrations by some fine artist on this particular poem. But we can talk about that later. They are very keen to do something of yours in this elegant format, and perhaps there is some other text that would be suitable, or they could settle on one of the stories. I don't think they want to do anything that is very long because of the handprinting aspect. They would, of course, consult with you about the suitability of the artist to be chosen.

As Bob may have told you, Ann's mother passed away the end of last week, so we have been much occupied with that. It was, as they say, "for the best," as she had a mass of ghastly ailments and certainly wasn't enjoying life at all. A really wonderful woman and we will miss her sorely.

As ever,

James Laughlin

≪ • ≫

untimely closing of Milk Train: A revival directed by Tony Richardson opened on January 1, 1964, and closed in less than a week.

the new poem, the one for Frank: TW wrote "A Separate Poem" for Frank Merlo. It was added to *In the Winter of Cities* when that volume was published as a paperbook in 1964.

David: David Ford was ND's production manager at the time.

143. TLS—1

3/6/64 [Key West]

DEAR JAY AND BOB:

I have a big favor to ask you in regard to the book of *Milk Train*. I've thought about it almost continually and it seems to me that inserting the "errata" slip is not an answer. I think the only answer is to insert new pages in the unbound books. The "errata" is too big and too damaging to be solved by a slip in the book, it is too terribly embarrassing to me and to you as the publishers of the book and of all my other books. This play is the last long play that I can possibly write, but it is an important play, and not just to me. It should not be degraded at birth. Please don't let it be.

What I suggest is that you withhold all royalties on this book, I don't need them, don't want them, I only need and want—desperately—a book that is the book of the play that I wrote over a period of several years, under the most awful difficulties, a play that tore me to pieces but which I did manage to create on paper regardless of its two disasters on stage.

It seems to me that it should be possible to insert the corrected pages as quickly as the "errata" slip, and that if I abjure royalties on the book-sales till its full cost has been recuperated, the just thing for you to do is to use for distribution the unbound copies and have them bound with the new pages, not the slip. A friend of mine who works in a New York bookshop tells me that "errata" slips are usually torn out of a book by the bookshop managers, since they discourage sales.

We have been together such a long time and we are not just business associates but trusted friends. Psychologically the mutilation of my last play in print is like a "coup de grace." Please don't let it happen. It would leave such a terrible scar. I have read so many of your books and there's never been a printer's mistake of any consequence in them before.

If you think I am making too much out of this, it's because you don't understand what I have been through these past two years, or more, and what I know is before me. But I know you must know that I devoted my life to my work and it isn't right for it to end with an "errata" slip that can't possibly clear up the errors.

[. . .]

Audrey told me that the publication date was the twentieth of February and it seems to me that setting it, now, in April, is, at least from my view-point, too much a delay. Can't it be earlier than that?

I will be in New York very soon, on my way to Europe, and if we can get together, I hope that something in this letter, or between the lines of it, will have persuaded you to make certain that the book goes out as a thing worth respecting. Yours,

10.

≪ · ≫

insert new pages in the unbound books: In a letter dated the same day, MacGregor wrote to TW that the manufacturer was taking responsibility and that instead of printing an errata slip, all copies from the warehouse and elsewhere that could be recovered would be sent to the bindery to have the four pages removed and corrected pages tipped in.

144. TLS—1

[before March 12, 1964] [Key West]

DEAR BOB:

I am very grateful to you for coming to the same conclusion as I did, in my letter crossing yours, about what to do with the book. I think it's the only thing that we could do, we couldn't let the book go out with an <u>errata</u> slip that would be so embarrassing to us both.

Please do try to push the insertion of the new pages ahead as fast as possible. I know there will be a problem of page numbering. When I make insertions in a script I use the addition of alphabetical letters such as 42A, 42B, 42C, 42D and so forth till I arrive at the following number. I don't think such an expedient would compromise the book as I dare say everyone knows that this play was beset with very special problems.

I am very ill and am starting north tomorrow. Mother is apparently in about the same condition as she wrote me yesterday that she had a nurse with her. So I am going to go north by way of Saint Louis. I feel that this will be our last meeting, and I think that I would feel awful if I didn't see her again.

How I hope that I will see this last long play come out as soon as possible without mistakes in its printing, it would mean so <u>very</u> much to me now!

I saw nothing wrong in the proof of "A Separate Poem." As for the publication of *Summer and Smoke* and *The Eccentricities of a Nightingale*, I would rather see the latter play put first because I think it is better, I mean put first on the cover and inside, too. I don't think the cover should say "Two Versions." I think the explanation of the two versions should be on the cover-flap or in a short introduction that one of us could write, saying that this was the re-write of the play that I had hoped to have performed in England, but that couldn't be performed because, by the time I arrived, the original version was already in production.

I'm afraid I couldn't stand more than four days in Saint Louis: then will fly on to New York: after that, London, Rome, or Athens. I plan to give my brother my power-of-attorney so that I won't be plagued with all that cheque-signing. I will be traveling alone, apparently no other way, but I have an old friend in Europe that I can turn to.

Frederick was pleased with the cover design for his poems and I think his anticipation of their coming out keeps him happy, as it should. He understands, he says, as well as I do why it is wrong for us to try to go on together. We can't help each other any longer, and if we tried to, we would probably do nothing but hurt each other. Sic transit.

Affectionately,

Tennessee

≪ • ≫

the publication of Summer and Smoke *and* The Eccentricities of a Nightingale: During rehearsals for the original 1948 Broadway run of *Summer and Smoke*, TW was in Rome writing a new version of the play he called *The Eccentricities of a Nightingale* but he arrived in New York too late for the new script to be used, so he put his revision away. The dual edition of *Eccentricities* and *Summer and Smoke* was published by ND in 1964.

145. TL—1

May 1964 [Key West] [received June 1, 1964] [New York]
DEAR BOB:

Thanks for the books. I'm back in Key West trying to decide, what, if anything, I ought to do or where I ought to go next. Marion [Vaccaro] is here with me but she's got to leave tomorrow and I might leave with her as this is not a happy place to be alone in. I guess no place is a good place to be alone in.

It seems that *The Eccentricities of a Nightingale* is going out on the summer circuit, opening in late June and if possible I'll come up and take a look at it, and also at the final version of the film, *Iguana*, which is going to open in Lincoln Center. Any excuse to keep on the move is welcome. It's already getting oppressively hot here.

Did you take a look at the crazy "novella" [*The Knightly Quest*]? You didn't mention it, so I'm wondering if you think it's a possible thing. Audrey didn't seem to realize that it was meant as a fantasy, but that is probably due to the difference in styles between the time when I first worked on it and my later attempt to complete it.

Yours,
Tenn.

≪ • ≫

146. TL—1

June 12, 1964 [New York]

DEAR TENN,

Bob gave me your novella, *The Knightly Quest*, to read, and I wanted to write you to tell you how much I liked it, how exciting I found it. You make those characters, who are fascinating people, completely vivid, and you really do have a wonderful narrative gift. I hope you will keep on writing a lot of stories because they really are unique and marvelous.

I do urge you, if you feel like it, to do some more work on *The Knightly Quest* to put it into final shape. Where I think it needs a little more filling in is in the transition from the "real" part to the "fantasy" part. This transition seems to me a little bit sudden now and needs more detail so that it is more gradual.

To move from the realistic to the fantasy requires great art, but you are the one who can do it, as proved by the way you carried it off so successfully in stories like "The Widow Holly" and "Yellow Bird."

I think also that the part about the plot to infiltrate and blow up the project needs a little more detail as you go into it to flesh it out. Perhaps a little more specific about how they are going to get in there and what they are going to do when they get in. But you will know best about this.

I hope you will not mind my making these suggestions. It's a really terrific story and I am so keen to have you finish it up so that we can publish it in due time, and make it just as good as it possibly can be.

Not much news around here except the usual complaint about too much work, which is nothing new. I hope it is nice down there and that you are feeling better all the time. Do be sure to let me know if you come back to New York so we can have lunch or something.

I hope that copies of *In the Winter of Cities* have reached you and that you like it as much as I do. I think it's a beautiful little book. I am so happy that we have finally persuaded you to put the poems into paperback because they are fine poems and I know they are going to get around much more widely now that they are available at a price where the young people who go for poetry can easily afford them. The advance sale on this paperback was the best of all the paperbacks in the current list, I am told, and I think this is a very good sign indeed. I'm sure it will do well.

With best from all here, as ever,
James Laughlin

« • »

147. TLS—1

12/16/64 [New York]

Dear Jay:

It was nice of you to write me encouragingly about the two plays. They open early in March and I haven't the least idea of how they will be received by the critics but I must confess that I have doubts and fears. Still, I think that absorption in another production, regardless of how it turns out, will help me to distract myself from the long period of depression I have been going through. It's somewhat better now but there is still a good distance to go. I am going to an analyst again, and I find him better than the strict Freudian one [Dr. Kubie] that I went to a few years back, who was so strict and severe that he reminded me of my parents and I dreaded the sessions. This new one puts a bottle of whiskey on the table beside me and he tries to persuade me that I am a reasonably good person, despite my self-contempt.

Did you know that Maria's mother died lately? I think it is better both for Maria and the mother, who was completely helpless in a nursing home for several years, her mind so gone that when I last saw her she didn't know me. I think that Maria would love it if you dropped her a condolence note, as she is still so very fond of you. Her address is #9 Gerald Road, London.

My life is quite routine and uninteresting. I am sharing a duplex apartment, next to City Center, with the grandson of my grandmother's sister. We go to the same analyst. His sister goes to him, too. I have finally decided that there is so much eccentricity in all branches of my family that I might as well resign myself to kook-hood forever.

I hope all is well in your life.

With love,

Tenn.

« • »

the two plays: The money to produce *The Mutilated* and *The Gnädiges Fräulein* could not be raised in time and so the production was postponed for a year. They opened on Broadway under the collective title *Slapstick Tragedy* on February 22, 1966.

a new analyst [. . .] grandson of my grandmother's sister: Ralph Harris was the analyst, whom TW's cousin Jim Adams had recommended.

148. TLS—1

3/3/65 [New York]

Dear Bob:

I have missed seeing and talking to you. I feel that while I am still "not out of the woods" I should stick to a simple daily program of getting up about eleven AM, working till it's time for my analyst appointment, taking a swim on the way home, having a drink when I get there and then going out to dinner in the neighborhood which fortunately has several good French or Italian restaurants. If I do more than that, I suffer from nervous exhaustion the next day. I felt sad about myself till I heard that the wealthy East Indian, Denishaw, has stayed in a silver bed for five years because his dearest friend died. He is now just beginning to get out of the silver bed, and a Baroness of some kind is taking us out to dinner tonight at a new place called "Ondine's" where we can compare notes on neurotic seclusion, and how to escape it, if escape it we can.

I thought it was rather mischievous of Mishima to write about my little book *Grand* and say nothing except comments on the binding and printing, but I suppose I had that coming to me as I failed to say a thing at all about *Killed by Roses*, which I enjoyed very much, I mean the pictures. Probably the text was even more beautiful and had I known the Japanese language I could have and would have been delighted to praise it.

I have written a new ending to *The Knightly Quest*, it is in the style of the rest and is only two pages. The MS. is now 64 pages in type. Perhaps with "Grand," "Man Bring This Up Road," and "Mama's Old Stucco House," there might be enough material for a little book, with *The Knightly Quest* as a title.

As Spring comes on, I long to get away from New York, but I have rented the house in Key West and really have no one to go abroad with. Perhaps "some enchanted evening" I will find someone. I am sure that Pangloss would assure me that this will come to pass.

With love,
Tenn.

« • »

my little book Grand: A short memoir of TW's maternal grandmother, whose full name was Rosina Maria Francesca von Albertzart-Otte Dakin, was published in a limited edition by House of Books, New York (1964), and later collected in *The Knightly Quest* (see below), *Collected Stories* (ND 1985), and *New Selected Essays: Where I Live* (ND 2009).

The Knightly Quest: *The Knightly Quest, a Novella and Four Short Stories* was eventually published by ND in 1967.

149. TLS—1

Sept. 26, 1965 [New York]

DEAR JAY AND BOB:

This is only to say hello. Nothing much to report except that I made a recording of Hart Crane's poems for Caedmon a few nights ago. I believe my reading voice has improved since I had that sibilant old bridge replaced. I have been asked to give a reading at the Poetry Center, a thousand dollars honorarium which is a nice bit of cash to pick up. I hope I have the guts to do it. My rental property in Coconut Grove was practically demolished by the hurricane down there. I don't think the tenants had battened it up properly. And I don't know how much insurance I have on it, the real estate firm is very vague about that, almost as vague as they have been about sending me rental cheques which is very vague indeed. So I need to pick up some of the hard stuff when offered a chance to.

A little catastrophe here in my new apartment. I was taking out the novella one morning and it all fell on the floor and the pages have to be re-assembled. Somehow it seems like a colossal undertaking, but gradually it will be accomplished, I guess. I don't think there is much more writing to be done on it right now.

I finished a film-script of *Milk Train*, all with my own fat little fingers and it is now at the mimeographer's. Columbia Pictures is interested in it. It seems to work much better as a film than as a play. I've also finished two more long-short plays [*The Mutilated* and *The Gnädiges Fräulein*] which are being mimeographed, too. I keep busy so that I won't be so conscious of being in New York.

Do you know my new address? It is 15 W. 72nd, Apt. 33B, and has a lovely view of the park and upper Manhattan. On a very clear day you can see the straits of Gibraltar. On a very clear night you can see just the lights, which is better. On a foggy day you can't see tomorrow. Oh, well. Sight-seeing was never my kick.

When I finally re-assemble the novella and get it typed up, I will run down to 333 Sixth Ave. Would you like me to give you a few hours advance notice so you can be in Connecticut or somewhere?

Ever yours, Tenn.

≪ • ≫

a film-script of Milk Train: The film adaptation, *Boom!*, was directed by Joseph Losey and released in 1968. It starred Elizabeth Taylor (1932–2011), British-born film actress, who had previously played the leads in the movie versions of *Cat on a Hot Tin Roof* (1958) and *Suddenly Last Summer* (1959).

150. TN—2

10/9/65 Saturday

J—

Tenn was just fine, but, my what a lot of time it always takes, and yet noon is the time to see him, before he's had much to drink. (He had three martinis at lunch, but this mellowed him.) I think that part of it is that he's really very lonely. The apartment does have a magnificent view north and to the Hudson, and it's more roomy and thus less cluttered. It was arranged by the cousin, young Adams, who lives there, with his own room and bath. T. seems to have another friend he'd like to have move in but doesn't know how to let Adams out. Am not sure I understand it all, but I guess there is no involvement with Adams.

T. says the plays [*Slapstick Tragedy*] are going ahead, now that Margaret Leighton has replaced Leween McGrath (who's furious but on whose name they couldn't raise the money). He has rewritten them somewhat. He will let us have them when the play opens "in final form."

About *Twenty-Seven Wagons Full* paperbound he said "Why not?" I'll talk to Audrey.

About poems, he said he hasn't written one since those several we put into the paperbound *In the Winter of Cities*. "They weren't very good," he said, "and I've decided I'm too old to write poetry." He didn't think he had anything else for the Annual but would think about it.

He seems serious about our doing in the spring the new book of short plays about which I'll enclose a memo—for other eyes.

Tenn talks of you with great affection, and asked a couple of times if you were "happy."

His age seems to preoccupy him a great deal, and when it turned out that he was four or five months even older than me this depressed him momentarily, but quickly I was able to kid him out of that.

He kept asking me what time it was and finally when it was after 3:20, he clapped his hands and said, "Oh, goodie." It turned out that he could get his swim at the Y nearby and go to meet the analyst. "I have a dream for him today," he said and we laughed about bringing an apple for the teacher. It turns out that it is the analyst who got him to go and see his mother at Easter, and then he had his mother and brother for her birthday for a week in Bermuda. He now writes her every week, "She's mellowed, you know." And this seems to give him much relief. He immediately then, as if it were a part of the free-floating anxiety, spoke of seeing Rose every two weeks, and how he admires Rose's dignity, the way she has taken her trouble.

Through his cousin, Adams, or someone he seems to have been going to parties at Andy Warhol's, and some friend of Andy's sent him a poem that Tenn liked very much. He'll send to us.

Did I tell you that Nicklaus has brought us a new "volume" of poems? I haven't had the courage to look at them, but will, and I guess you'll have to see them too. TW had seen Nicklaus the night before at the ballet and Freddie had been very drunk. Bob

« • »

SECTION XIV

——◦◦◦——

PF: Tennessee's "late plays," the plays after *Iguana*, have always been controversial. Early on New Directions published *27 Wagons Full of Cotton*, which collected the earlier, more realistic short plays, and then in 1970 you did *Dragon Country*, which included *In the Bar of a Tokyo Hotel* and others of the later short plays that were not as realistic. Now what did you really think of those plays like *Out Cry, The Two-Character Play*?

JL: Tennessee always said to me that that was his most important play, *The Two-Character Play*, and I could see what he was driving at. He was trying to get to a different kind of human relationship with almost a relationship of despair these two poor people were in, and then I think it was very important, though, that he had the sunflowers so prominently looking in the window.

≪ • ≫

151. TLS—1

Jan. 7, '67 [New York]

DEAR BOB:

Thanks for sending me an advance copy of the book [*The Knightly Quest*, published February 21, 1967]. Two friends read it for me and said they laughed out loud. I hope that will be a prevalent reaction. I mean I hope more will laugh than be outraged. Despite the delay in publication, it still seems topical. But please no further delay!

Glavin and I are passing a little time here in New Orleans till the Key West house will be vacated by its tenants. We are in the only New Orleans hotel that admits dogs. It is Maison de Ville, Toulouse Street. Last night, in the patio, our intrepid dog caught a large rat.

I am attempting the difficult transition from a finished play [*The Two-Character Play*] to a new one [*Kingdom of Earth*].

Love to you and Jay.

Tennessee

≪ • ≫

Glavin: Bill Glavin was TW's partner during the late 1960s.

152. TLS—1

1/18/67 [New York]

DEAR JAY:

Bob wrote me about the loss of your mother. I'm sorry. I would have heard of it sooner, I'm sure, but I have been on a moving kick, Saint Thomas, New Orleans, Chicago. I am now afflicted with flu or bronchitis or something that comes from exhaustion. Soon as I recover a bit I will be heading back South.

Maria is in town. Full of antibiotics, I went with her to see a lovely

musical, *Man of La Mancha*, about my favorite character, Don Quix-
ote. It was wonderful being with her again. My God, how the wind
is howling about this terrible, tacky building! I'm going back to bed
as the doctor ordered. The antibiotics make me feel a long way away,
and the only place to feel that way is in bed.

I hope all's going well with you, now.

Ever,

Tennessee

« • »

153. TL—1

2/19/67 [New York]

Dear Tennessee:

I was sorry to hear that you were troubled because the new book
[*The Knightly Quest and Other Stories*] was not included in the list ad
in the *Times* on February 12th. This was because the books were not
yet in the stores by that date, and it just makes the stores, and readers,
mad if we advertise a book before they have copies to sell. You probably thought the books were on sale because you had received your
copies, but let me explain there is always a period of about six weeks
between completed books and publication date in order to give the
reviewers time to write their reviews and the papers time to get them
set up in type. We try to have everything "break" at about the same
time: books in stores, reviews, and ads.

Please don't think for a moment that we don't like the book—I
like it VERY MUCH—or that we don't do right by it in the ads. It
is all planned, just a question of timing. It is in the ads in *Book Week*,
the joint section of *NY Tribune*, *Chicago Sun*, *Washington Post*, this
Sunday, the 26th; and then it will be in the *NY Times* on March 12th.
And then there will be some special ads on *Knightly Quest* alone when

we have some good review quotes to work with. Keep in touch where you are and I'll send along copies as these ads come along.

I hope it is nice down there in Key West and you are having some sun and fun. I always remember my nice visit with you down there, and your marvelous grandfather, I bet you miss him.

As ever,

[James Laughlin]

≪ • ≫

154. TLS—1

March 25, '67 [New York]

DEAR JAY AND BOB:

Here is the first poem I have completed in a long time. It's probably something to be put in the files.

I'm leaving today for a few weeks in Key West, then to Europe.

Sidney Lanier says that *The Two-Character Play* has been accepted for the Edinburgh Festival in September. With some luck, I'll go to England for the rehearsals in late July and the try-outs in provincial places.

Is the book selling at all? If there are any more reviews send them to me in Key West—1431 Duncan Street.

Now to pack.

Ciao!

Tenn.

≪ • ≫

first poem I have completed in a long time: "Young Men Waking at Daybreak" was first published in *Evergreen Review* 50, December 1967, and collected in *Androgyne, Mon Amour* (1977).

Sidney Lanier: (1923–2013). Rev. Lanier, who was an Episcopalian minister, referred to himself as a "theologically trained layman" after he left the priesthood. In 1963,

Lanier gutted the interior of St. Clements Church on West 46th Street in Manhattan and along with Wynn Handiman founded the American Place Theater. Lanier went on to produce Broadway plays, including TW's *The Slapstick Tragedy* in 1966, and later moved to Big Sur where he worked at the Esalen Institute. A cousin to TW—they were mutual descendants of the nineteenth-century Southern poet Sidney Lanier—Lanier was the model for the defrocked Episcopal priest, the Rev. Shannon, in *The Night of the Iguana* and he conducted the service at TW's funeral.

155. TL—1

3/30/67 [New York]

DEAR TENN -

"Young Men Waking at Daybreak" is a lovely poem, I think. It moves well and says some pretty profound things in its quiet way. I'm glad you're writing poems again, and hope you'll do more. I always love your poems, which seem to me very much the essential you in their directness, and yet so subtle.

When you have a few more new ones, let's think, perhaps, of a limited edition done by one of the fine handprinters, a really beautiful book, such as we did with *I Rise* [*I Rise in Flame, Cried the Phoenix*]. What about that wonderful one you wrote about Frank? Did that ever get published anywhere?

The Knightly Quest is moving along all right. Nothing sensational, and the reviews have been, as they say, "mixed," but I have confidence it will make its way by word of mouth. More ads early in April, if the papers don't get struck, as is now threatened by the printers.

Hope it's nice down there.

Very best, as ever,

[JL]

≪ • ≫

wonderful one you wrote about Frank: "A Separate Poem" was added to the paperback edition of *In the Winter of Cities* in 1964.

156. TLS—1

August 1, 1967 [New York]

DEAR BOB:

I've been wanting to see you and Jay. Do you remember the "will" made out by the <u>New Directions</u> lawyer? There are several changes I think should be made. Audrey Wood should function along with you and Jay in making out contracts for my work. You wouldn't want the responsibility alone. She has a malicious tongue, at times, but has been associated so long with my work that it would be unduly harsh to eliminate her altogether. Could the lawyer add a codicil restoring her (with you and Jay) to the making of post-humous contracts? There is another important matter in the will, if I remember it correctly, that I'd like to change or at least check up on. If you have the time, call me this week and I could come downtown to look the document over. I've made out no other will since that one. Since I'm feeling so far from well, it seems a thing of some urgency.

Poems in the files? The only good one I can think of is "Young Men Waking at Daybreak," but when I drop by to adjust the will, I could look at any other poems of any value you have on file.

I leave for Sardinia in about ten days to watch the shooting of the film made out of *Milk Train*—that is, if I feel able to make the trip.

I've seen Frederick Nicklaus several times lately and he's shown me new poems of his that I think are marvelous. Of course, I suppose he will always be "traditional" in his style. He's a desperate young man and I'm a desperate old one—a basis for some degree of communication, perhaps.

To you and Jay my warmest regards as ever,

Tennessee

≪ • ≫

157. TLS—1

[3/10/68] [Philadelphia]

DEAR JAY:

It was kind of you to send me the heartening review [of *The Two-Character Play*] from England. There was also an excellent review in the *Observer* and the *London Times*. Last night, for the first time, the play here, which they call *The Seven Descents of Myrtle* despite my protests, was as funny and touching as I had wanted it to be.

As for me, I am tired to the bone. Bone tired. It will be surprising to me if I survive the Philadelphia and New York openings.

Mother is coming up for the New York one. She wrote me that she had a dress of real lace and that she wanted me to buy her a feather boa and elbow length gloves, and I did. Whenever things collapse on the stage, if they do, there should be a small spotlight turned on her. I am sure she will make coquettish gestures with the boa, flipping it from right to left or left to right.

She is an apparition, perhaps you might say a terrifying apparition, but at the age of 84 I suppose it is her privilege to be one.

I'm sure you'll excuse me for not writing much of a letter just now. I feel as if I'd been ravaged, without vaseline, by a troop of elephants.

But Spring in Key West will pull me together again.

My love to you and Bob,

10.

≪ • ≫

England: The first version of *The Two-Character Play* opened in London in December of 1967.

the play here: The title of TW's play *Kingdom of Earth* was changed by producer David Merrick, and it opened as *The Seven Descents of Myrtle* on Broadway March 27, 1968.

158. TL—1

3/30/68 [New York]

DEAR TENN:

I do want to thank you so much for giving us the pleasure of the opening [of *The Seven Descents of Myrtle*]. Although you maintain that I didn't see the play—because they didn't do it the way you wrote it—I've got to confess that I found it completely absorbing and thoroughly enjoyed it.

But be assured that we will get it in the book the way you wrote it, and stress in the promotion that it is in the Gothick [sic] tradition.

Here is your little check for the poem in the annual. I trust copies of the book reached you safely and let me know if you need more.

I'll talk to you soon again about the idea of a signed, beautifully-printed edition of *The Two-Character Play*. I agree with the London critic that that is one of your masterpieces, and I think we should get it in print. There can be a trade edition later when it gets produced here.

I'm just off for a few days of spring skiing in Colorado, and will call you when I get back.

Very best,
[James Laughlin]

≪ • ≫

poem in the annual: TW's poem "You and I" was published in *NDPP 20* in 1968.

159. TLS—1

April [rcd. April 15] 1968 [Key West]

Dear Bob:

I am so pleased that you will publish the play [*Kingdom of Earth*] in its original long version and with its real title. I loved the jacket design on *Suddenly Last Summer.*

I am trying hard to recover from the play production but it's a sticky do. Can't sleep more than two or three hours and feel a terrible disinterest in everything of a social nature down here. I have a play script and a film-script to work on but so far the little creative work I do is very primitive painting.

Wasn't it lucky that Estelle Parsons got that Academy Award so the engagement can be extended a bit?

I can't tell you how tired I am. It is hard to move around. Well, I'm an old man now.

The weather of Key West remains as lovely as ever, and the pool I had constructed is also a help.

I wish I could think of somewhere to go next. Endsucht, maybe.

I don't believe God is dead but I think he is inclined to pointless brutalities.

You know how I feel so you won't mind the brevity of this letter.

My love as always to you and Jay,

10.

<One time Estelle came up on my blind side and gave me one of her fabulous smiles. I said, "Oh, Estelle, actors don't like playwrights." She said, "I love playwrights but not directors.">

《 • 》

jacket design: For the jacket of *Kingdom of Earth* MacGregor had suggested the same designer who had done the jacket for *Suddenly Last Summer,* Stefan Salter.

Estelle Parsons: (1927–). American stage and screen actress, Parsons created the role of Myrtle on Broadway and won the Academy Award for best supporting actress in the film *Bonnie and Clyde*.

Endsucht: Apparently TW's attempt to coin a German compound word meaning, approximately, "sickness unto death."

160. TLS—1

July 5, '68 [Key West]

DEAR JAY AND BOB:

How kind of you both to write me!

I am delighted by the idea of the limited publication of *The Two-Character Play*. About the songs, I should think you would release them in whatever manner you are accustomed to.

I am going to send you a somewhat primitive painting I did of Frankie. I call it *The Portrait of an Idol*—which it seems to be.

About the scandal—I am hysterical and my little brother whom I love very much is indiscreet.

Tony Richardson: "Tennessee, your life is complete hysteria."—No argument there. But it does strike back at you sometimes.

Bill [Glavin] flew down yesterday with Gigi, the precocious little dog.

It's fiendishly hot here. Perhaps I can persuade Marion [Vaccaro] to go to Taos with me. Fuck the altitude! The air is cool and pure. Heat prostration unheard of.

Every day I work slowly but carefully as possible on a middle-length play called *Two Scenes in the Bar of a Tokyo Hotel*. I drink much less, but sometimes I fall out of my chair in a restaurant. Do I have brain cancer?

Subject for objective speculation. Doctors seem to tell you anything but the truth.

En avant with much love,
Tennessee

≪ • ≫

my little brother . . . is indiscreet: After the deaths of his friends Carson McCullers and Lila von Saher, TW remained out of the public eye for six months in 1968, causing his brother Dakin to contact the police, which prompted the following headline in the *New York Post*, "TENNESSEE WILLIAMS DROPS FROM SIGHT HERE."

Tony Richardson: (1928–1991). English stage director, husband of Vanessa Redgrave and father of Natasha and Joely Richardson, he directed the second Broadway incarnation of *Milk Train*.

Gigi: Another of TW's many bulldogs.

161. TL—1

January 9, 1969 [New York]

Dear Tenn:

I was so sorry to hear from Bob that you had had a rough time with the flu. I only had a very light touch of it—knock on wood—and was pretty lucky. As Bob probably told you, we went out with the two little boys, between Christmas and New Year's, for some skiing in Utah, and had a very fine time. About six feet of snow out there. I find it hard now to get as excited about skiing as I used to, but the little boys are crazy over it, and it was fun to do it with them.

Thank you for approving the proof of "Crepe-de-Chine" for *The New Yorker*. I'm so pleased that it will be appearing there, it's a really wonderful poem. I thought that the new line you wrote in at the side of the proof was an improvement, and I passed that along to Howard Moss, and urged him to print it that way.

That's fine that we can get going on a volume of the shorter plays, *Dragon Country*, and I think it will be a strong collection. My only question about that list is whether to include *The Two-Character Play* in it. I feel it is different in tone, and so important—one of the most interesting things you have ever done, I feel—that it should have its own book. And, as you know, we had planned, with your blessing, to go ahead first with the signed, limited edition, to be beautifully printed by Joe Blumenthal at Spiral Press. I think we should press ahead with that, if you approve, and then it could have its own trade edition later.

I'm also pleased that you like the idea of our gradually assembling the other books into chronological volumes of a *Collected Plays* series [later *The Theatre of Tennessee Williams*], and we will get ahead with that as separate volumes go out of print.

I hope you are feeling better now, and will have fun in Rome if you get over there. But if you come back here to New York first, please be sure to let me know, so that we can get together for lunch or something.

Very best, as ever,

James Laughlin

≪ • ≫

the two little boys: Robert Laughlin (1957–1985) and Henry Laughlin (1960–2014), JL's sons by Ann Resor Laughlin.

162. TL—1

March 5, 1969 [New York]

DEAR TENN:

I thought you might very much like to see another review of *Kingdom of Earth*, again on the premise that very few people will ever review [the published text of a] play, particularly one that has been done on Broadway. This one is rather nice and gets your idea as I am afraid Mr. Merrick and a few others didn't!

Someone told me that you had had pneumonia since you were briefly in New York. It begins to sound like a scourge of an Old Testament Prophet! Anyway, I hope that you are feeling better by now.

In fact I hope that you will be showing up in New York one of these days. We have a few small questions about the short plays volume [*Dragon Country*] which I would like to put to you in person, or rather show you the problem and get the answer then and there.

In my childhood, people used to talk about someone who has been converted as you were having "gone over to Rome." Physically you don't seem to have stayed "over there" very long. How about religiously? Or denominationally? Or spiritually (the word I am trying to avoid)? Maybe I mean spiritualismly or spirituous (in the hard liquor sense). Anyway whatever your state or state of your soul, I would love to see you.

Yours,

Robert M. MacGregor

≪ • ≫

"gone over to Rome": TW's conversion to Roman Catholicism. See next letter.

163. TLS—1

[*Received March 10, 1969*] [*Key West*]

DEAR BOB:

Of the conversion: it was intense loneliness and a very kind Jesuit priest. Everything that I do seems to provoke notoriety.

I swear that is not what I want.

As for Catholicism, I have always been a Catholic in my work, in the broadest sense of it.

Don't be disturbed. I question the canons of all faiths. I love the chanted mass, and rich ceremony.

At best, I will remain a very eclectic Catholic.

My brother was down here, as he had heard I was dying. He arranged the meeting with the Jesuit and the baptism. I also received the last rites, assuring my ascension to heaven after a relatively short stay in purgatory.

Since I last saw you, I spent two weeks in Rome and had a private audience with the general of the Jesuits, sometimes called "The Black Pope."

I will be in New York soon for the production, off-Broadway, of a play in two scenes! A rather outrageous play, only a renegade Catholic would write it.

Fondly,

10.

≪ • ≫

a play in two scenes: *In the Bar of a Tokyo Hotel* opened off-Broadway on May 11, 1969.

164. TLS—1

3/16/69 [New York]

DEAR BOB:

My apologies, again, for waking you. I know how distressing it is to be waked before you're ready. Why don't you get one of those phones that can be turned off? I have one in Key West, but nobody calls me there anyway.

I am here in connection with the off-Broadway production of *Two Scenes in The Bar of a Tokyo Hotel*. H[erbert]. Machiz is directing, and Anne Meacham has been cast. There is a possibility of getting Donald Madden who has become a close friend of mine and Bill's. The script needs careful editing which I am trying to give it as I hear actors read it.

Miss Hooligan is here and sends you her warmest regards, along with mine.

I am making every effort to avoid personal notoriety, but yesterday evening went out to dinner in a double-breasted pin-stripe suit and a purple shirt and nearly white tie, very wide. I wanted to look like George Raft.

Ever,

Tenn.

≪ • ≫

Donald Madden: (1928–1983), American stage and television actor.

Miss Hooligan: Another of TW's bulldogs.

George Raft: (1901–1980), Hollywood character actor known for playing well-dressed gangsters.

165. TL—1

[April (?) 1969] [New York]

DEAR TENN:

I was quite disturbed when Audrey called us to say that the producers of Ken Tynan's review were trying to claim partial book publication rights on the piece you had written for them. I think this is a terrible idea, and I hope you won't let them do it. I think it would set a very bad precedent indeed. In all the books we have done for you, book rights have always been a separate matter, directly between you and us, and I think that's the way it should remain. The theatre, I think, should be one domain, and book publishing a separate one.

We are now battling hard on a similar situation for Ferlinghetti. The Apple people—that is the firm the Beatles set up in England—want to do a record of him reading his poetry, and they are trying to claim publication rights in what they record, which, as Ferlinghetti agrees, is all wrong.

I know that Ken Tynan is a good friend of yours—and he's a writer whom I greatly respect myself—but I do hope you can find a way to make it clear to him that publication rights are an entirely separate thing from theatre performance rights. By the way, I'd love to see what you have written for them if you have an extra copy around.

I hope the new play [*In the Bar of a Tokyo Hotel*] is going well, and that I'll be seeing you soon. Do call some day when you might be free for lunch or a drink. I don't like to bother you when I know you are in rehearsal, but would love to see you, so hope you will let me know when you might have a moment.

I think some of the new books on our spring list might interest you and I'll send a few up, hoping you will enjoy some of them.

Very best, as ever,

James Laughlin

≪ • ≫

Ken Tynan's review: The Broadway musical review about sex, *Oh, Calcutta!* was controversial for its vulgar humor and use of nudity.

Ferlinghetti: Lawrence Ferlinghetti (1919–), American poet, publisher, painter, and friend to the artists of the Beat Generation. ND has published over twenty-three titles by Ferlinghetti.

166. TLS—1

April, 1969 [New York]

DEAR JAY:

I understand that the whole matter about *Oh, Calcutta!* has been straightened out by A[udrey] W[ood]. My little contribution would only play for a couple of minutes. A.W. feels that it sets—I mean would set—a very bad precedent and she was very "up tight" about it. I only wrote the tiny piece to please Ken, it isn't of any consequence. Since you're against it, too, I'm sure the right decision has been made.

This week I take over the direction of *Tokyo*, as the actors are in open revolt against Machiz. I can't call the shots on this one but I'll do my damndest. My relations with the actors are excellent. At least I'll have that going for me. Bill [Glavin] and I are flying to Rome the day after the play opens.

Some evening, about seven, I hope we can get together. I'd like you to have a finalized copy of this very protean work, and I have another short play that may interest you.

> Affectionately,
>
> 10.

<Theatre is hell!@*>

≪ • ≫

My little contribution: Possibly a sketch by TW called *Short Short*.

167. TL—2

10/5/69 [New York]

DEAR TENN—

I was so sorry to hear that you were in the hospital and hope you will be better and out soon. My saintly Mother, now in Heaven, <u>loved</u> hospitals, and kept thinking up useless parts of her stomach which could be excised, so she could get back into the West Penn, but not me, though once, when I had busted my back skiing in New Hampshire and was in a cast, there was this really good-looking young nurse, I'm afraid I gave her a bad time, she didn't dare get in range or I would make a grab for her . . .

Thank you so much for signing the pages for *The Two-Character Play*, that must have been quite a chore, you were noble to do it.

It's going to be a BEAUTIFUL book. It's in the bindery now, but I've seen a set of sheets, and they are lovely, really perfect printing. Keep me posted where you are so I can send you the book as soon as it's finished.

Did you see a fine piece about you, an interview, in a magazine called *After Dark* by a fellow named Dan Isaac? I think it's very good. Audrey probably sent it to you, but if not, I can make a xerox for you.

I've sent you, there in St. Louis, Tom Merton's last long poem, *Geography of Lograire*, which we've just brought out. I think there's some marvelous stuff in it. He was getting better and better all the time as a poet, really getting down into his unconscious and bringing up some strange wonders. I miss him sorely.

Very best from all,
[James Laughlin]

≪ • ≫

in the hospital: The accumulative effect of at least half a dozen years of Dr. Max Jacobson's amphetamine cocktail injections, combined with antidepressants, sedatives, barbiturates, and alcohol had left TW unable to function most of the time, caused severe paranoia, and created dangerous levels of drug poisoning, from which the playwright was apparently dying. In September 1969, his brother, Dakin, had TW committed to the psychiatric division of Barnes Hospital in St. Louis where he stayed for nearly three months while he detoxified. Though TW eventually understood that his life had been saved and that he was given many more years to write, he was never able to entirely forgive Dakin and left him out of his will, except for a nominal amount.

signing the pages: A signed, limited edition of *The Two-Character Play* was published by ND in 1969.

Dan Isaac: Isaac is the Williams scholar who edited the published editions of TW's early full-length plays, *Candles to the Sun* (ND 2004) and *Spring Storm* (ND 1999).

Geography of Lograire: The long, last poem of Thomas Merton, which JL prepared for publication after Merton's untimely death in Thailand on December 10, 1968. Merton had, after years of isolation at the Abbey of Gethsemani in rural Kentucky, been allowed to travel in Asia where he met the Dalai Lama and other leaders of Eastern religions and attended an ecumenical conference. After giving a final address to the group in Bangkok, he returned to his lodgings to take a shower and was accidentally electrocuted when, standing on the wet floor, he touched a faulty direct-current electric fan. His body was returned to the United States on a military plane also carrying the bodies of soldiers who had died in Vietnam. A brown satchel containing all the books and papers that Merton had with him was marked to be given to JL. This contained the notebooks that were the basis for Merton's *The Asian Journal* on which JL worked for the next three years. Merton's death affected JL deeply.

SECTION XV

PF: What do you see as your major influence on Tennessee?

JL: Of course, I think where I helped him maybe the most was in boosting the poetry. You know, bringing it out, trying to talk it up, and I think it's wonderful romantic poetry. But you see nobody will take him seriously because the New Critics came along and everything had to be all these formalist structures, and Tennessee would just write down what came into his heart so that he didn't get the credit for it that he ought to have had, and then the stories the same. I loved the stories.

PF: The stories are wonderful.

JL: I kept pushing for more stories all the time. I think both of those things pleased him, and I talked to him about Tom Merton as somebody who didn't get the credit he should have for his poetry because he was so famous as a religious writer. So I told Tennessee, "If you weren't a great playwright you'd be a first-class poet and story writer, you'd be Chekhov." I think that kind of talk he liked. It was sincere with me, I thought the stories were just marvelous.

« • »

New Critics: The New Critics were an informal group of teachers and writers ascendant from the 1950s to the mid-1970s, inspired by the work of John Crowe Ransom, Allen Tate, Cleanth Brooks, and Robert Penn Warren. They championed "close reading" of the text, particularly of poetry, to determine its value, excluding such factors as the writer's intent, the reader's response, and social and political currents including the biography of the author. Because they focused so intently on the "formal" elements of verse such as rhyme and meter as well as the use of the tension-creating devices of paradox, ambiguity, and irony, JL felt that the New Critics missed the point of poetry—to touch the human soul and elevate it.

168. TLS—1

11/10/69 [Barnes Hospital, St. Louis]

DEAR JAY AND BOB:

I have little hope that this re-write and cut in *I Can't Imagine Tomorrow* will reach you in time to be used, but here they are anyway. I'm also enclosing the first proof-page of *The Frosted Glass Coffin*. Two beginnings are used; I've scratched out one. You'd probably caught that yourselves.

I'm afraid this collection of plays [*Dragon Country, A Book of Plays*, 1970] reflects the depression and fatigue of the writer. Of the new works, only *Confessional* seems to have much vitality, and even that is over-laden with loose verbiage.

I'm just beginning to get in contact with the world outside again. The doctors are nearly ready to release me from the hospital, but I'm far from well physically. I'm afraid my heart has been severely damaged. I plan to go directly from the hospital to the airport and board a plane to Key West. Whether or not I can stand a long plane-trip is anyone's guess. I wouldn't make book on it. If I can, it will be wonderful to be back in my little Key West compound. I might even get relatively well. In any case—I never could stand confinement! It's too bad that Dakin didn't realize that, and it's too bad that I didn't realize that Dakin didn't realize that. I am waking up rather late from a very bad dream . . .

How terribly I've abused myself and my talent in the years since—(?)*

Love,

10.

<*I suppose since Frankie's death.>

« • »

169. TL—1

November 12, 1969 [Norfolk]

DEAR TENN:

I was pleased indeed to hear that you were getting along well and might soon be out of the hospital. I hope it hasn't been too dismal for you there. But I imagine you have had your typewriter there and have been able to work. Have you written any new poems?

We now have the copies of the limited edition of *Two-Character Play* from the bindery, and I'm rushing one off to you there at the hospital today, and hope you will be as pleased with it as I am. I think Joe Blumenthal did a beautiful job with the printing and design. And thank you again for signing all the copies.

Please let me know where you would like your other author's copies to go. You're entitled to five and I've sent one to Audrey, of course, but that leaves three, if you want to let me know whom you would like to have them. No hurry about this, I'll just keep them here until you let me know where you want them to go.

I hope you received all right the copy of Tom Merton's last poem, *Geography of Lograire*, which I sent some weeks ago. I think it's his best thing in poetry, some marvelous passages in it, and I do want you to see it, so let me know if it didn't turn up, and I'll send another. I'm working now on the editing of Tom's *Asian Journal*, the diary which he kept on his trip to Asia, from which he never returned. It's very fascinating, some really marvelous passages. But needs a good deal of work on my part as he wrote in pretty much shorthand, and I have to fill in to make it read in proper sentences, as a published book should. He was a terrific guy.

Very best, as ever,
James Laughlin

≪ • ≫

Asian Journal: JL, along with Brother Patrick Hart, Merton's secretary at the Abbey of Gethsemani, and Naomi Burton Stone, who had been Merton's literary agent, worked for three years on deciphering the notebooks JL received after Merton's death and creating a coherent manuscript. *The Asian Journal* was published by ND in 1973 to great acclaim.

170. TLS—1

11/29/69 [Key West]

DEAR BOB:

After my two months' stay in the Saint Louis bin I am quite lucid mentally, but physically I am far from well. I want to add a codicil to my will, providing, as best I can, for Glavin who has no resources but me. I would not rest easy in my grave, which I'm afraid is something to be considered now, if he were cast upon the unreliable tenderness of the world. So would you please send me, in an envelope marked private and personal, a copy of the will. Soon as I've added the codicil I'll return it to you.

The special edition of *The Two-Character Play* is a <u>beautiful</u> piece of book publishing, but I am not at all pleased with the writing. I wrote it when I was very sick and the writing shows it. I am trying to make some improvements in the text.

I'll get a longer, more informative letter off to you and Jay as soon as I feel more settled in Key West and my skin.

Love,

Tenn.

≪ • ≫

171. TLS—1

5/12/70 [Key West]

DEAR BOB AND JAY:

[...]

It is now just about all set for me to attend the Rotterdam and London poetry festivals and I am trying to prepare a suitable program of poetry readings. I have written a long new prose-poem about my experiences in the "Bin." It is called "What's Next on the Agenda, Mr. Williams?" and is pretty rough stuff in its subject-matter. Now I believe you have a number of long poems of mine in your files that haven't been published and I wish you'd dig them out for me. I may be able to get them in shape for inclusion in the poetry readings abroad. I remember one in particular which began with the lines:

The day turns holy as though a god moved through it,
wanderingly, unknowing and unknown,
led by the sky as a child is led by its mother.

It was more or less an elegy for Merlo and ranged widely in geographical background, one section annotating my impressions of Bangkok.

Another poem I'd like to take another whack at is something about two brothers who were acrobats in a circus in Europe and I believe its title was "Les Etoiles d'un Cirque Etrange."

A third [as yet unidentified] was about a fantastically ancient woman who got up at 5 PM for nightly excursions to Tiger Town to pick up a black lover. It was a sprawling poem but I think it had some excellent passages and I could tighten it up for reading or for some future publication. I remember little about it because I was very heavily on pills and liquor at the time of its composition which may have been a couple of years ago, or nearly.

I would greatly appreciate your digging these poems up for me if you do, indeed, have copies of them.

I am very busy working on *The Two-Character Play* with which I hope to entice Margaret Leighton, and preparing four shorter plays for an evening's program. I still have cardiac symptoms but not so badly now and I suspect that I will die with my boots on, as it were, during the production of a play.

I am happy and well.

With affectionate best wishes,
Tenn.

« • »

The day turns holy: From "A Separate Poem," added to the paperbook edition of *In the Winter of Cities* (1964).

Margaret Leighton: (1922–1976), British stage and screen actress who won a Tony for her performance in *The Night of the Iguana*. Leighton did not play the role of Clare in any subsequent productions of this play or its variants.

four shorter plays: Possibly, *The Reading, Green Eyes, The Demolition Downtown*, and *Now and at the Hour of Our Death*, the latter an early draft of *Now the Cats with Jeweled Claws*.

172. TLS—2

10/28/70 [Singapore]

DEAR BOB:

It was very reassuring to get a letter from you in a place that is so frightfully remote from everything familiar to me. It's true I was here once before, when Frankie and I took our rather abortive trip around the world about ten years ago, but at that time I was working on a long play, probably *Iguana*, and only paid passing attention to anything else. My interest in places and people is much keener now that I am not committed to ambitious work-projects. I still work every morning for an hour or two but it no longer pre-empts other interests in life. It's too bad that it did for such a long time, it was obsessive and compulsive and finally it defeated itself and came very close to destroying me.

I had hoped I'd feel like settling in Bangkok for six months or so but I find it to be an ugly city, there is such an incongruous mixture of the East and the West, so much Pepsi-Cola and American type hotels and high-rise buildings and New York cut sirloin and hot dogs and hamburgers plopped down among the wats and the klongs with no assimilation, that I have a depressing sense of an old and graceful and simple way of life being overwhelmed by something only concerned with exploitation. It is enlightening, of course. Economic imperialism was just a phrase to me before this Oriental junket. Now it is shockingly defined and graphic and I feel that I know, now, what Vietnam is really about and I am embarrassed and guilty.

Oliver [Evans] thinks I'm being ridiculous but then Oliver is able to kid himself that his three silky catamites, at one hundred baht a throw, are romantically in love with him, and yet he will go to bed with the younger brother of Oot while Oot is exiled to the bathroom. I am also quite willing to enjoy these very easy and voluptuous little affairs but afterwards I don't feel that I have been valued for anything but the one hundred baht. Of course there is nothing more uncomfortable in the world than a decadent Puritan.

[. . .]

I had some surgery performed by an excellent Thai surgeon, it was for the "excision biopsy" of something called a "gynecomastia" which seems to be a growth of the mammary gland, a thing that is often associated with liver-damage when it occurs in men. I've known for years that my liver was not in a good shape, it couldn't be after all the abuse I've given it. But the liver is the largest organ in the body and with the practice of relative temperance, I mean like having Bristol Cream Sherry instead of a double martini, it may hold out a good while. Anyway, after those three months in that Saint Louis snake-pit which Dakin (with Audrey's advice and consent) threw me into, I no longer have much fear left in me. I had the surgery, complete removal of the left mammary gland, with just a local anesthesia and the operation lasted more than an hour and the local wore off and it was quite painful toward the end. But I learned that I was tougher than I had thought. I got right off the operating table, dressed and went to the best restaurant in town to celebrate with venison and vintage wine, and there was a lot to celebrate because I was convinced I had cancer, terminal, but the frozen section proved that the growth was benign and I don't think the Thai surgeon was lying to me about it. My heart was quite a matter of concern after the two coronaries I had in the snake-pit but now the cardiac symptoms are disappearing and I go to sleep at night with no apprehension of not waking up the next morning and I swim twenty or thirty lengths of a pool without a touch of angina. I am really a very tough old bird after all, and I am glad about that since I am more interested in life than I have been since Frankie's death. The big problem now is loneliness. I must find a new life-companion. This is especially urgent since, after five years with Glavin and an almost total celibacy, I have a strong libido again as well as a need to be close to someone. It's pretty hard to work out a problem like that in the States at my age with my minimal attractions, discounting what I hope is still a fair degree of financial security . . .

[. . .]

I hope you and Jay are both well. I'll be writing him soon. I know his interest in India and I'll give him a report on my reactions to it.

With love,

Tenn.

≪ • ≫

173. TLS—4

April 23, 1971 [London]

DEAR JAY:

It was nice hearing from you before sailing though I'm concerned over your indisposition. Bob had told me you were afflicted with "morning sickness" as if pregnant. I have the same complaint, usually feel nauseous the first half hour after waking. In my case it seems related to dinner wine. If I have more than two or three glasses it makes me liverish. I'm afraid we have entered into a time of life when we must engage in various delaying actions and strategic withdrawals from the front lines of our early years. I find it acceptable since it can't be denied.

I left word with some lady at your office that I was disturbed over the title "Collected Works of." It strikes me as a bad omen, especially since poor Jane Bowles had her paralytic stroke immediately after they came out with a volume called "Collected Works," I suspect it made her feel that her time was finished. Bob called me on the ship to suggest the alternate title of "The Theatre Of" which isn't perfect but I think less final-sounding. I have quite a number of works still on the bench, including the Bangkok Version of *The Two-Character Play* which is quite a bit different from the limited edition published so handsomely last year. At first it kept expanding but now it is contracting and after the Chicago gig this summer it ought to be in good shape and sufficiently different to be brought out in a paperback. I think we have a good cast in Eileen Herlie and Donald Madden and I have "good vibes" about this project, it seems to me purer than the work I did in the Sixties, that terrible decade when I was almost a Zombie.

I believe in regeneration, and I look forward to the next few years with an absolutely unrealistic relish. Among the mail which Audrey brought aboard the ship the morning we sailed was a letter from the Mayor of Greenville, Tennessee, asking me to contribute to "the rehabilitation of Old Harmony Graveyard" where several of my distinguished forebears are laid to rest, such as Valentine Sevier, Dr. Charles Coffin who was President of what is now The University of Tennessee, Dr. Francis McCorkle, pastor of Harmony Presbyterian Church and also a medical doctor, Thomas Lanier Williams I who was First Chancellor of Tennessee before it joined the union. All were active in the early anti-slave movement which gives me satisfaction, though not enough to wish to join them in Old Harmony. I want to be buried at sea. However I am going to donate a big piece of the new fence about the graveyard. Oh, and one of these ancestors was a Dr. Charles Laughlin—wonder if we're related.—I suppose I'm interested in my lineage because the popular notion is that I was dropped in a back alley, due to my usually raffish behavior. Of course I can sometimes "come on" like a colonial dame, but it's pretty boring.

Maria has said she will join me in Italy. Her Mother-in-law, the Dowager Lady Saint Just, died a couple of weeks ago and it may be that Maria has benefitted financially from this sad event, in which case it would not be completely sad. For some time Maria, and even her daughters, had been banished from the Dowager's county seat.

Maria has been a devoted friend to me all these years despite her present attachment to Gore Vidal. I think he uses her as a "front" for his dissolute activities in Rome but she is impressed by the grandeur of his penthouse on a Roman palazzo and his undeniable wit. (I thought *Myra Breckinridge* was more disgusting than funny.)

I love the Pound *Cantos*, there is a true fineness of spirit in his work as in his nature when I met him at St. Elizabeths hospital.

Did you know that Oliver Evans and I had dinner with Yukio Mishima in Japan a few weeks before his dreadful end? He came out to Yokohama by taxi from Tokyo and signed a book for me and gave me a touchingly grave lecture on the virtue of sobriety. Although our social (political) attitudes were almost opposite, we always had a good relationship and he spoke admiringly of *In the Bar of a Tokyo Hotel.* I explained to him that it was an allegory on Western Imperialism in the Orient. I am now reading a lovely early novel of his, *Thirst for Love.* I felt at that last meeting that something was deeply wrong with him and in retrospect I think he had already decided upon the ritual suicide and was telling me goodbye.—We first met in New York under very odd circumstances, neither of us knowing the professional identity of the other.

Time to start packing as we land this afternoon in Naples. I believe there is a mail-strike in Italy now which may delay your reception of this letter some time.

All the best,

Love,

10.

≪ • ≫

"morning sickness": During the second half of 1970, JL began to feel unwell in both body and spirit. As his depression deepened, he was subject to frequent bouts of nausea that he called "morning sickness." He was referred to Dr. Benjamin Wiesel, director of psychiatry at the Hartford Hospital. Once he was sure, in early 1971, that JL's problem was bipolar disorder, Dr. Wiesel prescribed lithium, which had only been approved as a treatment for manic depression the year before. JL would continue to take lithium until his death. However, neither JL nor MacGregor mentioned to TW that the "morning sickness" was related to a mental problem.

I was disturbed over the title: The series was brought out as *The Theatre of Tennessee Williams* from 1971 to 1992 in eight volumes. TW has a character recount the debate about what to call the collection in his novel *Moise and the World of Reason* (Simon and Schuster 1975 and ND 2016).

Chicago gig: A revised version of *The Two-Character Play* opened in Chicago on July 8, 1971, at the Ivanhoe Theater, directed by George Keathley and starring Donald Madden and Eileen Herlie.

Dowager's county seat: Wilbury Park, near Salisbury, Wiltshire, England.

at St. Elizabeths hospital: See note to JL's letter to TW of 11/10/56.

[Mishima's] dreadful end: In November 1970, Mishima took over the office of the commandant of the Eastern Command of Japan's Self Defense Forces to give a speech on the balcony that he hoped would inspire a coup d'état. When it did not, Mishima went back into the commandant's office and committed the ritual suicide, seppuku.

174. TN—1

September 27, 1971 [Norfolk]

MEMO:

TO: RMM

RE: TENNESSEE WILLIAMS

I hope that you have a good session with the new young agent, thanks for giving me his name which I'll put on my records here, and that all goes smoothly, and that Floria Lasky won't prove a problem on contracts. I met her a few times years ago, and I think we always got on all right, and I believe she knows that I am sort of a friend of her brother Mel.

I have read through the three little one-act plays that Audrey sent over to you on September 17, and I think they are rather slight, particularly the first one, called *The Reading*, but the second one, *Green Eyes*, is rather strong, in the way that *Kingdom of Earth* was, and the last one, *The Demolition Downtown* has a quality rather like that of *The Two-Character Play*, the sense of the world falling apart. I don't see that these three plays would make a very strong book by themselves, or do much for Tennessee's reputation at this stage. But certainly they should be added to one of the other volumes of short plays at some point, either 27 *Wagons* or *Dragon Country*, whichever worked out best technically. Probably that would be the thing to propose to the new young agent. Then we would add them at the next printing of one of these paperbacks. Or, if he would rather, wait until Tennessee has done a few more one-acters, and make a third collection of them. I'll bring the script back down to New York when I come this week.

J. L.

≪ • ≫

the new young agent: Bill Barnes took over from Audrey Wood as TW's agent from 1971 to 1978.

Floria Lasky [. . .] her brother Mel: Floria Lasky (1923–2007), TW's lawyer at the time, was an influential American lawyer whose practice included many theater people. She was also the younger sister of American journalist and intellectual Melvin J. Lasky, prominent on the anti-Communist left.

Audrey sent over: During a rehearsal for the Chicago production of *The Two-Character Play*, TW broke off the working relationship he had had with Audrey Wood for more than thirty years. According to director George Keathley, on July 7, 1971, during a notes session in the dressing room of Donald Madden, TW turned on Wood and said, " . . . you've been against me from the beginning, I'm through with you. You're fired." The two never spoke again, and although TW stayed with the same agency, initially assigned to work with Bill Barnes, Wood continued to oversee TW's affairs until she suffered a stroke in 1981.

175. TLS—2

9/28/71 <in transit> [received, Oct. 4, 1971]

DEAR BOB:

Thanks for your warm note delivered by Henry [sic] Martin, along with the striking dust-jackets for the plays. Like the colors and print but the photo on the back is reproduced much too darkly so I seem to have a long black Bolshevist beard and no neck. It would be good if you could give it a lighter exposure. I suggested that the projected fourth volume—why doesn't it appear with these?—should have a bright yellow color. Another suggestion: I would like to use the sub-title *Hi-Point Over a Cavern* as the <u>title</u> of *Period of Adjustment* with <u>that</u> as the <u>sub</u>-title. Forgive this scrambled writing, I've had a sleepless night.

October first Maria and I are flying to Paris for the French premiere of *Le Doux Oiseau de la Jeunesse* with Edwige Feuillère.—then somewhere to rest by some warm sea for a while, perhaps Tunis or Marrakesh which I've never visited.

Mr. Martin told me that Jay is better and I'm very relieved about that. Please give him my love and thank Gertrude for the great job on the jackets.

Ever,

10.

Paul Scofield seems quite seriously interested in "Out Cry" but Margaret Leighton is still "dragging her foot" a bit, I think because of ill health, hers and her husband's. I hope to see her today. Meanwhile I keep refining the texture. I'm thinking of emigrating to England as I feel that there is no longer much chance for me in the American theatre. Too much awful personal publicity and hostile press. I'm looking for a country place, a cottage, in Sussex: could build a heated pool: keep a cow and a goat and get Mary Poppins (my latest secretary) into a dairy-maid's outfit.

This afternoon I met Harold Pinter and he was very charming and gave us tickets to his new play this evening. I feel that over here I could maintain stimulating contact with a theatre which is so much better than ours.

I'm very happy with my new agent at IFA, Bill Barnes. He is young and "with it" and, unlike Audrey, wants me to remain active in the scene.

Of course, the primary and ultimate object is to remain alive.

≪ • ≫

Henry [sic] Martin: Frederick R. Martin, then managing editor of ND.

dust-jackets for the plays: The jackets for the first three volumes of *The Theatre of Tennessee Williams*.

I would like to use the sub-title: This change was never made though it is not clear whether the request was overlooked or TW changed his mind.

"Le Doux Oiseau de la Jeunesse" with Edwige Feuillère: The French premiere of *Sweet Bird of Youth* starred Edwige Feuillère (1907–1998).

Paul Scofield: (1922–2008), English stage and film actor.

(my latest secretary): Most likely Victor Campbell.

Harold Pinter: (1930–2008), English playwright and director.

176. TLS—1

<P.S. My sister is seriously ill.>

1/22/72 [New York]

DEAR BOB:

I'm glad you liked the story but I'm afraid this does not presage a new vital era in my life as a writer as you kindly profess to think. Actually I am just about through with writing and after this last production at—guess where?—"The Truck & Warehouse Theatre" off-Broadway—I'm going to pull up stakes in America and settle somewhere abroad and face up to the fact that things are approaching a conclusion.

I have been a writer nearly all my life, well, from before puberty, even, but it adds up to almost nothing. I mean I've discovered nothing. There's been no answer to the questions. I am sure this must be the feeling of nearly all writers when they sense that their work is finished. Probably all of them, as I did, had hoped that the Sphinx at the edge of the desert would reply to their shouts, but she remains a silent stone enigma at the edge of the desert.

(Rilke, Duino Elegies, #10.)

However—

I have no complaints to make in sharing a common experience. There's been a lot of satisfactory encounters along the way.

I don't mean to sound elegiacal. Take that back. I probably do. Last summer's experience in Chicago was shattering and I want no more. I won't let this off-Broadway bit bother me much, in fact I plan to stay through the early pre-views and leave before the opening.

The Two-Character Play will be done with a pair of fine actors someday, here or in England, but it doesn't seem at all likely that I will see the production although I continue work on it.—

Love—

10.

≪ • ≫

this last production: *Small Craft Warnings* opened off-Broadway April 2, 1971, at the Truck and Warehouse Theatre, moving that June to the New Theatre, and ran for a total of six months. TW often declared that any given upcoming production would be his "last."

(Rilke, Duino Elegies, #10.): TW loved Rilke and had the character of August paraphrase from this elegy at the end of *Something Cloudy, Something Clear.*

experience in Chicago: The second incarnation of *The Two-Character Play* (after London in 1967) was in Chicago, under the title *Out Cry*. It opened July 8, 1971, with Donald Madden and Eileen Herlie in the principal roles, directed by George Keathley. Not only was the Chicago run unsuccessful, but it was also the occasion of TW's break with his agent Audrey Wood. See note to memo from RM to JL of September 27, 1971.

177. TN—2

3/29/72 [New York]

J—

As you know Tenn's new play [*Small Craft Warnings*] (*Confessional*, now expanded, with one new character and a second act) is going great guns and will open next Sunday night, April 1, Easter night. Bill Barnes has been keeping everyone from Tenn, and I guess rightly, for at least last week he was acting as director and also rewriting every night, and he had moved Tenn from the Plaza because so many people knew he was there.

Last Sunday night Barnes invited up to 8 ND people to a dress rehearsal, but I seem to have been the only one able to go (and I had come in from the country). I expect I made people like Peter and Carla and even Eleanora who "just couldn't get to it" feel that they missed a theatrical event, for the theatre was crowded with stars of all kinds, mainly young, and the run through was without break and excellent. I got there late and had to stand at the back, but it was where TW passed at the intermission, and he hugged me warmly and said he wanted to see me.

Barnes then called Monday, gave me Tenn's number at the Elysée, said he wanted to see me after the opening for lunch "to talk about everything." Audrey in the meantime called to say she had heard a rumor that "Barnes was negotiating with a big publisher for TW's *Memoirs*." She didn't know anything about it but just thought we'd like to know and perhaps ask at some point.

Today I was up there "for lunch." This turned out to be something of a misnomer, but I did have a steak sandwich and some coffee while Tenn phoned new speeches for the principal lady (I heard them first from the hallway, and thought for a while that he was in trouble and calling for the police himself and then remembered that this fit into the play). Then people kept arriving and leaving, and Maria was phoning from London. (She presumably has gotten Paul Scofield to play in *Out Cry* which is of course *Two-Character Play*, and she and Bowden are to be co-producers, to which Bill Barnes is very opposed.) Then at 12:50 exactly there arrived Mel Gussow and a photographer from the *NY Times* for an interview. I just stayed on and listened, took part in fact, trying to get the interview which lasted until after 3:00 back from attacks on the critics and on the interviews last year in *Esquire* & in the *Atlantic* (Tenn said he fired his lawyer "because he wouldn't sue the *Atlantic*"). I think I helped for TW was very edgy about the interview and learned many things about which I'll tell you in time.

One thing though I'd like your reaction about. Gussow asked TW if it were true that Doubleday had offered him $50,000 for his *Memoirs*, and Tenn said it was true, but he hadn't agreed yet. [. . .]

However, he is going to write a beginning for *Esquire* he said. I expect of course this is what Barnes wants to talk about.

My own feeling is that we should not stand in his way, as long as it is clear that all other books come to us. For I don't imagine we want to get into a sensational kind of work, nor equal this kind of advance, and this is obviously what they want. I can also imagine that Barnes wants some feather in his cap, as indeed this production of *Small Craft Warnings* (the new title of *Confessional* of course) [is].

Barnes had said that he had had inquiries "from other publishers" about this play, and I said that of course we wanted to publish it.

However, I would like your earliest reaction about the *Memoirs*. We could of course pony up the advance. Even though sales are behind we have lots of "reserve."

After learning of a real fight in the office on Monday between Gertrude [Huston] and Carla, with Gertrude leaving in the elevator with George [Zournas] and saying she was "Resigning," I called her Tuesday AM and asked to go to the opening with me (and Fred and Kathy [Martin]). They are all coming for an early supper at 77 Washington Place. Audrey by the way tells me she's going to be "out of town."

Bob

« • »

Peter: Peter Glassgold began work as an editor at New Directions in 1970 and helped MacGregor put together the five initial volumes of *The Theatre of Tennessee Williams*. Made editor in chief in 1983, Glassgold left to pursue his own writing in 1993 but remained editor at large and was JL's preferred editor for his own poetry books, including *The Collected Poems of James Laughlin 1935–1997*, published by ND in 2014. Glassgold and his wife did, in fact, attend a performance of *Small Craft Warnings* with Robert MacGregor and George Zournas sometime after the opening.

Carla: Carla Packer, production manager for New Directions at the time.

Eleanora: Ellie Sassani, publicity director for New Directions at the time.

Bowden: Charles Bowden produced several TW plays.

Mel Gussow: Gussow was a theater critic for the *New York Times*.

178. TLS—1

4/4/72 [Norfolk]

DEAR BOB—

Many thanks for your report on Tenn's affairs. Called office this AM but you were at home so gave the message for you to Fred that I'm sure we don't want to get into "uptown" bidding on Tenn's autobiography IF he writes it. But I certainly hope you can hold on to the plays, the present one, and those to come. Also poems and stories. Please let me know what to say if you think I ought to write him anything. I don't know quite how to put it, I mean we must be sure he understands that we'd love to do the auto if it were in our price range, but we must conserve cash or we wouldn't be able to do young poets and translations that don't sell . . .

JL

≪ • ≫

179. TL—2

May 22, 1972 [Norfolk]

DEAR TENNESSEE:

I'm sorry to have been such a lousy correspondent for so long a time. As Bob may have reported to you, I have been deeply engaged in the editing of Tom Merton's *Asian Journal*, which he left in a very rough state, almost stenographic, but I know he wanted it to be published, and so I have been trying to do what he would have done with it to finish it, and also trying to get all of the Asian terms spelled right—he spelled phonetically in the handwritten journal—which has meant all kinds of correspondence all over the East. Then, on top of that, we went out to Utah, as usual, for some skiing with the children, during their Easter holiday, and I managed to take a slide on some ice, and ran into a big direction post, about four inches square, at high velocity, and why I wasn't killed I don't know, I guess because it didn't hit my head, and no bones were broken, but I had a sore muscle which kept me crippled for about a month. But, happily, that is over now, and I was able to get down to New York the other day, and one of the first things I did, of course, was to take in a performance of *Small Craft Warnings*, and I wanted you to know at once what a wonderful play I think it is, and how both Ann and I liked it enormously. It held us absolutely absorbed, and not only because of that remarkable performance by the girl who played Leona. She is terrific, and I think this is one of your greatest character studies. But all of the characters are good, and each one very moving in his or her own way, and the way you alternate between action and poetic revery, or "confessional" as you first called it in the original version, is very beautiful, and I think most effective theatre. There is great poetic beauty in many of the passages, and also a great deal of human wisdom, and beyond that the touching effect of one's feelings of your compassion for suffering humanity. I think it is a very beautiful play, one of your finest, and I am happy that it is getting the recognition it deserves. I talked a little bit with the boy in the ticket window and he said they were getting good audiences and expected to be running right through the summer. And, needless to say, I'm very happy that we will be bringing out the book, and I believe it is already in composition, and that Fred and Bob are pushing it as rapidly as possible.

Are you writing any poetry these days? You know how I love your poetry. I know you have sometimes felt discouraged because of the neglect it has suffered at the hands of the academic critics, but surely you must understand that their hearts are as constipated as their bellies, and not let it upset you. Your poems move me in a way that those of no one else do, and I know that my feeling is shared by many readers. So, while I don't want to push you, I think it is time we should be thinking about another volume of poetry, when you have enough gathered together that you like. Do let me know how matters stand, on this, if you have a moment. I know that between us, Bob and I have in our folders half a dozen poems which haven't been in books but I suspect that you may have a great many others around, in various stages of completion, which you could perhaps finish up without too much difficulty.

[. . .]

I do hope that I will have a chance to see you the next time you are back in New York. And, meanwhile, do think about more poems, and congratulations again on *Small Craft Warnings*, which is a beautiful, beautiful play.

As ever,

[James Laughlin]

≪ • ≫

180. TLS—1

<7/?[sic]/72> [New York]

DEAR JAY:

It was such a joy to receive that long, wonderful letter from you. You know how badly I need reassurance about my work. I always have and more so now than ever as the work becomes more difficult with age despite the fact there seems so much more to say.

"S.C.W." [*Small Craft Warnings*] is minor. But I have corrected the proofs, I hope accurately, and I know that you will make of it an attractive looking book. Sometimes someone will bring me all the old first editions from New Directions (of my work) and I am always thrilled by the beauty of the way the books look—at least before opened for readings. . . .

I am working, now, on a long play. Wish me luck. And I wish you all the best.

Love,

Tenn.

« • »

a long play: At about this time TW began drafts of what would eventually become *The Red Devil Battery Sign*.

181. TL—2

August 11, 1972 [Norfolk]

DEAR TENN:

It was so good to have your letter, not long ago, you sounded well and happy, and I hope that work is going along well on the long play. Needless to say, I'm all eagerness to see it when you have it completed.

I think you underrate *Small Craft Warnings* when you pass it off as being just "minor." To me so much of life, both its tragedies and its heroism, and above all its pathos, and whatever it is that keeps people going in the face of it all, is right there, "in cameo," if you will, but all crystallized in such a wonderfully poetic way. I came away from the theatre that evening both saddened—because it seemed so unjust that life has to be so rough on so many people—and yet wonderfully heartened, by the very fact that they do find ways to make it meaningful to themselves, small, pathetic ways, perhaps, but nevertheless ways that work—and all this you have understood and put down so delicately, and yet so strongly.

I've not been down too much to the New York office this

summer—I was finishing up the work on the Merton *Asian Journal*, which is finished now, and then starting to pitch in on the selection of material for the next Annual—but I gather from Fred and Bob that things are on schedule with the book, and that we ought to have it out in the early fall, and I hope you'll be pleased with it.

You made me very happy saying what the books meant to you, and let me reply, in turn, that they mean just as much, and perhaps even more, to me. I love the original editions, remembering something special about each one, and then when I look at the sturdy volumes of the "theatre" set, it makes me feel that I have been part of something very important in the course of American drama and literature, something which was only possible because of your friendship and loyalty.

Could I come back to asking whether you've been writing any new poems? Just the other day, there came up a copy of Fred's memo to the production department that *In the Winter of Cities* was soon to go into its fourth printing in paperback, so you really must think of yourself, always, seriously, as a poet, and write poems when you can. Is there by any chance some new one you may have around that we could put into next spring's Annual, *ND 26*, that will be, for which I'm assembling material now? I would love to have you in the Annual again, it seems some years since you have been there, and you belong there so much.

[. . .]

Very best, as ever,
James Laughlin

≪ • ≫

182. TLS—1

12/15/72 [New Orleans]

DEAR JAY AND BOB:

This last time I got a letter from you all, you asked if I had a new poem. Well, here is one, a grim celebration of the festive season.

I leave here (New Orleans) for Key West tomorrow but expect to be in New York on or about Christmas, skipping the first week or ten days of rehearsals of *Out Cry*—my nerves are in no condition to encourage the director and cast.

I plan to emigrate to England the day before the play opens, and I do mean <u>emigrate</u>.

Four more years is eight too many for me, since a bit of humanity still survives in my heart.

I'm also hoping to find a place in England for Rose.

I saw her just before I flew down here. She arrived at my door with the chauffeur and said: "Tom, this is Charlie, I've invited him to dinner!"

—Always a great lady . . .

Love and Xmas cheers,
Tenn.

<P.S. S.C.W. very handsome book—next time please omit the actor's drunken ad-libs pp. 59–62—worse than <u>mine</u>.>

≪ • ≫

a grim celebration of the festive season: Possibly "I Think the Strange, the Crazed, the Queer."

Out Cry: The revised version of *The Two-Character Play* titled *Out Cry* opened on Broadway March 1, 1973, and closed after twelve performances. Directed by Peter Glenville, the play starred Michael York and Cara Duff-McCormick.

Four more years: A reference to Richard Nixon's reelection as president the preceding month.

P.S. S.C.W.: A copy of this letter was not placed in the corrections file and the requested changes were not made to the published editions of *Small Craft Warnings*.

183. TL—2

March 6, 1973 [Norfolk]

DEAR TENN:

What a beautiful—and powerful—play [*Out Cry*]! I was sorry that you had rushed away before the end of the opening so that I couldn't give you a big abrazo of congratulations. I had loved it too, as you know, in the somewhat more spare, abstract version that we did as *Two-Character Play* in the limited edition, but I think the new version, with so many new good touches, is even stronger: the abstract quality is not lost, but there is more fleshing out to dramatize the ideas, and it certainly is that, a play of ideas as well as human passion, and I use the word passion here in the religious sense, what man suffers just to exist, and must suffer all the more intensively if he is driven by the daemon of the instinct to create. I think *Out Cry* is one of your most important statements, and best plays, because it's all there, crystallized, the basic ontological problems: what is "being," what are we here for, and what do we do about it if we are more than mere animals going through the motions without doubt or question.

We want, of course, to get out the book as soon as possible, and I think it should be paperback as well as cloth, because the students will eat it up and I'm sure many professors will want to teach it in their classes. I hope Bob can get a final script from Bill Barnes before he (Bob) takes off for his vacation in Spain next week, so that we can have it ready for the fall list.

And that was a very graceful piece you had in the Sunday *Times* about *Cat* and other matters. You sound relaxed and happy, and I hope it stays that way for you now, you've been through some rough seas, I know.

It's good to have you back again in the annual with the fine poem, "Old Men Go Mad at Night." Many thanks for that. The *ND* 27 will be out in the fall if all goes well. And I liked the story in *Playboy*, too, "The Inventory at Fontana Bella,"—very randy and almost Guignol, your own special blend of black humor, but with so much more color and wit than most of them, the Barths & Roths, can manage in that genre. I trust that Bill Barnes is keeping track and a file of stories and will let us know when there are enough for another collection of them.

It's been a lousy winter here in Connecticut for snow, mostly just ice and rain, but we'll soon be getting off for some skiing in Utah with the kids, and they report nearly a hundred inches out there. Hope to see you when we get back in April if you're around New York at any time then, do be sure to let me know.

Very best, as ever,

[James Laughlin]

≪ • ≫

very graceful piece: TW's pre-Broadway essay for *Out Cry*, "Let Me Hang It All Out," was published in the *New York Times* on March 4, 1973.

Guignol: Reference to the French puppet shows whose main character is Guignol. Using sharp wit and linguistic playfulness, the shows, like their near relative the English Punch and Judy, were often bawdy and sometimes violent.

[John] Barths & [Philip] Roths: Disparaging reference to John Barth (1930–) and Philip Roth (1933–) who were considered among the "best and the brightest" American novelists of their generation.

184. TLS—2

3/9/73 [Key West]

DEAR JAY:

It is beautifully kind of you to write me about the play [*Out Cry*]. Its stage-history, at least in this production, seems to be almost finished, so it is a comfort to know that you'll bring it out as a book: something will survive the holocaust of these years of half-crazed, often impotent effort.

I must prepare a copy for printing myself as I am afraid the only copies available now are the always-mutilated stage-manager copies, in which the original description of business is omitted.

Honestly, I don't know how much of me has survived, but luckily, I have the retreat of the little compound in Key West to try to put the pieces together again into a simulation of something, and luckily Maria was with me the last two weeks and a young companion, now, Robert Carroll, a veteran of three years in Vietnam who is himself a writer. Maria took an immediate dislike to him but didn't know his work nor his kindness when alone with me.

I was to have gone to the West Coast almost immediately for various publicity things in connection with *Streetcar* out there but knew, after reading the magazine notices, that I had to stay in hiding for a while longer. The plan is now for Robert and I to fly out with Barnes from New York about the Seventeenth. After the opening, I hope to catch another one of those "slow boats to China"—the Orient brings out the latent Buddhist in me and the wounded ego is gently medicated.

Sometimes it seems to me that the past twelve years or so has been one long sick ego trip and I don't see the end of it yet.

The simple natural thing of doing my work was slowly shattered through my collision with the false intensities and pressures of "show-business"—for which I was not cut out. Thank God I have accumulated some capital to carry me through the time of retreat that now seems imperative to me.

I often think of a visit that Maria and I made to Ezra Pound in St. Elizabeths hospital, the humanity and dignity of the man in prison: but then I think of his end in Venice and I hope it wasn't as desolate as reported.—That was a very lovely interview that you recently gave about him.—People of his stature don't seem to exist anymore in the fever of these times and the cheapness of them.

There is a variation to that poem for the anthology.—the last two lines.—

Was that a board that creaked as he took leave of us
or did he speak—"I'm going to sleep, good night . . ."

<Regards to Bob,
Ever, Tenn>

≪ • ≫

with Streetcar *out there*: A twenty-fifth-anniversary revival of *A Streetcar Named Desire* opened at the Ahmanson Theater in Los Angeles on March 21, 1973, starring Faye Dunaway and Jon Voight, directed by James Bridges.

Robert Carroll: TW's last regular boyfriend. They had a volatile on-again/off-again relationship through much of the 1970s. Aside from his housekeeper Leoncia McKee, Carroll was the only individual for whom TW provided a monthly stipend in his final will.

a visit that Maria and I made to Ezra Pound: See note to JL to TW letter of 11/10/56. TW also refers to this episode in his letter to JL of 4/23/71.

SECTION XVI

—◦—

PF: When I came to New Directions in 1975, Peter Glass-gold had been doing all the work on the first five volumes of *The Theatre of Tennessee Williams*, and he was ready to move on from Tennessee—he'd had Tennessee up to here—and once I started doing editorial work, he turned Tennessee over to me and the first thing I worked on was the *Androgyne* volume.

JL: *Androgyne, Mon Amour*, the poetry.

PF: And a few years later they had the London production of *Vieux Carré*, and I just happened to be going to England on vacation, this would have been '78, and I picked up the Direc-tor's Script of the London production from the agent in Lon-don and brought it back and then worked from the Director's Script so that we would have the play . . .

JL: To get a real text.

« • »

Vieux Carré: Born out of the journals TW kept during his stay in the French Quar-ter of New Orleans in 1938 to 1939, the play evolved over the decades in the form of poems, short stories, essays, and one-act plays. The ND edition of *Vieux Carré* was based on the Nottingham Playhouse Production, which premiered in London in August 1978 (ND 1979). It starred Sylvia Miles as Mrs. Wire and was directed by Keith Hack.

185. TLS—2

6/24/73 [Positano, Italy]

DEAR JAY AND BOB:

Bill Barnes has just told me, to my joy, that you will bring out the latest little collection of stories next Spring. And that this time it will be not only a beautiful publication but one that will be brought more immediately to public attention.

As a token of my pleasure, I thought of titles this morning and here is one that seems right to me, since the stories deal with six ladies, all of them mortal and all of them possessed in one sense or another.

I have taken a big apartment in Positano for the summer. The young gentle (?) man sharing with me has taken flight to a little commune in the town, and among other projects in London, I am looking and hoping for a replacement, since the apartment is too big for a man alone. It's a good place to work. The water is clear and cold and I have made some charming friends there, including John Cromwell who knew Jay at Harvard and is a very unusual and talented playwright—I'm hoping Barnes will help him get one produced.

Positano is built rather precipitately between the sea and volcanic (inactive) mountains—but I take my time on the steps and the palazzo isn't far from the beach.

Maria came down there for a week, staying at film-director Zefferelli's show-place "The Ville." She's returning to London before I leave this week.

Meanwhile she is getting Positano society into shape like a drill-sergeant, to its—I guess the _mot juste_ is dismay . . .

> With love & thanks ever,
> Tennessee

≪ • ≫

little collection of stories: "Six Mortal Ladies Possessed," which became *Eight Mortal Ladies Possessed* by the time it was published in 1974.

John Cromwell: (1914–1979). Minor actor and playwright, his Broadway debut occurred in *The Old Maid* in 1935. He was the Harvard roommate of another of JL's friends, Joe Pulitzer.

186. TL—3

October 3, 1973 [Norfolk]

DEAR TENN:

I was so very pleased when I got back from Wyoming, and managed to sort through the great stacks of mail which had accumulated on the hall table, to find copies which Bob had sent of your three very interesting poems. I think you know how happy I am when you get to writing poetry, I love your poetry, and I hope that before too long we will have enough of it to gather together for another book. I liked "Night Visit" especially, but they are all good.

Would you like me to hold these for the next available Annual, which, actually, wouldn't be till *ND 29* in the fall of 1974, since *ND 28* is already at the printer. We would certainly love to have them in the Annual, or would you like to have Bill, or I can work at it if he is too busy, try to place them first for you in magazines? There would be plenty of time for them to come out in magazines before we needed to use them in the Annual.

From all the rumors that I have heard, your new full-length play must be quite a blockbuster, and naturally I'm happy about that, too, and hope that all will go well with it.

As you may have heard, our return from the ranch was considerably delayed, because I managed to involve myself in a stupid accident while out fishing. I guess I must really face up to the fact now that I am no longer the stripling who won the high jump in prep school.

I was out fishing on the ranch, and in a big hurry to get to a certain hole on the stream where the day before I had seen a simply enormous cutthroat trout, and came to a cattle fence which had to be crossed, and instead of doing what I usually do, and should do, and certainly will always do in the future, which is to humbly get down on my stomach and shimmy under the lowest strand of barbed wire, I tried to vault over it, and something slipped, and I landed with all my weight on top of the fence post, crushing in three ribs and slightly puncturing the lung. Fortunately, this was fairly near one of the roads on the ranch, and I was able to crawl back to the road, and pretty quickly was picked up and carted off to the hospital, where they kept me for nearly a week, to make certain that I hadn't ruptured any of my organs.

Actually, the hospital experience wasn't too bad. The place was full of nymphet Florence Nightingales, some of them very good-looking and quite funny [. . .]

Another good by-product of the hospital was that, for the first time in several years, I began writing some poems again, I would wake up in the night, with the ideas for the poems floating around in my head, and then put them down before I called one of the nymphets for a pill to go back to sleep again. Actually, they are all about my experiences as an 18-year-old when I first went to Rapallo, to study with Ezra Pound, and about my romance there with the bank janitor's daughter. It was as if the shock of the accident had somehow thrown my unconscious back about 40 years in time, so that I was able to remember feelings and details which had been buried, for the most part, in the intervening period. The poems are written partly in English and partly in Italian, as we neither of us really spoke the other's language, and whether it is corn or Porn or what it is I'm not quite sure yet, I still have several sections to finish to complete the cycle. Since the juicier bits are in Italian, I imagine I can get the new Supreme Court ruling if anybody is foolish enough to want to publish them when I get them finished. Anyway, it's a new venture for me, as I've never tried to do anything of extended length, or rather, as this is, a kind of sequence that tells a story from start to finish. Maybe I can send them along to you for inspection later on, if I do get them finished. You have such an extraordinary sense of how people interact, especially when they are in love, or think they are in love, I'm sure you would be able to spot it immediately if I had gotten off the psychological beam, so to speak, at any point. I want them to be naive, as both of us were at the time, but, I hope, true. But I won't put in the sequel. I ran into her again about ten years ago in Rome, where she had married a journalist, and she had gotten very fat, and seemed rather stupid. But if you could have seen her at 15, as she was then in her tight white bathing suit!

> Very best, as ever,
> James Laughlin

« • »

about my experiences: The long poem "In Another Country."

187. TLS—1

4/30/74 [Norfolk]

Dear Tenn—

I'm so sorry about the mix-up over the poems for *ND 29* and mighty glad that you caught that in the proofs.

The mistake was mine—culpa mea—I had them up here, and decided, from my reading of the texts, that these were two separate poems, and I marked them that way for Peter, so don't blame him.

By the way, it's time already for me to start assembling the material for the next number, *ND 30*, and hope you will have something for that. Would the new poem I hear you sent Fred be suitable for that, or do you have something else you'd prefer? I hope there will be something and I promise to be more careful and to check with you if in any doubt.

I think it's terrific you're going to go down to the ABA convention to sign *Mortal Ladies* for the adoring Book Ladies. That really will send them! Wonderful of you to do it.

I should be getting down to the city one of these days and will call ahead to see if there is any chance you are free for lunch or something.

Very best,

JL

« • »

ABA convention: The American Booksellers Association is a trade association that promotes independent booksellers in the United States. Its annual "convention" (now called BookExpo America) allows publishers and authors to showcase their new titles for the coming year.

188. TLS—1

May 16, 1974 [New York]

DEAR JAY:

It's characteristic of you to assume blame for the mix-up in the poems for ND annual but I know you are just being chivalrous, or as Bob puts it—"saintly." You are the one at ND who is interested in my poetry and who would notice—despite my mistake of putting them in caps—that it was the end of the poem, not another.

I have an advance copy of *Eight Mortal Ladies Possessed*. It is becomingly modest with no color at all, as if pretending not to be there: at least a great improvement over that malignant cell blow-up with which Gertrude graced the dust-jacket of *Dragon Country*.

(What's that girl got against me?)

I hope you and I will be in the city at the same time someday.

When I was in New Orleans last week I found a volume of your poems with a particularly lovely poem in which a lady is wryly compared to a trout. I have met some that reminded me of more aggressive water-creatures—but the image was used very charmingly.

With best wishes always,

Tennessee

[P.S.] Particularly want to discuss with you the next volume of the "on-going" series—you know, there is a new version of *Kingdom of Earth* which ought to be in it. I don't think *Milk Train* deserves total exclusion. And then there are all my one-acts and my next season's long play, *The Red Devil Battery Sign*.

≪ • ≫

dust-jacket of Dragon Country: In an ongoing feud of his own making, TW mistakenly attributes the jacket—and later cover—design of *Dragon Country* to Gertrude Huston, when in fact the cover image was by F. H. Horn and the design was by David Ford.

lovely poem [. . .] compared to a trout: JL's poem "The Trout" originally appeared in a small book of his poems, *The Wild Anemone & Other Poems* (1957), printed by JL's friend, the fine printer and publisher of limited editions, Giovanni Mardersteig, at the Stamperia Valdonega, Verona.

a new version of Kingdom of Earth: TW revised the play for a production produced by Michael Kahn at the McCarter Theater in 1975, which is now published in *The Theatre of Tennessee Williams*, Vol. 5.

189. TLS—3

June 12, 1974 [New York]

DEAR TENNESSEE:

Please forgive my being so slow in answering your wonderfully kind letter of May 16. I've been rather snowed under, trying to assemble the material for the next Annual that is to go to the printer in a few weeks, and also trying to "vet" some translations of Montale, done by an Indian professor who teaches Italian in Ireland, if you can believe that combination, and Montale is certainly the most difficult and strange poet writing today, so it has been quite a job. Montale is so "hermetic" now it is really almost impossible to translate him at all, but I think the Indian gent has made a good stab at it, and I'm just trying to make his version sound a bit more American and less Indian.

You were, as always very forgiving about my "goof" on the poems for *ND 29*, but it really was my fault, I just read them that way. But at least we were able to fix it in proofs.

[. . .]

I'm sorry that I wasn't be able to get down to Washington for the ABA, but I've had most enthusiastic reports, both from our people, and from the Sales Manager of Lippincott, who says you were absolutely terrific, and charmed the pants (if that is the right word) off all the bookstore ladies, of whom I would have been completely terrified, I think you were very brave to undertake it, and I just hope that it wasn't too wearing. I think there's no question that this sort of appearance with the people who actually do the ordering and selling of books is terribly important, and will help greatly not only with *Mortal Ladies* but with all of your books. We are all most grateful to you for having done it.

I'm glad that you were pleased with the way the cover for *Mortal Ladies* came out. In the end, that is. I had my doubts, too, about that first color that Gertrude used, but she was so insistent about it, that it was right for the book, that I didn't argue. But you're quite wrong to imagine that she has anything against you and was trying to sabotage. To the contrary, she absolutely worships you. She would rather work on a book by you than those of any other author.

[. . .]

I was touched and pleased that you like my poem about the trout. It's always been one of my favorites. The lady was very elusive, but she certainly was a knock-out, but all that was long, long ago. Part of my skiing days in Switzerland. Actually, I think she liked automobiles better than people, as she went off with a very stupid Romanian who had an absolutely magnificent, Italian sports car. At least, I like to tell myself it was that.

I think that at various times, over the years, I've sent you some of my little books, but probably with all the moving around you have done, you may have lost them, and I'd love to replace them; if you can let me know which ones you have, I can send you the others. Not, as you know, that I take my poetry very seriously, but I have fun with it and am always terribly pleased when a friend likes some of it.

Very best, as ever,

J.

James Laughlin

≪ • ≫

Montale: Eugenio Montale (1896–1981), Italian poet and translator. ND published three volumes by Montale. The book JL is working on is *New Poems: A Selection from Satura and Diario del '71 e del '72*, translated by G. Singh (ND 1976).

190. TL—2

January 17, 1975 [Norfolk]

DEAR TENN:

I am not exactly sure whether you are in Key West or back in New York, so I'll send copies of this letter to both places, and hope one will reach you.

I hope that you had a very good Christmas, and am glad that Maria was able to come over for part of the time to keep you company. I am sorry I missed seeing her. We got out to Utah with the kids for a week of skiing and it was very fine indeed, as far as weather and snow were concerned, but many too many people. Alta is just getting too big and crowded to suit me. Of course, it's good for the ski lift business, but I miss the old days when it was wild and lonely. I don't have the stamina that I used to have for the sport, but managed to get out for a few hours each day, and particularly enjoyed the cross-country trips, up the old mining roads on the mountainsides, away from the lift crowds.

I have just finished reading the draft of *The Red Devil Battery Sign*, which Bill Barnes was kind enough to lend us, and wanted to let you know right away that I think it is quite a blockbuster. Five really memorable and marvelous characters, and I just hope that you can find actors good enough to do them full justice. It won't be easy, as there is a blending of tenderness and toughness in them which would be very hard to do, I would think.

I am so out of things, you must fill me in on Presentational Theatre. No matter, I read it for the stories and characters and loved it. From the stylistic point of view, I was much interested in the "shortening" of your cadences in the speeches. Or in many of them. The shorter phrases, more staccato, more elliptical. This should make for a very interesting and exciting kind of "pace" in the dramatic action. Of course, it doesn't lend itself so readily to the "poetic passage," for which you are so famous, and which I have always particularly admired, but the poetry is still there under the sharp bite of the faster rhythm. It's a powerful piece of work, and a very moving one, both frightening and compassionate, and I hope that you are pleased with it, and that it will bring you a lot of satisfaction.

[. . .]

As you can imagine, we are missing dear Old Bob very sorely. He trained up a good staff, and they are all working like Trojans, but it just isn't the same place down there in the Village without Bob there, we miss his wisdom, and all his professional knowledge, and his wonderful sense of humor, and so many other little things each day.

[. . .]

Very best as ever,

James Laughlin

« • »

Presentational Theatre: See TW's letter of 2/3/75 below.

missing dear Old Bob: Robert MacGregor died of lung cancer on November 22, 1974. His deterioration had been very quick and JL was prepared for neither the effect of his loss on New Directions nor his own personal sense of bereavement. To one ND author, Kay Boyle, he wrote: "He was my right hand at New Directions for 20 years, and he took all of the dirty work off my back, such a kind and generous and understanding man, we will not see his like again."

191. TLS—1

2/3/75 [Key West]

DEAR JAY:

The staccato style of "Red Devil" is attributable mostly to my nervous state and the urgency of getting through a heavy piece of work in a delicate state of health. I know that Claire Bloom, who is to play the Woman Downtown, can handle the hysteria. She made a clean sweep of the awards in London as Blanche. I am dubious about Anthony Quinn, however, because he is getting so long in the tooth to project sexuality, at least from my point of view. As for "presentational theatre," it is the kind in which powerful and innovative production values—music (the <u>mariachis</u>), unusual freedom of style, cinematic quickness, startling effects—are employed. I hope you are right that the characters themselves are vivid enough to hold an audience which is now conditioned to sensation.

I'm very happy that you are giving thought to the shorter works in the "Theatre of" series. I prefer some of them to the long plays.

Now I must get to work. You know, you ought to come South sometime in the winters. The past two weeks here have been warm and golden as late Spring.

Love,

Tenn

≪ • ≫

Claire Bloom: (1931–), English stage and film actress who created the role of the Woman Downtown in *The Red Devil Battery Sign*.

Anthony Quinn: (1915–2001), Mexican-born American stage and film actor who followed Marlon Brando playing Stanley in the original run of *A Streetcar Named Desire* on Broadway and created the role of King in *The Red Devil Battery Sign*.

192. TL—1

July 5, 1975 [Norfolk]

DEAR TENN:

Many thanks for your and Maria's card from Boston. If she is there with you, please give her my best love.

I was so upset when I read about the troubles with *Red Devil* in Boston. The "Hub of the Universe," as I believe they used to call it in Emerson's day, must be a jinxtown for you. I remember your telling me about when the stage caught fire at the opening of *Battle of Angels*.

From the newspaper account, I couldn't figure just what happened but it sounded like a fight among the producers more than anything wrong with the play. As you know, I read the script some months ago and thought it very good indeed, moving, powerful, good characters and many fine poetic passages.

Tenn, what about letting us do the book of *Red Devil* without waiting for another production. I think it reads very well and I like it a lot, the themes and the way you handle them, and the dramatic method. What about it?

Also, have you had a chance to look at that selection of essays these two kids in Detroit made? I gave the typescript to Bill some months ago, but know you were busy with rehearsals, etc. That's another book I'd like to do, so I hope you'll look over what they have assembled.

I envy you being in Italy, wish I could get back there myself, but Leila is having a baby and Paul is getting married in August.

Best, as ever,

[James Laughlin]

≪ • ≫

selection of essays: This became *Where I Live: Selected Essays*, edited by Christine R. Day and Bob Wood (ND 1978).

193. TLS—2

1/17/76 [San Francisco]

DEAR JAY:

I received bound proofs of a book from <u>New Directions</u> just before leaving for the Coast and in the flurry of departure I left it at the Elysée. I'll read it soon as I return middle of this week. I've written a new long poem that I like very much and have revised several others: I think there will be enough to justify another book, at least paperback. The title could be that of the new poem—*The Lady with No One at All*. Or it could be *Stones Are Thrown* or *Old Men Go Mad at Night*. I hope you'll help me choose one.

[. . .]

I know how difficult it must be for you, as well as sad, without dear Bob in the office. There'll never be another MacGregor but I think that Mr. Martin is very nice—and also a gentleman, which I'm afraid is somewhat a rarity in the publishing world.

This Is is being given a great production by A.C.T. but I suspect that both the leading newspapers here are violently allergic to works of an anarchistic nature, especially the *Examiner* which is a Hearst paper.

Did you know that Maria has returned to the Boards in Vienna's English Theatre? She is excellent as the fiery Mexican wife of the male lead, Keith Baxter [in *The Red Devil Battery Sign*].

[. . .]

> With affection always,
> Tennessee

≪ • ≫

A.C.T.: The American Conservatory Theater is San Francisco's Tony Award–winning regional theater. Set up as a nonprofit organization, the theater stages both classical and contemporary productions and maintains an acting school.

Keith Baxter: (1933–), Welsh actor and director, who staged the first London production of *The Red Devil Battery Sign* in 1977.

194. TLS—3

February 17, 1976 [Norfolk]

DEAR TENN:

[. . .]

The little poem that you put at the end of the letter, "Winter Smoke Is Blue and Bitter," is a lovely one, and that certainly ought to be included in the new volume. Of the titles which you suggest for it, I think that I like *Old Men Go Mad at Night* the best, that is very strong, though the other ones are good, too.

Yes, it is very hard without Bob MacGregor. There isn't a day that I don't think of him, with gratitude for his loyalty and affection and enormous competence. Fred Martin is doing a splendid job of taking things over in the New York office, but there just never will be anybody quite like Bob, with his remarkable combination of human qualities.

I'm so glad that the new play *This Is [An Entertainment]* has been doing well out in California, and will be eager to have a look at the script when you have finished with the rewriting work. And, of course, also, to see what you have done with *Red Devil Battery Sign*. We will be eager to bring out both of these, when you have them ready, and don't feel that it is necessary to wait for a New York production to do the books, if you have the scripts in shape that satisfy you.

And I haven't forgotten about the little book of your introductions and literary essays [*Where I Live*] which you approved. Peggy Fox, the copyright lady in our office now, has been working with Floria Lasky and Bill Barnes to pick up the necessary copyright assignments into your name from the various newspapers and magazines which first ran the pieces. Once this is in order, and we are certain that there are no problems with permissions, then we can proceed with that book, too, and that should be fairly soon.

[. . .]

With very best wishes, as ever,

J.

James Laughlin

≪ • ≫

Peggy Fox: (1946–). While looking for a job in college teaching, Peggy Fox began working at ND in the summer of 1975 doing copyrights, contracts, and foreign rights. She began doing editorial work in 1977, becoming senior editor in 1983, then vice president in 1994, and president and publisher in 2004. She retired in 2011 but remains a trustee of the New Directions Ownership Trust, along with JL's son-in-law, Daniel Javitch, and Donald S. Lamm and is JL's literary coexecutor with Javitch.

195. TLS—2

<April 7, 1976 and 5/7/76> [New York]

DEAR JAY:

I'm expecting my sister in about an hour for a matinee at Ring-ling's, the circus, then dinner at the National Institute's Annual bash which she attends as head of The Rose Isabel Williams Foundation, though I'm not sure she is altogether cognizant of this position: she digs the circus much more, standing at salute, formally as a queen inspecting a regiment, when an act particularly pleases her, such as performing polar bears, dogs, clowns, etc.

About the poems: I suppose there are enough to warrant a paperbound sheaf called "Later Poems" or whatever title you select for it, I'd best leave that to you. As for "Prudence in Kings," it is the longest poem in the collection called "Drunken Fiddler" and probably the only one of consequence. It has a recurrent refrain which would become monotonous if repeated in full each time. I suggest it be reduced at its recurrent intervals to

> It is prudent, Menelaus, etc.
> (the full refrain is:)
> It is prudent, Menelaus, for even a king
> To watch a young wife when the season is Spring

Of course it is more conventional in style and content than most contemporary verse, even mine, but there are several lyric passages which have the intensity of youth, which compensates for a good deal in the POV of a poet now at the age of retirement.

Poor Oliver Evans is in a New Orleans nursing-home and his octogenarian lady-friend, Ardis Blackburn, says that he is rarely coherent—so it is good that UCLA has this depository of MSS which would otherwise have been in his hands.—I trust this doesn't sound like a callously selfish consideration: my feelings are not.

If there is room in the envelope I will include 2 of the recent poems I've been at work on.

Ever,
Tennessee

(over)
P.S. I've taken a new suite here at the Elysée, mainly because it has a small terrace for my new bull-dog, Madam. Bill Barnes said he had

negotiated a good deal for the place: but I just now signed a cheque for $2500. A month! Frankly, I think that's extortionary, considering how little time I spend in New York. The best play I've written in a long time is the version of *Red Devil Battery Sign* as revised for Vienna's English Theatre—but Barnes has not placed it with a New York management. I have no real reason, then, for remaining here at all, or, for that matter, not retiring to Italy.—What do you think?—The problem is my sister. She is increasingly frail—and discontented with the sanitarium in Ossining. I think I could take her abroad.

« • »

National Institute's Annual bash: The National Institute of Arts and Letters is now known as the American Academy of Arts and Letters. On the strength of JL's recommendation, the institute awarded TW a grant of one thousand dollars in 1944 (see letter of TW to JL [March 1944]). In 1969, TW received a Gold Medal for Drama from the Academy. The Gold Medals are occasional awards of "special distinction" given for an entire body of work.

the collection called "Drunken Fiddler": In the early 1940s, TW bound together a collection of his poems from the previous decade and called the manuscript *The Drunken Fiddler*. Some of the poems were later published in *FYAP* (1944). Although JL queried the UCLA Library several times, the manuscript for the poem "Prudence in Kings" was never located.

Elysée: The Hotel Elysée, 60 East 54th Street in New York City, where TW regularly stayed and where he died in 1983.

sanitarium in Ossining: TW arranged for Rose Williams to be transferred to Stoney Lodge sanitarium in Ossining, New York, in 1950. Rose was later moved to the Bethel Methodist Home in Ossining and died at the Phelps Memorial Hospital in Tarrytown, New York, in 1996.

196. TL—3

April 29, 1976 [Norfolk]

DEAR TENN:

Please forgive my delay in thanking you for your fine letter of April 7 and the two beautiful new poems, which are really lovely, I think "The Lady with No One at All" is one of your very finest, terribly moving, and "Stones Are Thrown" is a good one, too. (I note that you sent your only copies, so I will take these down to the city with me on the next visit to the office, and get Xeroxes made for you so that you will have safety copies.)

I should have written sooner, I am so enthusiastic about the new book of poems project [*Androgyne, Mon Amour*], but have been much harassed with various out-of-town visitors and other routine, editorial problems.

[. . .]

Your new apartment at the Elysée sounds very grand—and it certainly ought to be at that price! I hope I'll have the opportunity to meet the new bulldog, "Madam," soon, and that she is as nice as the one you had before.

I can well understand your wanting to live most of the time in Italy—I love it there, too—but this would be pretty hard on your friends, as we wouldn't see you very much.

I'm sorry to hear that problems have developed with the sanitarium at Ossining. But if Rose has been there for so long, and gotten used to it, would it be good for her to move somewhere else, even with you, to Italy? She might feel disoriented if she made such a big change. And I would think, if you took her there, you would have to find someone very reliable and good to help you look after her. Which might not be easy in Italy, the way things are so disturbed over there now, from what one reads in the papers.

I was sorry to hear that Bill hadn't as yet found a producer for the revised version of *Red Devil Battery Sign*. I haven't seen the revised version—I'd love to if you have an extra copy—but I liked the first one very much, and thought it was extremely powerful, and should play well. And I'm also eager, of course, to see the play that was put on in California, on which we had such good reports. Any chance of having a look at that one?

Now that spring has finally come to the northwest corner of Connecticut, and it's very lovely here now, we don't get down to the city as much as we did, but I hope I will have a chance to see you soon, and will try to give a call next time I get down to see if you are there and have a little free time.

Very best, as ever,

James Laughlin

≪ • ≫

the play that was put on in California: *This Is (An Entertainment)* premiered at the American Conservatory Theatre in San Francisco on January 20, 1976, for a limited run.

197. TLS—1

[June] 1976 [New York]

DEAR JAY:

Here, finally, is another batch of poems and a list that includes a few that aren't in my hands right now.

Well, I deliver them to yours.

I haven't yet thought of a title for this new collection. Maybe one will occur to you before it does to me.

I leave this afternoon for San Francisco with my bull-dog bitch, Madam Sophia, and a very gifted young photographer, Christopher Makos—had to leave poor Robert [Carroll] in Key West where he had submerged himself all but completely into the drug scene.

More anon. Must get on with packing.

As ever,

Tennessee

≪ • ≫

Christopher Makos: American photographer who apprenticed with Man Ray and collaborated with Andy Warhol.

198. TL—1

June 22, 1976 [Norfolk]

DEAR TENN—

Many thanks for your letter written just as you were leaving for San Francisco and the fine batch of poems, some new and some old, and all very good. I think we must nearly have enough now for a book. My next visit down to the New York office I'll pick up the ones that are there and go over them all again.

For a title, what about "A Liturgy of Roses" or "The Speechless Summer" or "The Brain's Dissection"? I think one of those would be good.

I found a copy of the first number of *Antaeus* so we have the text of "The Speechless Summer" all right. And I think there is a copy of "What's Next on the Agenda, Mr. Williams?" at the office. If not, we'll hunt for the *Meditarraneo* magazine. Do you recall where that was published or who edited it? I've never seen it.

[. . .]

A rather humid summer here in Connecticut, but we'll be getting out to Ann's family's ranch in Wyoming about the middle of August and the air is wonderful there.

Very best, as ever,

[James Laughlin]

≪ • ≫

199. TLS—1

[received 10/4/76] [New York]

DEAR JAY:

Here is a re-written and expanded version of "Wolf's Hour" which was published, I believe in *ND 30*. I feel that it may contain too many qualifying words—I mean like adjectives and adverbs. If it strikes you that way, too, would you mind scratching the most dispensable ones out and sending the original back to me for further repairs?

A curious little Gypsy band takes off tomorrow for slightly less than a week in New Orleans, its members being Maria, the Lady St. Just, one Shone Dunigan, the latest and by far the most efficient of three traveling companions I've had this bitch of a summer. Our primary objective is to remove Oliver Evans from a nightmare nursing-home in a wasteland outside New Orleans and establish him in one of my rental apartments. It seems that poor Oliver, who had quite despaired of continuing his existence when I saw him a month ago, has now rallied and is in a mood to go on with his life under improved conditions. Of course he will need an almost constant attendant to see he is fed and medicated: it will be a costly enterprise but fortunately he does have a pension of $800 a month from the University in California at which he taught literature and creative writing—assuming that the latter can be taught.

Ever,

10.

Tenn.

≪ • ≫

Shone Dunigan: Possibly Mickey Shone Dunigan (1942–1984).

200. TLS—1

[received 12/27/76] [London]

DEAR FRED [MARTIN]:

HOLD PRESSES ON THAT SCANDALOUS DUST-JACKET FOR POEMS. IT WOULD DISGRACE US ALL!

I know that I am not a good draughtsman but I don't draw as badly as that. Head, feet, totally misshapen.

And that horrible accentuation of the genitalia with lurid rust color!

Is this the work of Miss Gertrude Huston? Dearly as I once loved her and admired her spirit, if she is responsible for this cover, I will then know that when she sent me a cover of 27 *Wagons* containing a compilation of recipes for a smorgasbord—freak accident she called it—it was with malicious intent.

I am returning to New York before Xmas. A proper jacket might involve my painting with no color at all on genitalia and no linear distortions. Failing that, why not just put the title in bold black print on a glossy white background? Please, Fred. There are living members of my family to be considered including myself!

Returning by Concorde mid-week and will call you at once about this freak accident #2. I have a very gifted painter-friend in New York who would immediately set the jacket right without a fee for it.

Yours sincerely,

Tenn.

« • »

containing a compilation of recipes: TW had previously received a reprint of 27 *Wagons Full of Cotton* in which pages from a recipe book had been bound. It was a mistake made at the bindery that Gertrude Huston could not have caused.

201. TLS—1

12/31/76 [Key West]

DEAR FRED:

The second phase of the poetry book cover is a distinct improvement but I still think a lot can be done. Only one blue eye is apparent to me and the hair color is barely apparent and the little toe on the left foot looks more like a big toe. Please set my anxieties at rest by getting a more finished version soon as you can. I have enough to worry about, here, with an old jazz-singer and her loutish swain on the premises.

Bill Barnes promised me on the phone yesterday he would visit your offices to have a look at the painting. I am <u>not</u> a good draughtsman but I'm not quite as bad as I seem in these preliminary designs—not when I have a live model as I did in this case.

I gave Bill a new poem, one I like, called "Snowfall" to return to you with the proofs. Hope it's not too late to include it.

It was awfully kind of you and your wife to visit Rose. She is awfully withdrawn but I'm sure she appreciated the visit.

Fondest regards to you all,

10.

≪ • ≫

please set my anxieties at rest: Despite all of his reservations about the reproduction of his painting on the jacket, sometime after he had received finished copies of *Androgyne, Mon Amour* (published 4/28/77), TW would add a P.S. to an undated note to JL, "Charmed by your editions [cloth and paper] of *Androgyne*."

"Snowfall": The poem "Snowfall" was not included in *Androgyne, Mon Amour* but instead was published as a limited edition broadside in 1980.

202. TLS—1

Nov. 26, '77 and 12/8/77 [Key West]

DEAR JAY AND FRED:

[. . .]

There are a couple of things I'd like to discuss with you. One, a collection of my one-acts for a new volume of the continuing series *"Theatre of."** The other bringing out a selection of the better poems in *Winter* and *Androgyne* along with a few unprinted.

Perhaps we could also discuss bringing out a little book of my essays.

Have you seen Robert Brustein's vitriolic review of my letters to Donald Windham? I've had to spend days composing a suitable reply, exposing the true circumstances (shocking) that surround the two publications. Harvey Shapiro, who edits the Book Review section of the Sunday *Times*, promised me on the phone that he would publish my reply to the piece but I have a feeling that he may not do it. I think the reply is good and honest and must be published even if I have to publish it myself in a pamphlet to be handled by a few selected bookstores like Gotham Book Mart at a price no higher than needed to recover the cost. I'd appreciate your advice: it has to be done quickly to be effective.

In about a week I'm flying to New Orleans. A young English director is arriving in the States. I revised *Vieux Carré* under his supervision in London: he was brilliant at cutting and re-arranging material. He says that he plans to do the play in London in the early Spring and that he wants to know New Orleans first.

Warmest regards,

Tennessee

<*Including several new ones.>

P.S. Would like to contribute a couple of these poems to *Antaeus* as I am still listed as a contributing editor and it's been a long time since I made any contribution.

≪ • ≫

Robert Brustein's vitriolic review: Brustein's review of the letters for the *New York Times* included, among other unfavorable observations, "If revenge is a dish that tastes best cold, then Donald Windham has certainly fixed himself a satisfying frozen dinner."

A young English director: Keith Hack.

203. TLS—1

August 13, 1978 [Wilbury Park, Wilshire, England]

DEAR JAY:

This distillation of your poetry has been a great joy to me and to Maria. You've never shown an adequate confidence in the unique quality and beauty of your work. Please recognize it and take deserved joy in it as I always have.

I have very little time as I must return with Maria from Wilbury Park to London to cope with an hysterical leading lady and an irate narcissan of a leading-man.

For once, perhaps for the first time, I cut a play [*Vieux Carré*] beyond expectations—the scene involving these two.

Sometimes I feel that I should confine the *Theatre of Tennessee Williams* to my studio in Key West, for there's little time or strength left.

Very briefly and truly, I want to say this. You're the greatest friend that I have had in my life, and the most trusted.

With love,
Tennessee

« • »

distillation of your poetry: The 1978 City Lights publication of JL's *In Another Country: Poems 1935–1975*.

an hysterical leading lady and an irate narcissan of a leading-man: See following memo from Peggy Fox to JL of August 30, 1978.

204. TN—1

August 30, 1978 [New York]

To: JL
Re: London production of *Vieux Carré*

Since I was going to England on vacation I had arranged with Bill Barnes to take in the new London production of *Vieux Carré*. Else [Albrecht-Carrié, ND permissions editor and JL's personal assistant at the time] thought I might be able to shed some light on the cryptic sections of TW's letter [of August 13, 1978] as I got the latest gossip at the London ICM office.

The "hysterical leading lady" would be Sheila Gish in the part of Jane. Evidently after the opening night, TW decided to rewrite a scene, cutting out a page or so of dialogue and substituting about 20 new lines. Well, Miss Gish just refused to do it saying it would destroy her conception of the part and she would fluff her lines and look like an incompetent actress—and TW refused to let her go on unless she did learn the new lines. The upshot was that the understudy, Di Trevis, took over the part and was playing it when I saw the play—she was excellent. I assume that the "narcissan" is the young man playing Jane's lover Tye [Jonathan Kent].

I thought the play, too, was excellent. From what Fred said about the New York production, I think the character of "The Writer" has been made more prominent and the "education" of the young, naïve writer becomes the focus of the play (the actor playing this role—Karl Johnson—was first-rate). The character of the landlady was not as overpowering as I understand it was in the NY production although it was certainly well played by Sylvia Miles. The set was a simple revolving one divided into the different rooms of the boarding house and was used very effectively—the play is episodic but the separate stories are all clearly related to the emotional and artistic growth (in some ways hardening) of the young writer. And the angel in the alcove was treated with ironic affection and didn't seem to be overly sentimental. The play seems now to have a coherence that it lacked before, and, of course, the dialogue is vintage TW. I found it quite moving.

peg
[Peggy Fox]

205. ANS—1

[September 1978] [Norfolk]

Peggy—

<u>Many</u> thanks for the run-down on the London production of *Vieux Carré*. I'm so glad TW got it in better shape and hope there will be another US production.

J

« • »

Many thanks: This is just one example of what the ND staff called "Norfolk confetti" referred to in the Introduction. JL responded to queries, memos, and copies of staff letters with short typed or handwritten notes on pieces of scrap paper and sent them to the New York office every few days. These notes ranged from substantive statements: "I don't want to publish this book" to praise "Nice letter [to a particular author]" to requests for more stationery.

SECTION XVII

———

PF: How often did you see Tennessee in, say, the last ten years of his life?

JL: Well, not a great deal. Tennessee liked to go to the Century, and that was good for me because it meant that I could see him without any hangers-on around. He got a real kick out of the Century. He liked the old building; he liked the old boys, you know, sleeping in the library under their newspapers. It meant something to him. We'd go there very often.

PF: Sounds like a posh British club atmosphere.

JL: And talk about things. We talked a lot about what he was to do with his papers. I think if he had followed . . . I don't know. I've actually talked Harvard to him—that it would be a good place for his papers to go—and then we talked a lot about fellowships, and that meant a lot to him. Of course, he loved his grandfather's alma mater, The University of the South, and I think the way it ended up is that the papers are divided between Harvard and The University of the South. Then he would have liked his income, which continued to be very good . . .

PF: It still continues to be . . .

JL: And he would have liked that to go to into fellowships.

≪ • ≫

Century: The Century Association (more commonly called the Century Club) is a private club in New York with its headquarters on West 43rd Street, just off Fifth Avenue. It is noted for its literary, theater, and artistic members as well as "la crème de la crème" of professionals. At the time that JL would have taken TW there, it was a male-only bastion, but women were admitted to full membership in 1989.

206. TLS—1

April '79 [New Orleans]

DEAR FRED:

The one time I've seen you since you so patiently helped me assemble that rather tired group of poems brought out in *Androgyne, Mon Amour* was the occasion on which Jay received the citation from PEN.

Lately I retrieved an astonishingly large collection of personal papers and Mss. from a safe in the "Railroad Museum" of my late gardener, Frank Fontis, shot mysteriously during the production of *A Lovely Sunday for Creve Coeur.*

Among the papers I found so many letters sent me from dear old 333 Sixth Ave.,* including some especially touching ones from Bob.

I hope they've come home to stay here in Key West.

I know it is my fault that we have so little communication and if there's an excuse, it is just that I wear myself out working as long as I can each morning.

I've accumulated a number of poems and a couple of long prose-poems, perhaps enough to interest you in bringing out a pamphlet of them, and when I was last in New York I left a batch of early writings which I titled *Pieces of My Youth* at Studio Duplicating to be typed for you. I may enclose a little more verse with this letter.

When is *Vieux Carré* coming out? I think Mitch Douglas said it was scheduled for this spring.

Best regards,
Tennessee

*What's the <u>new</u> address?
<P.S. Am to give a poetry reading at N.Y.U. towards middle of May.>

« • »

citation from PEN: In early 1979, JL received a citation from PEN, the international literary organization that champions "the freedom to write and the universal power of literature" in recognition of his publishing that so clearly supported its aims.

Frank Fontis: Gardener and caretaker of TW's Key West property. Fontis was murdered on January 5, 1979, the same night of a break-in and robbery at TW's home. The murder was never solved, though dozens of original manuscripts stolen from TW were later found in the victim's safe.

A Lovely Sunday for Creve Coeur: This play premiered in New York at the Hudson Guild Theatre on January 10, 1979, starring Shirley Knight and directed by Keith Hack. It was published by ND in 1980. The play uses the same basic plot as the screenplay *All Gaul Is Divided* (published in *Stopped Rocking & Other Screenplays*, ND, 1984, but written at least twenty years before *Creve Coeur*). In an "Author's Note" accompanying the published screenplay, TW comments: "The most remarkable thing about the teleplay is that I had *totally* forgotten its existence when I wrote *Creve Coeur* in San Francisco about three years ago [. . .] The screenplay rectifies the major defect dilemma of the recent play: the giving away of the 'plot' in the very first scene."

Pieces of My Youth: TW submitted a typescript of odds and ends to New Directions in 1979 entitled "Pieces of My Youth." While not strong enough to stand on its own as a collection, the various "Pieces" were all eventually published in volumes such as the *Collected Stories* (1984), *Collected Poems* (2002), and various one-act collections. At least two of the pieces in this group, the one-act plays *The Parade* and *Steps Must Be Gentle*, were begun in TW's youth but heavily revised in the 1970s.

Mitch Douglas: TW's agent from September 1978 through October 1981. Douglas was a strong advocate for Williams and his later plays; however, he was forced to draw strict boundaries due to TW's overwhelming personal demands.

207. TL—2

May 4, 1979 [New York]

DEAR TENN:

Yes, it has been a long time, and that makes hearing from you all the more a pleasure! It was awfully good to see you at the J.L. P.E.N. session and I know he really appreciated your presence, too.

Mitch [Douglas] told me about the strange shooting of your gardener, Frank Fontis, and the cache of papers which showed up in the aftermath, down in Key West. I can only begin to imagine how "touching" Bob's letters must have been from 333 Sixth Avenue. He was a correspondent in the 19th Century sense and his letters were absolutely superb.

[...]

Vieux Carré will be coming out this May, although the exact publication date is still a little fuzzy, I'm afraid. Once things are in sharper focus, I'll let either you or Mitch know, of course. There's a pretty good chance that I'll have reasonably firm dates from our binder just before your N.Y.U. reading, on May 10th. I hope to see you there and was delighted to learn from Mitch that you had accepted the invitation.

[...]

Yes, after all of thirty years, we've finally been "turfed out" of our old quarters at 333. It was quite a traumatic experience for us all—that is, taking on a new distributor (the nice W. W. Nortons) and having to move our quarters almost simultaneously. Our new offices are at 80 Eighth Avenue (New York, N.Y. 10011), in a charming Art Deco building which was once owned by none other than Joseph P. Kennedy. We're on the nineteenth floor and have absolutely sensational views of the Hudson River, harbor, Statue of Liberty, and Staten Island on a clear day. Next time when you're in town, and it's sunny, perhaps you'd like to come visit and enjoy our sensational vistas. [...]

With all best wishes,

Frederick R. Martin

≪ • ≫

the nice W. W. Nortons: ND's new distributor, employee-owned W. W. Norton & Company. In 1978 ND's longtime distributor, J. B. Lippincott & Company, was acquired by Harper & Row, Publishers, Inc. Alarmed when the Harper salespeople called his books "products," JL began looking elsewhere and soon formed an alliance with W. W. Norton president George Brockway, a fellow member of the Century Club, for distribution, warehousing, and certain financial services. The association is ongoing.

208. TLS—1

9/26/79 [Norfolk]

DEAR TENN:

Just watched you on the Cavett show and I thought you were in great form. Who else of our friends can give off so much human warmth and mellowness. Somehow you have triumphed over the vicissitudes.

When can we see the script of the play about the Fitzgeralds [*Clothes for a Summer Hotel*]? He is one of my favorites in this century. I agree with you that *The Last Tycoon* was potentially his greatest, but I can always read *Tender Is the Night* with enormous emotion. And some of the short stories.

We had a quiet summer, here in July and then on Ann's family's ranch in Wyoming, but it was all nice, as I had time to read a lot of good books I had missed in college.

I want to thank you again for coming to the affair at the PEN. I was in a state of nerves and you really helped me get through it.

Very best,

[James Laughlin]

≪ • ≫

Cavett show: TW appeared at least three times on Dick Cavett's talk show in the 1970s as well as two special programs in which Cavett interviewed TW in New Orleans.

209. TL—1

1.16.80 [Norfolk]

DEAR TENN:

I just read *Clothes for a Summer Hotel* and wanted to rush you my congratulations. It's a beautiful and very moving play. And most ingenious the way you have worked out the flashbacks and double roles. You certainly did a lot of research. I have read quite a bit about Zelda and Scott, but you've come up with a lot of things I didn't know about them. They come through as very real people.

Congratulations, too, on your Washington medal. Now if you were English you'd be Sir Tennessee. We watched the ceremony on the tube and were so happy for you.

As ever,

[James Laughlin]

« • »

your Washington medal: TW was presented with a Lifetime Achievement Award by President Carter at the Kennedy Center Honors on December 2, 1979. JL is referring to when the event was televised December 29, 1979. TW was also awarded the Presidential Medal of Freedom at the White House by President Jimmy Carter on June 9, 1980.

210. ALS—3

[rc'd 1/31/80] [Chicago]

DEAR JAY—

Conrad Hilton does not provide a rental typewriter nor even pen and stationery in their $50 a night hotel rooms, just TV and a "Rainbow Cinema box" that offers a bunch of "R" rated movies at $5 a selection.

I'm back in Chicago with my final batch of re-writes. The Company is recalcitrant. I feel apologetic about every effort I'm obliged to make to protect them and the play [*Clothes for a Summer Hotel*] and myself from the wolves waiting for us on Broadway.

All anybody told me about the script before it was rushed into rehearsal was that it was beautiful. That beautiful things may be damned was something that even Fitzgerald knew in his early romantic youth.

The hazards of writing about real-life characters, re-assembled for a ghost play, was never mentioned. And I had not anticipated them. Consequently, the hectic revisions have been more demanding than the original work.

Latest development is that Sheilah Graham (Lily Shiel) is threatening to sue me for depicting her as vulgar. I refer you to her autobiography called "A State of Heat!"—passages from it would throw the case out of court at once.

The script for publication will be as different from the playing script as was *Camino Real*.

Thanks for your supportive letter.—Business has been excellent despite negative notice in *Washington Post* and almost continual snow in Chicago.

Maria is joining me for first preview in New York. Please let me know if you wish to attend the opening March 26.

Love,

10.

« • »

Sheilah Graham: (1904–1988), English-born, as Lily Shiel, to Ukrainian immigrants, American gossip columnist during Hollywood's "Golden Age." She is best known for her intimate relationship with F. Scott Fitzgerald in the several years before his death in 1940, a relationship immortalized in her 1958 book (and the subsequent movie) *Beloved Infidel*. Her memoir, *A State of Heat*, was published in 1972.

opening March 26: Also TW's sixty-ninth birthday.

211. TL—1

May 29, 1980 [Norfolk]

DEAR TENN:

I am more grateful than I can say for the wonderfully warm message which you sent to the Rochester presentation. It meant so much to me.

The event was somewhat chaotic because of dear old Rexroth's condition. He has a hiatal hernia and gets a lot of pain from it. At times I thought he was going to pass out, but we managed to find a wheelchair for him, and so he completed the event. Actually, when he got on his feet and talking, he was as wonderful as ever.

I was pleased to see from the office envelope that Mitch had approved the contract for the Fitzgerald play. Whatever its fate on Broadway, I like it as much as ever, and will be proud to publish it.

With best wishes, as ever,

James Laughlin

≪ • ≫

the Rochester presentation: JL was honored for his publishing by the New York State Literary Center in Rochester, New York, in April 1980. The ailing Kenneth Rexroth was brought in from California as one of the main speakers. TW had sent an encomium to be read at the event: "The recipient of your award, Mr. James Laughlin, was my first publisher and will undoubtedly be my last, should his tolerance endure to that point. Kindly extend to him my congratulations on this important event. Tennessee Williams" (TW to A. Poulin at the New York State Literary Center, 4/20/80).

Whatever its fate on Broadway: After opening on TW's sixty-ninth birthday, March 26, 1980, at the Cort Theater, his last play produced on Broadway, *Clothes for a Summer Hotel*, ran for only fifteen performances.

212. TLS—1

2/17/81 [Key West]

DEAR FRED:

Mitch Douglas tells me that you plan to continue the volumes of *Theatre of T.W.* Of the long plays not published, there are nearly complete revisions of *Clothes for a Summer Hotel*, the definitive edition of *The Red Devil Battery Sign* as performed last Fall in Vancouver (Brit. Col.) and now there is one yet to be performed [*A House Not Meant to Stand*] at The Goodman Institute [sic] in Chicago, scheduled to start rehearsals on March 10. As of the moment I haven't settled upon a title—probably one will occur to me before we open—the subtitle is *A Gothic Comedy*. Oh—and *Something Cloudy, Something Clear.*

As for the one-acts or short plays, I think all the plays in the two published volumes, *27 Wagons* and *Dragon Country*, should be included and in addition there are a few not yet published. They are more experimental. The ones I prefer are *Demolition Downtown*, *The Traveling Companion*, *A Cavalier for Milady*, *Green Eyes*. By the time you go to press—hopefully before—the list will increase.

I guess you are pretty much "keeping shop" at N.D.—Remember me to Jay. I hope he's well and enjoying his relative leisure.

With every good wish,
Tennessee

≪ • ≫

The Red Devil Battery Sign: After its failure in Boston in 1975, *Red Devil* was revised and presented at the English Theater in Vienna in 1976 with Keith Baxter and Maria Britneva St. Just in the leading roles. Baxter was instrumental in shaping the new version and both directed and played the role of King in the 1977 London production, which was the basis for ND's 1988 published version. The play is dedicated "To Keith Baxter." Although TW says that the "Vancouver" script is "definitive," Maria St. Just, acting as TW's literary executor at the time of the play's preparation for publication, insisted on the use of the London script since it was the same version in which she had appeared in Vienna.

213. TL—1

March 5, 1981 [Norfolk]

DEAR TENN:

What happiness for me to be able to wish you joy and a long life on your 70th Birthday. It seems only yesterday, though it must be nearly 35 years, that we first met at Lincoln Kirstein's party, and became friends. And how much pleasure you have given me in those years: the opening night in Chicago of *Glass Menagerie*; and then of so many other wonderful plays; visits in Key West and encounters in various parts of Europe; your beautiful poems; and above all your loyalty to New Directions which has made possible the publication of so many young and unknown authors.

Long may you flourish!

[James Laughlin]

≪ • ≫

to wish you joy: This note was likely written in advance for a birthday party thrown for TW at the Goodman Theater in Chicago, by Artistic Director Gregory Mosher, where *A House Not Meant to Stand* was rehearsing. Very few out-of-town guests attended.

214. TL—1

3/26/81 [Norfolk]

DEAR TENN -

I have just been reading those 4 TV or film scripts that Mitch sent over to Fred, and I think they are very fine. You have added so many good new parts to the old ones, and I think that *Stopped Rocking* is one of the most powerful and moving things you ever did. It really shook me.

I hope we can do a book of them.

Best, as ever,

[JL]

≪ • ≫

film scripts: Published as *Stopped Rocking and Other Screenplays* (ND 1984), this volume includes *All Gaul Is Divided, The Loss of a Teardrop Diamond, One Arm*, and *Stopped Rocking*.

215. ALS—3

[March 1981] [Orlando, Florida]

DEAR FRED:

How could you imagine that I (of all people) would not want to contribute some words of homage to Jay? The delay has been due to extraordinary pressures as I prepare (2 work sessions a day) for at least one more full-length new play production at The Goodman Theatre in Chicago. Please feel free to edit this. I am flying to Chicago from a most exhausting sort of "festschrift" in a preposterously ultra-conservative place—Orlando. Don't know how I got through it but it now appears that I did . . .

Homage to "Jay"

It was "Jay" Laughlin who first took a serious interest in my work as a writer. My first notable appearance in print was in an N.D. volume called *Five Young American Poets* in 1944. True, I had suffered an abortive play production in 1940, which collapsed in Boston. It appeared to me that this failure was conclusive. Jay thought otherwise. Consistently over the years his sense of whatever was valuable in my work was my one invariable criterion.

Among all the multitude of persons I've encountered in the world of letters and theatre (if that distinction is permissible), "Jay" Laughlin remains the one I regard with the deepest respect and affection. My gratitude to him is an inexpressible thing and I trust that he knows it always.

Ever,

Tennessee

≪ • ≫

homage to Jay: A slightly revised version of this tribute appeared in *Conjunctions: I, Inaugural Double-Issue, A Festschrift in Honor of James Laughlin, Publisher of New Directions*, edited by Bradford Morrow (1981).

full-length new play: The first production of *A House Not Meant to Stand* at the Goodman Theater.

216. TLS—2

[received 10/30/81] [New York]

DEAR FRED:

Very regrettably Mitch Douglas didn't let you know that I was not releasing *Now the Cats with Jeweled Claws* but was holding it back for re-writes of a considerable nature and all quite essential. This play was written while I was quite ill in the Sixties and the fact is embarrassingly evident in the text, especially as I read it in print. I'm afraid that everything about my professional relationship with Douglas was regrettable.

With any luck it is now terminated.

I don't suppose there is any way that—in this volume Seven—you could indicate that the inclusion of the particular play was due to this misunderstanding? I am well aware that I have failed to keep in direct personal touch with you. These past few years the work-load has been much greater than Douglas appears to have understood: consequently long works as well as this particular short one were thrown into production before ready.

Clothes for a Summer Hotel was already cast, except for a supporting role, when I arrived in New York for rehearsals.

And confidentially two plays [*Kirche, Küche, Kinder (An Outrage for the Stage)* and *Something Cloudy, Something Clear*] were placed with the Jean Cocteau Repertory Company while I thought they were still in reserve—for second drafts—at Studio Duplicating.

I am a slow and conscientious writer if permitted to be. Not an electric rabbit at a dog race.—Of course these misapprehensions are finally set right. I've done two versions of *Clothes* since the one thrown with such cavalier haste onto Broadway. One is being held by a good management in London and if you wish a copy, just call the Dramatists Play Service.

The semi-retirement of dear Jay and the loss of Bob MacGregor somehow interrupted the flow of communications between N.D. and me. Let's now try to restore it.

A serious writer needs serious contacts to keep on the right track.

Yours faithfully,
Tennessee

<Please remember me to Jay who introduced me to the "world of Letters." I never want him to be ashamed of a work of mine that bears the N.D. imprimatur. P.P.S. There is also a now definitive *Red Devil Battery Sign*—a controversial but major work.>

≪ • ≫

Now the Cats with Jeweled Claws: TW was upset about the inclusion of *The Youthfully Departed* in Volume 7 of *The Theatre of Tennessee Williams* and so it was replaced with *Now the Cats with Jeweled Claws*, which TW had revised and sent to his agent Mitch Douglas to submit for publication or production. Peggy Fox sent all proof pages to TW c/o Mitch Douglas early in 1981 and TW had then approved them, prior to this letter of protest.

written while I was quite ill in the Sixties: In the late 1960s TW wrote multiple drafts of a play he called "Now and at the Hour of Our Death." Through his agent Bill Barnes he submitted a new version of that play to ND in 1977 with the working title "Urban Problems Confronting." A revised version, with the play's current title, *Now the Cats with Jeweled Claws*, was sent to ND in 1980 by Mitch Douglas, along with *The Youthfully Departed* and *A Cavalier for Milady*, under the collective title "Three Plays for the Lyric Theatre."

two plays were placed with the Jean Cocteau Repertory Company: *Kirche, Kutchen, und Kinder* (1979) (published by New Directions in 2008 under the title *Kirche, Küche, Kinder*) and *Something Cloudy, Something Clear* (1981). According to Mitch Douglas and director Eve Adamson, TW was well aware that these titles were offered to Jean Cocteau Repertory Company and pleased by the company's desire to produce them.

217. TL—2

November 24, 1981 [Norfolk]

DEAR TENN:

Fred showed me a copy of your last letter to him, and I am very grateful for your kind postscript to me on the letter. I have always had great faith in your high artistic standards, and I don't think you have ever let me down, or ever will.

You speak of me as being in "semi-retirement," and I just wish that that were true. I seem to be working as hard as ever. I don't come down to the office as much as I used to, as I really don't like New York any more, but I am very busy reading manuscripts and keeping up correspondence. In addition, this late in life, I have taken on a kind of new career as lecturer and literary entertainer at colleges. This means a lot of work doing the research to get up the lectures. I think I did ten of them this year, and have six more scheduled between now and the end of spring. I don't know exactly why I do this, except that it rejuvenates me to get out in the college world and meet the young students, who are so wonderful. They really are bright and keep me on my toes.

Then, this fall, I was over in Italy working on a documentary film about Ezra Pound which is being produced by the New York Center for Visual History. It was a most educational experience for me, but hard work. I had never realized what a technical business film making is. But I guess you do. I found the long sitting around while they changed lights and lenses between shots very frustrating. My role in the picture is to be interviewer, narrator, and reader of poems. I did eight hours of interview with Olga Rudge, Ezra's mistress, who is still alive in Venice, and also helped the crew to locate beauty spots in Venice which Ezra had written about in the *Cantos*. Happily, Venice is just as beautiful as ever, although it seems to be sinking into the mud on which it was built. On days of high tide the water was coming up over the sidewalks. And the boats couldn't get under some of the bridges. It will probably take another year to finish the film, as we will have to go back and do other places in Italy where Ezra lived, or about which he wrote, and then go to Provence, for the troubadour towns, and probably to Paris and London as well.

I am afraid that I won't be able to get to the big celebration for you, because I have a college lecture engagement that same date, but I will be thinking of you.

Very best, as ever,
James Laughlin

≪ • ≫

new career as lecturer: As part of JL's treatment for bipolar disorder, his psychiatrist, Dr. Benjamin Wiesel, enjoined his patient: "You have so much to tell, to teach the coming generations, *give of yourself*." Beginning hesitantly, JL spoke at Indiana University in the fall of 1971, launching a lecturing "career" that would last for more than two decades and include numerous college appearances, semester-long college courses (as at Brown University), and star turns at places like the New York Public Library.

documentary film about Ezra Pound: *Ezra Pound: American Odyssey* was a film made for the Voices & Visions Series—separate films on thirteen American poets were shown on PBS television in the late eighties. JL also participated in the film on William Carlos Williams. Both films can be viewed on the Internet under Voices & Visions.

218. TN—1

To: JL

Subject: Tennessee Williams, *Clothes*

Here is a xerox of Tennessee's "corrections" for *Clothes*. His pen markings come through a bit light on the copy but I think you can get the general idea—he has taken out anything to do with a "ghost" play. Fred and I both think that in doing so he has destroyed what is special about the play.

I also enclose a clean copy of the Dramatists Play Service edition. When Tennessee first came into the office he said he was satisfied with this version and that we could just publish our edition using it and making just the corrections necessary to put it into our play style. If we can proceed on this basis, I could get the manuscript ready very quickly and we could have the book on next spring's list.

If we are going to do the play in the spring, we need an answer rather quickly or we won't be able to get anything into the catalogue.

As I understand it you are going to write to TW at his Key West address.

PLF [Peggy Fox]

≪ • ≫

219. TL—2

10/31/82 [Norfolk]

DEAR TENN:

I hope this finds you well and working. I am just back from England where I was working again on the Pound documentary film in which I am the commentator. I have found this film work very interesting—we were in Italy for a month in the summer—but it is certainly different from ordinary writing. I found it easier, actually, just to talk off the cuff rather than write a script.

Thank you for sending in that very interesting poem. It came just in time. We were able to get it into the anthology just going to the printer, which will be out in about six months. I am always pleased when you write poems, and wish you would do more.

This spring, for my annual reading or lecture for the Academy of American Poets, I've decided to read eight or ten poems which I have published at New Directions, by different poets, and try to do a few minutes talk about each poet. Which of your poems would you suggest I read? Do let me know. And if there is any background story to go with it, something I wouldn't know about, please give me that. Many thanks.

I'm glad that we can go ahead now with *Clothes for a Summer Hotel*, a wonderful play and one of my favorites, perhaps because I have always liked Fitzgerald so much, and Zelda's book, too. Fred and Peggy asked me to look over the corrections you had marked in the DPS edition. I think many of the small corrections are excellent, they tighten it up. But I'm much troubled by your taking off "A Ghost Play" as subtitle and the deletions and changes which play down or even eliminate that important part of the structure. It just isn't the same play if you take that out. I like the comparison with the Japanese Noh plays, where ghosts are so important. And I like what the ghost concept enables you to do with time, making past and present contemporaneous. I think this is very strong.

So I hope you will reconsider and let us know if we can keep as much as possible of the ghost concept, though, of course, using the other good small changes that you made. Forgive me if I am being professorial—I never like to fuss with your work—but it may be the influence of my new old-age career. I have now lectured, mostly on Pound and Williams, at about twenty colleges, and this fall I have

Harvard, Princeton and Maine to do. Then a course at Brown in the spring. I don't do anything very scholarly. It is more hortatory, trying to get the kids to like and read good modern poetry.

I keep busy trying to increase the principal of Rose's trust, the one for which Dakin and I are trustees. By moving around in money market instruments, all safe ones of course, I think I have nearly doubled the value in ten years. So that is in order.

Very best, as ever,

[James Laughlin]

≪ • ≫

very interesting poem: "The Color of a House" was the first contribution in *ND 46* (1983). The volume was dedicated: In Memoriam / TENNESSEE WILLIAMS / 1911–1983. JL's poem in response to TW's death, "Tennessee," was published in the following annual, *ND 47* (1983); the first line of the poem, which follows from the title, read "called death the sudden subway and now he has taken that train."

220. TL—1

January 26, 1983 [New York]

DEAR MR. WILLIAMS:

I am enclosing the galleys for *Clothes for a Summer Hotel,* and I have marked my queries in the usual way. If you remember, you gave Fred Martin a marked copy of the Dramatists Play Service version of the play in which you had made some cuts—these we have restored in the main (per J. Laughlin's letter and your discussion with Fred), but Mr. Laughlin did like some of the minor changes and most of my queries concern these and the wording that you prefer in certain cases where changes had been made. Other than those few questions, the galleys look very clean.

I have taped a copy of the "Author's Note" at the head of the galleys. If you have time to expand upon this, I think it would be helpful to the reader (just a paragraph or two), but if you don't we will use the original "Author's Note" as is. (I remember Mr. Laughlin saying that your technique in this play reminded him of Noh dramas.)

Is there any dedication for this play?

It's too bad that you won't be in town for the tribute dinner for Mr. Laughlin at the National Arts Club on February 25. If you have time to do a letter that can be read at the festivities, I know it will be most appreciated.

If you would just give either me or Fred a call when you have finished the galleys, we will immediately dispatch someone to pick them up.

After working on *Clothes*, I am very much looking forward to a really good production that can capture the intensity and pathos of Scott and Zelda's relationship.

I certainly hope you have a productive and enjoyable stay in Europe.

All best wishes,
Peggy L. Fox

≪ • ≫

tribute dinner [. . .] at the National Arts Club: The National Arts Club is a private club in Gramercy Park, New York City, founded in 1898 to "stimulate, foster, and promote public interest in the arts." It regularly honors those it feels have contributed to the artistic education of the American people, and it hosted a dinner in honor of James Laughlin and his contributions to literature on February 25, 1983. When JL found out on the morning of the 25th that Tennessee had been found dead in the early hours of that day, he closeted himself in his office at ND and composed the poem "Tennessee," which he read at the dinner that night, turning an occasion to honor him into an impromptu memorial for his friend of forty years.

221. ALS—1

[received February 4, 1983] [New York]

DEAR PEGGY,

Only serious mistake in galley was a bit of confusion at end of Scott-Hemingway scene—I trust my pen correction is clear.

Love & thanks, TW

≪ • ≫

222. TLS—1

[received February 4, 1983] [New York]

[to be read at the National Arts Club Award ceremony in honor of James Laughlin, February 25, 1983]

It was James Laughlin in the beginning and it remains James Laughlin now, with never a disruption or moment of misunderstanding in a friendship and professional relationship that has now lasted for forty years or more.

By nature I was meant more for the quieter and purer world of poetry than for the theatre into which necessity drew me.

And now as a time for reckoning seems near, I know that it is the poetry that distinguishes the writing when it is distinguished, that of the plays and of the stories, yes, that is what I had primarily to offer you.

I am in no position to assess the value of this offering but I do trust that James Laughlin is able to view it without regret.

If he can, I cannot imagine a more rewarding accolade.

Tennessee Williams

January, 1983

≪ • ≫

February 25, 1983: The morning of February 25, 1983, TW was found dead in his bedroom at the Hotel Elysée in New York City. The cause of death, initially attributed to "asphyxia caused by an obstruction in the opening of his larynx" from choking on the cap of a medicine bottle, was reported in the press and was repeated in articles and biographies for decades. However, six months after his initial report, Dr. Eliot M. Gross, the city's chief medical examiner, corrected the cause of death in his report, indicating that a toxic level of the barbiturate Seconal (secobarbital sodium) in the playwright's blood had brought about his death. Following a 1985 exposé in the *New York Times*, an acknowledgment of Gross's malfeasance was published in *Unnatural Death: Confessions of a Medical Examiner* (Random House, 1989) by forensic pathologist Michael Baden.

to be read at the National Arts Club . . . : JL typed the following sentence at the top of TW's tribute to him that he then copied and shared with friends: "The last message that I had from Tennessee, which touched me more than I can say, was what he wrote to be read at the awards dinner of the National Arts Club in New York."

Selected Bibliography

JAMES LAUGHLIN

The River. Norfolk, CT: New Directions, 1938.
Some Natural Things. New York: New Directions, 1945.
Skiing East and West. New York: Hastings House, 1946.
Report on a Visit to Germany (American Zone). New York: New Directions, 1948.
A Small Book of Poems. Milan: New Directions, 1948.
The Wild Anemone & Other Poems. New York: New Directions, 1957.
Confidential Report and Other Poems. London: Gaberbocchus Press, 1959.
The Pig. Mt. Horeb, WI: Th Prshbl Prss, 1970.
In Another Country. San Francisco: City Lights Books, 1978.
The Deconstructed Man. Iowa City, IA: Windhover Press, 1985.
Stolen and Contaminated Poems. Isla Vista, CA: Turkey Press, 1985.
House of Light. New York: Grenfell Press, 1986. (with Vanessa Jackson)
Selected Poems, 1935–1985. San Francisco: City Lights Books, 1986.
The Master of Those Who Know: Pound the Teacher. San Francisco: City Lights Books, 1986.
Tabellae. New York: Grenfell Press, 1986.
The Owl of Minerva. Port Townsend, WA: Copper Canyon Press, 1987.
Pound as Wuz: Essays and Lectures on Ezra Pound. St. Paul, MN: Graywolf Press, 1987. *Collemata.* Lunenburg, VT: Stinehour Press, 1988.
This Is My Blood. Covelo, CA: Yolla Bolly Press, 1989.
The Bird of Endless Time. Port Townsend, WA: Copper Canyon Press, 1989.
Random Essays. Mt. Kisco, NY: Moyer Bell, 1989.
Random Stories. Mt. Kisco, NY: Moyer Bell, 1990.
Angelica: Fragment from an Autobiography. New York: Grenfell Press, 1992.
The Man in the Wall. Mt. Kisco, NY: Moyer Bell, 1993.
Collected Poems. Mt. Kisco, NY: Moyer Bell, 1994.

The Country Road. Cambridge, MA: Zoland Books, 1995.

The Empty Space: Twelve Poems. Ellsworth, ME: Backwoods Broadsides, 1995.

Heart Island and Other Epigrams. Isla Vista, CA: Turkey Press, 1995.

The Music of Ideas. Waldron Island, WA: Brooding Heron Press, 1995.

Remembering William Carlos Williams. New York: New Directions, 1995.

The Secret Words: Poems. Coffeyville, KS: Zauberberg Press, 1995.

The Lost Fragments. Dublin: Dedalus Press, 1997.

The Love Poems of James Laughlin. New York: New Directions, 1997.

The Secret Room. New York: New Directions, 1997.

Poems New and Selected. New York: New Directions, 1998.

A Commonplace Book of Pentastichs. New York: New Directions, 1998.

Byways: A Memoir. New York: New Directions, 2005.

The Collected Poems of James Laughlin 1935–1997. New York: New Directions, 2014.

TENNESSEE WILLIAMS

For Williams titles in this section, years refer only to year of book publication and not to original productions of plays or completion of texts.

Battle of Angels. New York: New Directions, 1945.

27 Wagons Full of Cotton and Other Plays. New York: New Directions, 1945.

The Glass Menagerie. New York: Random House, 1945; New Directions, 1949.

A Streetcar Named Desire. New York: New Directions, 1947.

American Blues, five short plays. New York: Dramatists Play Service, 1948.

Summer and Smoke. New York: New Directions, 1948.

One Arm and Other Stories. New York: New Directions, 1948.

The Roman Spring of Mrs. Stone. New York: New Directions, 1950.

The Rose Tattoo. New York: New Directions, 1951.

Camino Real. New York: New Directions, 1953.

Hard Candy, stories. New York: New Directions, 1954.

Cat on a Hot Tin Roof. New York: New Directions, 1955.

Baby Doll. New York: New Directions, 1956.

In the Winter of Cities. New York: New Directions, 1956.

Orpheus Descending. New York: New Directions, 1958.

Suddenly Last Summer. New York: New Directions, 1958.

Sweet Birth of Youth. New York: New Directions, 1959.

Period of Adjustment. New York: New Directions, 1960.

The Night of the Iguana. New York: New Directions, 1962.

The Milk Train Doesn't Stop Here Anymore. New York: New Directions, 1964.

The Eccentricities of a Nightingale. New York: New Directions, 1965.

The Knight Quest, stories. New York: New Directions, 1967.

Kingdom of Earth. New York: New Directions, 1968.

Dragon Country, A Book of Plays. New York: New Directions, 1970.

Small Craft Warnings. New York: New Directions, 1972.

Eight Mortal Ladies Possessed, stories. New York: New Directions, 1974.

Memoirs. New York: Random House, 1975.

Moise and the World of Reason. New York: Simon and Schuster, 1975.

The Two-Character Play. New York: New Directions, 1976.

Androgyne, Mon Amour. New York: New Directions, 1977.

Where I Live: Selected Essays. New York: New Directions, 1978.

Vieux Carré. New York: New Directions, 1979.

A Lovely Sunday for Creve Coeur. New York: New Directions, 1980.

Clothes for a Summer Hotel. New York: New Directions, 1983.

Stopped Rocking and Other Screenplays. New York: New Directions, 1984.

The Collected Stories of Tennessee Williams. New York: New Directions, 1985.

The Red Devil Battery Sign. New York: New Directions, 1988.

Tiger Tail. New York: New Directions, 1991.

Something Cloudy, Something Clear. New York: New Directions, 1995.

The Notebook of Trigorin. New York: New Directions, 1997.

Not About Nightingales. New York: New Directions, 1998.

Spring Storm. New York: New Directions, 1999.

The Selected Letters of Tennessee Williams, Volume I. New York: New Directions, 2000.

Stairs to the Roof. New York: New Directions, 2000.

Fugitive Kind. New York: New Directions, 2001.

The Collected Poems of Tennessee Williams. New York: New Directions, 2002.

Candles to the Sun. New York: New Directions, 2004.

The Selected Letters of Tennessee Williams, Volume II. New York: New Directions, 2004.

Mister Paradise and Other One-Act Plays. New York: New Directions, 2005.

The Traveling Companion and Other Plays. New York: New Directions, 2008.

A House Not Meant to Stand. New York: New Directions, 2008.

New Selected Essays: Where I Live. New York: New Directions, 2009.

The Magic Tower and Other One-Act Plays. New York: New Directions, 2011.

Now the Cats with Jeweled Claws and Other One-Act Plays. New York: New Directions, 2016.

Index

Ford, David, 261, 262*n*, 331*n*
Ford, Ruth, 27*n*, 251*n*
Ford Foundation, xxi, xxiii, 177, 188*n*, 195*n*,
    198*n*–99*n*, 204*n*, 214
Fordham University, 244
Forest Service, U.S., 11*n*
Forster, E. M., 10
    The Longest Journey, 11*n*
    A Room with a View, 11*n*
Four by Tennessee (TV show), 229*n*
Fox, James, 129*n*
Fox, Peggy L., xxx, 339, 350–51, 366*n*, 369,
    370–72, 373
    excerpts from interviews with JL by, xiv*n*,
    3–4, 27, 51–52, 71, 83, 95, 109, 119, 141–
    42, 177, 221–22, 239, 275, 295, 353–54
France, 180
    Provence, 368
Franco, Francisco, 209
Frost, Robert, 213*n*–14*n*
Fundación García Lorca, 210*n*

Gabel, Martin, 7*n*
Gandhi, Mohandas K. "Mahatma," 240,
    241*n*
García Lorca, Federico, 54, 209–10
    The Butterfly's Evil Spell, 210
    Five Plays, 54*n*
    The House of Bernarda Alba, 81
    Selected Poems, 54*n*
García Lorca, Francisco, 209
    In the Green Morning: Memories of Federico,
    210*n*
Gauguin, Paul:
    Nave Nave Mahana "The Careless Days,"
    22, 24*n*, 46
Gazzara, Ben, 203*n*
Germany, 209, 210
Gibraltar, 195, 271
Gide, André, *Theseus*, 136*n*, 137*n*
Gielgud, John, 104*n*, 112*n*
Gigi (dog), 284, 285*n*
Giraudoux, Jean, 80, 81
Girodias, Maurice, 113*n*
Giroux, Robert, 129*n*
Gish, Lillian, 75
Gish, Sheila, 350
Glassgold, Peter, xxvi, 312, 313*n*, 325, 329
Glass Menagerie, The (film), 123, 126, 131, 227
Glavin, Bill, 276, 284, 285*n*, 288, 291, 299,
    303
Glenville, Peter, 319*n*
"God Bless America" (Berlin), 72*n*
Goethe, Johann Wolfgang von, *Faust*, 132
Goethe Festival, 131, 132, 198*n*
Goodman, Paul, 13, 61
    The Break-Up of Our Camp, 14*n*
Gotham Book Mart, 107*n*, 242*n*, 348

Graham, Sheilah:
    Beloved Infidel, 360*n*
    A State of Heat, 360
Gray, Morris, 65*n*
Great Books Program, 198*n*
Greenville, Tenn.:
    Harmony Presbyterian Church in, 305
    Old Harmony Graveyard in, 305
Griffin, Alice, 207
Grindel, Eugène, *see* Éluard, Paul
Gross, Eliot M., 374*n*
Group Theatre, xii, xv, 7*n*, 55*n*, 130*n*, 136*n*,
    164*n*
Grove Press, 48*n*
Gulf of Mexico, 4*n*, 80
Gulf Oil Playhouse, 89*n*
Gussow, Mel, 312, 313*n*
Guttusu, Renato, 117, 127–28
Gwenn, Edmund, 63, 64*n*

Hack, Keith, 325*n*, 349*n*, 356*n*
Hagen, Uta, 38*n*
Hamburg, 180–81
Handiman, Wynn, 279*n*
Harcourt, Brace, 129*n*, 165*n*, 236*n*, 245
Harper & Row, Publishers, Inc., 236*n*, 357*n*
Harper's Bazaar, 102, 137
Harris, Julie, 231
Harris, Ralph, 269*n*
Hart, Patrick, 299*n*
Harvard University, xi, xii, 3, 47, 70*n*, 125,
    138, 247, 249, 326, 327*n*, 353, 371
    Gray Fund poetry series at, 65
Hauge, Gabriel, 214*n*
Haussman, Sonja, 98*n*
Hawkes, John:
    The Beetle Leg, 174
    The Cannibal, 128, 129*n*, 174
Hayes, Helen, 101, 104*n*
Hearst, William Randolf, 337
Heine, Heinrich, 219
    The North Sea, 219*n*
Heinz, Doreen Mary English "Drue," 193
Heinz, H. J. "Jack," 193
Hemingway, Ernest, 117*n*, 140, 213*n*, 373
Hepburn, Audrey, 205, 206*n*
Herlie, Eileen, 304, 306*n*, 311*n*
Hill, George Roy, 225
Hillyer, Robert, 125, 128*n*
Hollywood, Calif., xvii, 14–16, 18, 21, 23, 30,
    43, 46, 85, 126–27, 131, 135, 182, 183,
    188*n*, 202, 203*n*, 215, 246, 360*n*
Holman, Libby, 233
Holt, Rinehart & Winston, 7*n*
Hopkins, Miriam, 35*n*
Hotel Elysée, 337, 340, 341*n*, 342, 374*n*
Houghton Mifflin, 104*n*, 107
Hound and Horn, 3

Poe, Edgar Allan, 79
Porter, Katherine Anne, 23, 24*n*, 25
Pound, Ezra, 3, 8*n*, 61*n*, 88, 125, 166*n*, 213*n*–14*n*, 323, 328, 367–70
   The Cantos, 305, 368
   The Letters of Ezra Pound, 165*n*
   as mentor to JL, 4
   The Pisan Cantos, 128*n*
   Selected Letters, 165
Powell, Dilys, 224*n*
Powers, J. F., 87, 88*n*
Pratt Institute of Art, 75*n*
   Graphic Arts Center of, 261
Prescott, Orville, 156, 157*n*
Presentational Theatre, 334, 335
Princeton, N.J., 155
Princeton Triangle, 39
Princeton University, 371
Prokosch, Frederic, 101, 103*n*
Proust, Marcel, 30
Provincetown, Mass., 35*n*, 45–48, 89, 109*n*
Publishers Weekly, 155, 223
Pulitzer, Joseph, 327*n*
Pulitzer Prizes, 133*n*
Punch and Judy shows, 321*n*
Purdy, James, 215, 218
   Children Is All, 216*n*
   Color of Darkness, 216*n*

Quinn, Anthony, 335, 336*n*
Quintero, José, 220*n*, 223, 224*n*

Radcliffe College, xxiii, 213*n*
Raft, George, 289
Rainbow, The (film), 53
Random House, xv, xix, 52*n*, 53*n*, 58, 99*n*, 165, 166*n*, 229*n*
Ransom, John Crowe, 296*n*
Rapper, Irving, 124*n*
Ray, Man, 343*n*
Redgrave, Vanessa, 285*n*
Resor, Ann Clark, *see* Laughlin, Ann Clark Resor
Resor, Stanley Burnet, 27
Rexroth, Kenneth, 86, 88*n*, 174, 361
Richardson, Joely, 285*n*
Richardson, Natasha, 285*n*
Richardson, Sandy, 236
Richardson, Tony, 251*n*, 262*n*, 284, 285*n*
Rilke, Rainer Maria, 209
   Duino Elegies, 310, 311*n*
Rimbaud, Arthur, 10
   Illuminations and Other Prose Poems, 11*n*
   A Season in Hell & The Drunken Boat, 11*n*, 57
Ringling Brothers Circus, 339–40
Robeson, Paul, 38
Rochester, N.Y., xxvi, 361

Rodríguez y González, Amado "Pancho," 78, 79*n*, 80, 96
Roebling, Paul, 250, 251*n*
Roman Catholicism, 54, 129*n*, 144, 256, 287–88
Roman Spring of Mrs. Stone, The (film), 223, 224*n*
Romantic movement, 161
Rome, xxi, 86, 96, 98–99, 101–3, 106, 117, 119, 124, 130, 133, 145, 148, 155–56, 180, 195, 209, 223, 286–88, 291, 329
Roosevelt, Franklin Delano, 84
Rose Isabel Williams Foundation, 254–56, 339, 371
Rose Tattoo, The (film), 206*n*
Ross, Tony, 60, 61*n*
Rossellini, Roberto, 105, 106*n*, 135, 136*n*
Rosset, Barney, 48*n*
Roth, Philip, 321
Rothschild, Adolf, 96
Royal Court Theatre, 257
Rudge, Olga, 368
Russell, John, 137*n*
Russia, 78, 87
Ryder, Alfred, 229*n*

Saher, Lila von, 285*n*
St. Clements Church, 279*n*
St. Elizabeths Hospital, 213*n*–14*n*, 305, 306*n*, 323
St. Just, Lord Peter, 112*n*, 211*n*, 232, 255
St. Just, Maria, *see* Britneva, Maria
St. Louis, Mo., xii, xxiv, 4*n*, 37, 41, 52, 76, 108, 110, 194, 199, 264–65, 292, 303
Salter, Stefan, 219, 283*n*
Salt Lake City, Utah, 11*n*, 14–16, 36*n*
San Francisco, Calif., 86–87, 343, 344, 356*n*
   American Conservatory Theatre (ACT) in, 337, 338*n*, 343*n*
San Francisco *Examiner*, 337
Santa Fe, N.Mex., 16, 17
Santa Monica, Calif., 24, 29
Sarasota, Fla., 249, 252
Saroyan, William, 34
   The Daring Young Man on the Flying Trapeze, 34*n*
   Madness in the Family, 34*n*
   The Man with the Heart in the Highlands, 34*n*
Sartre, Jean-Paul, 184
   Crime Passions (Mains Sales), 105
   No Exit (Huis Clos), 80, 81*n*
Sassani, Eleanora, 312, 313*n*
Saturday Review of Literature, 125, 128*n*, 140, 165
School of American Ballet, 4*n*
Schwartz, Alan, 245, 247*n*, 256
Schwartz, Delmore, xiii, 54, 156–57
   Dr. Bergen's Belief, 34*n*